Women, Religion and Sexuality

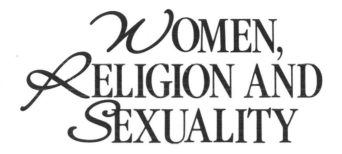

Women, Religion and Sexuality

Studies on the Impact of Religious Teachings on Women

Edited by Jeanne Becher

WCC Publications, Geneva

A US edition will be published in April 1991 by
Trinity Press International, Philadelphia.

Cover design: Rob Lucas

ISBN 2-8254-0991-X

Printed in Switzerland

Contents

Foreword

Many people have contributed to the dialogue which has made the publication of this volume possible. Marie Assaad, during her years of service as staff moderator of the WCC Unit on Education and Renewal, initiated the project, and worked with the original group of writers as they developed their papers. We are grateful for her vision which helped to launch this enquiry.

During the course of this project two women served in the position of director of the Sub-unit on Women. Bärbel von Wartenberg-Potter was director during the early stages of the study. Most recently, Anna Karin Hammar assured the continuity of staff support for the second stage of the project, promoting the inclusion of the diverse perspectives presented in this volume.

Many others have shared their responses to the papers and participated in reflection on the subject in various parts of the world, thereby sharpening the questions and issues the writers have incorporated into their papers. This has indeed been a process which has drawn on the interest and expertise of many people. For this the Sub-unit is grateful, and believes that as a result this volume is a rich resource.

For her commitment through this process of obtaining the papers and for the attention to the editorial help, we are grateful to Jeanne Becher of the Sub-unit staff.

Bertrice Wood
Moderator, Working Group
Sub-unit on Women in Church and Society

Introduction

The limited multi-faith, multi-culture study on "Female Sexuality and Bodily Functions in Different Religions" grew out of a deep concern for women's role and status and the inequalities experienced by women in most societies. The idea was born following the UN Mid-decade Forum in Copenhagen in 1980 and the World Council of Churches (WCC) four-year study on the "Community of Women and Men in the Church (CWMC)." At the Copenhagen meeting a seminar on Women and Religion attracted a large audience. Many participants in this seminar spoke of the impact of religious teachings on women, and expressed the desire to pursue those teachings and examine the extent to which they influence woman's perception of herself and society's perception of her role and status. The findings of the WCC study on CWMC revealed the need for a follow-up study to reach a clearer understanding of male/female identity and relationship, a clearer definition of human sexuality, and an interpretation of scriptures in the light of women's experience and the changing situations.

Therefore, in preparation for the 1985 Forum of the UN Decade for Women in Nairobi, it was felt that knowledge about religious teachings which either inspired or reinforced social values was a necessary basis for promoting the participation of women in decision-making, and for recognizing their significant role and contribution to public life. It was noted that very often cultural taboos have been reinforced by religious teachings, or perpetuated by the absence of positive teachings. Unless these taboos are brought to light and the negative teachings are dealt with through reinterpretations of scripture and tradition, most projects attempting to ameliorate woman's status would stop short of their objectives.

Some time after the initiation of this study project in November 1983, the result of the UN survey summarizing the response of governments to the long questionnaire on women around the theme "Equality, Development, Peace" was published. The answers revealed that by far the greatest barriers against women's participation in public life were traditional beliefs and values. This result further justified the purpose of our study.

The original proposal for this study was "to enlist the help of a small international group of women theologians and anthropologists, each belonging to one of the major religions (Christianity: Roman Catholic, Orthodox, Anglican, Reformed; Buddhism; Hinduism, Islam; Judaism) to examine their respective religious teachings relating to female sexuality and bodily functions. The aim was to understand how these teachings affect the public conception of femaleness (as something beneficial, inferior, dangerous, unclean, etc.) and try to discover possible common elements among the different religions. Further, the study was to provide basic information which might help to overcome the taboos that surround the subject and encourage further study and reflection by various local groups to understand the effect of those teachings on the status of women in contemporary society."

It took almost a year of enquiry and conferring to find eight women from Uruguay, Romania, New Zealand, Ghana, Japan, India, Egypt and the USA, recommended for their expertise in theology or social research, to accept to join in this venture.

It was a courageous venture, and the researchers soon realized the significance of such a risky decision to study a "taboo" subject and to delve into an enormous amount of complex material capable of a variety of interpretations.

The researchers agreed on a methodology: they would consult the original and authoritative sources of their respective religions to learn the teachings and attitudes regarding female sexuality, attempting to cover the following issues: definition and understanding of the nature of woman and her relation to man; ways in which the stages of the female life cycle are observed; roles prescribed and accepted for women in family, religious community and society; ritual practices associated with or pertaining to women; expectations and limitations on female sexual behaviour and relationships.

To be credible to the large number of women who tend to follow official religious teachings without questioning, it was agreed that this study limit itself to an investigation of the authoritative sources as they pertain to the topic. Any interpretation of the sources should be avoided at this stage. This was agreed upon in the hope that local groups would be sufficiently interested in the topic to make their own interpretations as they study their religious teachings in their respective contexts and analyze the impact of these teachings on their own lives. Thus the material provided by the researchers was to be considered as a pioneering step to be followed up by local groups in various parts of the world.

As the researchers listened to each other's reports they noted that in spite of the great differences separating their cultures and their religious faiths, there were similarities that could only be explained by the common patriarchal values of their societies and the dominant impact of these values on religious teachings. Among the conclusions they arrived at are the following:

1. Women need to be more involved in the study and interpretation of their religious scriptures and tradition, especially when they deal with woman's role and sexuality.

2. Women need to be more articulate in defining themselves and their faith experience, rather than letting others define them.

3. Women need to discriminate between the central and unchanging givens in religious teaching, and what has been incorporated in each religion through the powerful impact of culture, in particular the seemingly universal patriarchal values relegating women to inferior positions because of their being women.

4. Perhaps, women may need to scrutinize with greater care the deep psychological, social, and maybe economic reasons behind the perpetuation of those negative patriarchal values.

Realizing the significance of the topic following the Nairobi presentation, groups of women in various parts of the world took up the study of religious attitudes towards female sexuality in their own settings. These groups often went a step farther than the WCC project to look at actual practices pertaining to women in various faith communities, in addition to examining scripture and scriptural interpretation. It became clear that experiences and outlook varied, even among women of the same religious confession. Because of the richness and diversity of such findings, the Sub-unit on Women felt that it would be worthwhile to try to find a second group of researchers from the faith communities involved who would either react to the original papers or contribute new findings that would add to the reflection on the subject. This project was carried out over the next several years (although we did not succeed in obtaining a second paper from the Reformed tradition and from the Buddhist faith). The studies on Hinduism and Islam included here are in fact from the second group, since the original researchers from these faith communities decided not to publish their findings in their original form.

The Sub-unit hopes that the papers presented here will throw some light on the origins of discriminatory practices based on gender, expose some of the time-honoured taboos about female sexuality, and contribute to the on-going discussion of women's role in religion. If readers are thereby encouraged to continue the study and interpretation of scripture, then this volume would have served its purpose.

Marie Assaad

Female Sexuality
and Bodily Functions
in the Jewish Tradition

Blu Greenberg

I. Definitions of the female sex

a) *The historical context*

In the eighteenth century B.C.E., Abraham embraced monotheism and entered into a covenant with God, thereby binding himself and his descendants in an everlasting relationship with one God. Thus was the Jewish people established, through the lives of a patriarchal clan.

The Jewish religion, however, does not take on its fuller shape until some 600 years later. In the twelfth century B.C.E., Moses is selected to be God's agent in the liberation of Abraham's descendants, the tribe of Hebrews who had become enslaved in ancient Egypt. Immediately following the Exodus from Egypt, this band of ex-slaves encounters God in Sinai. The theophany at Sinai is the core of the Jewish religion, the basis of all Jewish law and theology. At Sinai, the Jews received the Ten Commandments and the corpus of sacred writings known as the Torah.[1]

As is true of all ancient regions that are still alive today, Judaism did not stop with the revelation at Sinai — or with the Torah. It continued to develop through history, the product of an interplay of three forces: explication of scriptures and tradition; incorporation of new historical events; and the impact of parallel cultures and value systems that Jews encountered along the way through history.

A vast and varied literature was developed to contain and transmit Jewish life and religion. Primary among the texts is the Talmud, a great body of Rabbinic literature known as the oral Torah. The Talmud, from which many of the sources below are cited, spanned more than six centuries of Rabbinic thought, and was redacted in the year 499 C.E.[2]

Following the Talmudic period, and in every century, new texts were added to the existing body of religious literature. These were works of *halacha* (Jewish law), philosophy, theology and exegesis. In almost every volume of religious literature, there can be found some reference, however brief, to women and their personhood.

It is no surprise, then, that because of this extended process of unfolding through time, there is no singular definition of female sexuality and bodily functions. On the contrary, at times conflicting values are registered. There are differences, for example, between the Bible and the Talmud regarding menstrual taboos; different definitions of a wife's responsibilities to her husband in the halacha formulated in Christian France from that in Moslem Spain; differing interpretations of sexual pleasure within different tractates of the Talmud itself.

To a twentieth century investigator, then, the Jewish traditional view of women emerges as a rich dialectic. Rather than begin with a bias and then select sources to suit it, I shall attempt to convey to the reader the dialectic regarding female bodily functions, life cycle ceremonies and role definitions. It is my hope that the dialectic will enable us, in summation, to draw conclusions with relevance to contemporary and future times.

b) *Biblical definitions and an emergent dialectic*

Everything in Judaism flows from the Torah. Thus the Torah is the appropriate place to look for an overarching theory of woman's personhood. We find it in the very first chapter of Genesis: "And God created Adam (humankind) in His image... male and female He created them" (Gen.1:27). There it is — man and woman, created equal to each other, in the image of God. One must ask: what does it mean to be created in the image of God, for God has no likeness and no image? The answer given by the sages is that human beings are created with godly attributes, with dignity and an ability to walk in God's ways. The human body is to be kept holy and fit for it is the spiritual, mental and moral likeness of God".[3] Thus, male and female are created as biologically and sexually distinctive, yet having the same godly attributes and strengths — a perfect paradigm for sexual equality if ever there was one.[4]

Yet, almost immediately, we encounter the dialectic. A second version of creation unfolds: after giving life to man *(Adam)* and planting him in the Garden of Eden, God reflects: "It is not good for man to live alone. I shall make a helpmeet unto him"... Then God caused unconsciousness to fall upon the man and he slept; and he removed one of his ribs and he closed the flesh ... and from the rib that he had taken from the man He formed a woman. And he brought her unto the man and the man spoke: "At last, this is it! Bone of my bone, flesh of my flesh, this one shall be called woman *(ishah)* because out of man*(ish)* she was taken..." (Gen.2:18-14).

What is the relationship between the two pericopes and what are the implications for female sexuality? The first version is divine-oriented, with overtones of sacredness, perfection, majesty, mysterium. The second is earthy, human-oriented, romantic; it is also existentially correct regarding human vulnerability, loneliness and interdependence. But it is also a derivative definition of femaleness. And yes, man needs woman, but here he also has the power of naming her.

Is the first creation story a description of male and female status in the eyes of God — as equals — while the second a description of male-female inter-relationships structured in hierarchy? If so, does embedding the human-relational pericope in a creation story imply that differential status between male and female is divinely conferred and is God's will? Does ranking in relation to each other mean to be ranked in the eyes of God, and for all time?

How shall we understand the phrase *e'zer K'negdo*, a "helpmeet opposite him"? — as enabler, a classic role for women in the Jewish tradition, or as the Talmud explains, "a helpmeet if he is worthy, an antagonist if he so deserves"?[5]

Should the creation story be interpreted as placing woman at the top of the hierarchy, created last on the ontological scale from lowest to highest form, woman as the perfection and perfectability of humankind?[6]

Or is the whole purpose of this second creation story simply a backdrop to the single most romantic verse in the Bible: "Therefore shall a man leave his mother and father and cling to his wife and they shall be as one flesh" (Gen. 2:24)? May we put aside questions of hierarchy and instead concentrate on themes of intimacy, romance, sexuality, procreation and eternal love?

These are some of the questions the dialectic poses.

Let us turn to the next biblical definition of female-ness which appears in the story of the fall and exile from the Garden of Eden. Is Eve, the mother of all human life, a temptress, progenitor of disobedience, and source of human downfall — as a surface reading would indicate? Or is she "more appealing than her husband... the more intelligent one, the more aggressive one... By contrast the man is a silent and bland recipient... not a decision-maker... follows his wife without question or comment, thereby denying his own individuality."[7]

More complex than the tale, perhaps, is the punishment. "And I will increase your pain... in giving birth, and you shall hunger after your husband, and he shall rule over you" (Gen. 3:16). Shall a 20th-century woman interpret the passage "and he shall rule over you" as a paradigm for all male-female relationships in post-lapsarian times — or shall we focus on it as curse/punishment, an imperfect model to be set aside as we strive to achieve equality? If we focus on it as a curse, must we focus the same on the phrase "and you shall hunger after your husband"? In so doing, would we not be obliterating a magnificent contribution of Judaism — the affirmation of women's sexual passions to be accounted for in a relationship? Indeed, many of the rabbinic laws acknowledging and protecting female sexual impulses are based on this very passage in Genesis, wedged between two curses — of pain in childbirth and of subordination to a husband.

So the dialectic comes through, in the very first definitions of women in the Jewish tradition and it continues throughout the sources, from Bible to Talmud, to Midrash (exegesis), to medieval commentary and philosophy, to legal codes such as the Shulkhan Aruch (14th century), to modern halachic (Jewish religion-legal) decisions. Always there exist two poles of thought vis-à-vis women — as distinctive, special, and equal on the one hand, as subordinate and inferior on the other.[8] At times one definition surfaces, at times the other. Almost side by side we read the magnificent and magnanimous paean of praise to the perfect wife (Prov. 31:10-31) and Ecclesiastes musing that "women are more bitter than death" (7:26). In one place the Talmud describes women as "greedy, eavesdroppers, lazy and jealous",[9] and elsewhere as "noble"[10] and "the source of all blessing and goodness";[11] as "lightminded" and therefore unreliable,[12] and as "endowed with greater powers of discernment".[13]

So much for the ambiguities of definition. Let us turn our attention elsewhere for further clarification.

II. Life cycles and ceremonies

a) *Birth and covenant*

Perhaps in no other area is the dialectical attitude towards females seen more clearly than at birth. In Judaism, to be born is not simply a biological fact. It is also entry into the covenantal community. A powerful theme, it signifies that this new life is not merely the child of a particular family but is a child of the whole Jewish people. Every Jewish child becomes a member of the covenantal community at birth. The attendant ceremony for males is circumcision which takes place on the eighth day after birth. The Hebrew word for circumcision is *brit*, which means covenant. There is no female circumcision, a happy circumstance for, unlike male circumcision, female circumcision may reduce sexual satisfaction. On the other hand, while males are accessed to the covenant with communal ceremony, females enter without any manner of rite, ritual, or public acknowledgment. An additional paradox is that males carry the sign of the covenant in their flesh, yet females are the pivotal figures in carrying on the covenantal line; a Jew, by definition, is one born to a Jewish mother, regardless of the father's faith.

Again, many questions come to mind: is it a higher state to be accessed automatically, without benefit of ritual, or does the tradition celebrate publicly the addition of males to the community because males are more highly valued?[14]

Moreover, one must wonder whether the silent ritual-less entry of women into covenant has had a domino effect on (a) women's place in community, (b) women and property, (c) women and Torah, (d) women and other rites of passage. This question of domino effect has significant political implications, for while we would prefer not to take on all the battles at once and to leave alone certain matters of benign inequity or harmless imbalance, we do not have the luxury of doing so, inasmuch as each matter is connected to the other.

(a) For example, in the Grace recited after meals, in which we thank God for sustaining us and all living things, we also express our gratitude "for your covenant which you have signed in our flesh".[15] Because of the fact that "our flesh" cannot possibly refer to females, women are not included in the quorum of three males that convenes the recitation of Grace-after-Meals, even though women are fully obligated to recite the Grace. Such is the ruling in the Talmud.[16] And yet, several centuries later, a medieval rabbi rules that three women may constitute the necessary quorum, if there are not three males to do so.[17]

(b) Inasmuch as the land of Israel was also a symbol of covenant — ("And I shall give to you this day the land as an eternal sign (of the covenant) between Me and thee") — women did not inherit the land. However, if there were no male heirs women did receive their portion of the land (Num. 17). Moreover, women could and did become landholders and property owners, by means of wills and gifts, a process that circumvented biblical law.[18] Further, if an inheritance was too small to divide up, the Talmudic decision was that it be given wholly to the daughter and let the son fend for himself.[19]

(c) The Torah is another symbol of the covenant. Women are not obligated in the daily study of Torah, a *mitzvah* (commandment/good deed) required of Jewish males. While no reason is offered and no explicit connection is made between covenant and Torah in exempting women it seems a possible line of reasoning. By means of the exemption from Torah, the access route to religious authority and leadership was virtually sealed off. This explains why women were never ordained.

And yet, the Sabbath is also a symbol of covenant, and women are as fully bound and blessed by its observances as are the Jewish males.

(d) Finally, we must ask whether the silent entry into covenant at birth muted women's celebration of other rites of passage. For that answer, let us examine the stage of puberty.

b) *Puberty/menarche*

Puberty rites, as birth rites, are focused on the spiritual, communal and covenantal dimensions and not on bodily functions. Because of this, the rabbis established a uniform age for marking puberty and celebrating its rites rather than depending on the appearance of individual signs (whose onset they understood to be two pubic hairs for males and the enlargement of breasts for females). I am not sure whether the process of spiritualizing this stage of growth contributed to a climate of modesty about female bodily functions or vice versa, but it carried over into many other areas. This modesty also explains why there is no formal ritual marking menarche, menstruation, conception, pregnancy, lactation and menopause, even though each one of these bodily functions figures significantly in certain areas of Jewish law.

The puberty rite in Judaism is known as *bar-mitzvah* (lit., a son of the commandments) and *bat-mitzvah* (lit., a daughter of the commandments). When a male reaches age thirteen and a female twelve (the rabbis were well aware of differing rates of maturity), he/she becomes fully obligated as an adult in all of the precepts of the Torah. In other words, all obligations of an adult Jew accrue at puberty.

For males, this rite of passage is celebrated with the public recitation of the blessing over the Torah, a portion of which is read each Sabbath in the synagogue. Oftentimes, the bar-mitzvah boy will also read, before the entire congregation and with proper cantilation, the particular portion of the Torah for the Sabbath of his thirteenth birthday. The celebration of the child becoming bar-mitzvah and confirming his acceptance of responsibility as a member of the covenantal community is a memorable event in the life of the young man, his family and the community. Jewish females at age twelve assume all of the adult female responsibilities in Judaism — the Sabbaths, the feasts and fasts, kosher food laws and many liturgical and ritual obligations. But, again, a Jewish girl enters this stage without benefit of ritual or rite. Perhaps all this has something to do with her quiet access to covenant at birth; perhaps to her lack of obligation in the study of Torah; perhaps to the generally more passive and inconspicuous role of women in liturgical celebrations.

The Psalmist's phrase: "The honour of the King's daughter is within", (Ps. 45-14) was frequently used in rabbinic literature to support women's primary role within the home away from the public eye. [20]

c) *Marriage*

In all cultures, marriage was the optimal adult relationship, particularly so for women, who historically have had few other options. Thus marriage becomes almost an exclusive definition of women's adulthood.

Oddly enough, there is no biblical commandment to marry. Rather, it comes in the form of description: "It is not good for man to live alone" Genesis 2:18. The entire Book of Genesis is an explicit story of three patriarchal marriages. Why all this attention focused on marriage and family? Because marriage and family life are the vehicles of transmitting the covenant, generation to generation, until the end of days. Thus, the family unit is central not only to Jewish history and survival but also to Jewish theology.

Marriage serves three functions: intimacy, procreation and the channelling of erotic desires. The Talmud recognizes these needs in both men and women; yet, in establishing a specific requirement to marry, the rabbis of the Talmud levy the obligation on men only. [21] While this would seem strange, it can be understood through the following rabbinic statements: "A woman wants to marry more than a man wants to marry." [22] "A woman prefers to be impoverished and married rather than be wealthy and unmarried." [23] In other words, a woman did not need a commandment to marry; she would do so quite naturally.

Some of the laws of polygamy, levirate marriage and divorce must be understood in the context of a woman's desire to be married. Polygyny provided that no woman would ever remain unmarried for reasons of demographic imbalance between males and females. The laws of the levirate marriage (Deut. 25:5-10) were established to protect the childless widow. If her husband died and left her without children, her situation was precarious. If she had already been married and was no longer a virgin she was not as desirable a commodity. Therefore, the brother of her deceased husband was required to marry her. If he refused, he had to go through a ceremony known as *halitzah* in order to be released from his obligation to her. In the presence of a *bet din* (Court of Law) he had to put a special shoe on his right foot. The widow would then say, in front of him: "My brother-in-law refuses to marry me." The levir would repeat: "I do not want to marry her." The widow then removed the shoe and spat on the ground in front of him, saying: "This is done to the man who does not build his brother's house." We understand, from the story of Ruth, that levirate marriages were welcomed by women.

Even the divorce procedures are geared to remarriage. The central part of divorce proceedings is the transmission of a divorce bill to the wife by the husband who states: "I release you and you are now free to marry another man."

Sexuality and marriage are highly interwoven in the sources: "Eighteen to the wedding canopy."[24] "If a man has reached age twenty and has not married a wife, he will spend all the day long in sin. Is this really so? No, not sin, but erotic thoughts."[25] "An unmarried woman runs the risk of becoming promiscuous."[26] It was considered optimal to marry off children, both sons and daughters, close to puberty in order to prevent promiscuity. "He who marries off sons and daughters close to puberty, of him it is said: 'You shall know that your tent is at peace'."[27]

It must be said, however, that the marriage age amongst Jews was of a wide range. It largely depended on practices of host cultures and parallel societies, as well as on historical events that affected Jews directly. For example, in the late medieval period in Eastern Europe there was a quota levied by the government on the number of Jewish marriages that could be performed in any given year. Since this quota was far less than the number of Jewish couples waiting to be married, parents were anxious to marry off their children as early as possible.

Although it was a father's responsibility to marry off his daughter, he was not permitted to do so without her consent. "He should wait until she grows up and says 'I want to marry Mr so and so'."[28] This rabbinic decision was based on the story of Rebecca who was asked by her brother whether she wished to go off with Eliezer, Abraham's chargé d'affaires, to Canaan to marry Isaac (Gen. 24).

Although a woman's consent was needed, marriage was clearly a man's initiative. The the Bible describes marriage as "a man taking a wife" (Deut. 14:5, 22:13). The Mishnah* asks what does "take" mean? The answer: "A woman is acquired in three ways and acquires herself (her independence) in two. She is acquired by means of money, deed or intercourse... and acquires herself (her independence) through divorce or death of her husband".[29] The Gemara* goes on to a lengthy discussion of why the word "acquired" is used when elsewhere "kiddushin" (sanctification) is the word for marriage. In the discussion, we learn that money is not purchase but rather a symbol of setting aside, just as kiddushin (holiness) is the act of setting one thing apart from another. A woman is set aside exclusively for her husband, and the money is simply a confirmation of the transfer of status. One reason the rabbis arrive at this conclusion is that the money specified is so insignificant — the equivalent of a few pennies — that it could only be a symbolic transfer. We also learn that deed means a document and that intercourse is ruled out by the rabbis as a valid means of contracting a marriage.

Still, it is the man who takes the woman in marriage. It followed naturally, then, that authority in marriage resides in the husband, the assumption being that authority over her was transferred from her father to her husband.[30] It is no coincidence that the Hebrew word for husband is *ba'al*, which also means master. For example, a husband had the power to annul his wife's vows.[31] On the other hand, both husband and wife had duties towards each other in marriage;[32] the relationship was understood to be a complementary one. Indeed, we find in the Talmud statements where the husband must defer to his wife's wishes and judgment. "If your wife is small bend down and whisper in her ear", which is interpreted in the tradition as "take counsel with her in all matters and follow her advice".[33] The value of a wife was not underestimated. "Whoever lives without a wife lives without well-being, blessing, without a home, without Torah, without protection and security, without peace."[34] Certain scholars have pointed out the fact that all positive statements about women are with reference to their status as wives.[35]

The marriage ceremony reflects the male initiative. The core act of the ceremony, which is a transaction between the two parties, is when the man places a ring on the woman's finger and recites the marriage verse:

---

* The Talmud consisted of two primary layers: the *Mishnah* is the earliest layer, the work of scholars and rabbis who lived between the second century B.C.E. and the second century C.E. The *Gemara* is the later and larger layer that interprets and expands the Mishnah. It contains the thoughts and statements of the rabbis who are quoted in the Mishnah, as well as those who lived in the third to sixth centuries C.E.

"Behold, with this ring thou art consecrated unto me according to the laws of Moses and of Israel." This formula is recited in the presence of two witnesses. Built up around the core ceremony are the recitation of the betrothal and marriage blessings, the reading of the *Ketubah* (the marriage contract) and other traditional customs. A woman is silent in the traditional marriage ceremony.

d) *Childbirth*

Although we shall deal below in detail with the subject of procreation, a word about childbirth ceremonies is in order here: at times we learn as much from the spaces as from the lines filled in. It is a curious matter that, in a religion as finely attuned to ritual and celebration as is Judaism, there exists no formal rite, not even a blessing, celebrating the most miraculous experience in a woman's life — the act of giving birth. This speaks volumes about the place, or rather lack thereof, of public celebration of women's experiences. It also makes a strong statement about the utter lack of self-perception and self-appreciation on the part of women throughout the ages. (Imagine for a moment what a glorious celebration the tradition would have developed by now, had Jewish men been the ones to give birth during these past four millennia!)

e) *Divorce*

In traditional Jewish law, divorce is not a court procedure, but rather a transaction between the two parties. This, despite the fact that it takes place in the presence of two witnesses and before a *bet din*, a religious court of law consisting of three rabbis. The essence of a Jewish divorce is the act of a man giving the *gett* (Aramaic for writ of divorce) and the woman accepting it. On the positive side, the procedure lends an important ingredient of psychological closure, which is often lacking when divorce comes in the mail.

While there is a certain imbalance in the procedure — one gives and one receives — and some women who have gone through the experience feel an indignity about the ceremony, the problem lies not so much in the brief proceedings as in the overall legal status of women in Jewish divorce law.

Divorce law is a significant issue because it is one of the few remaining areas of vulnerability and potential disability for a woman; also because it has broader implications for the marital relationship itself.

Jewish divorce law highlights four points: (a) it confirms the dialectical stance towards women in the tradition; (b) it shows that even an ambiguous or seemingly harmless hierarchy of male and female can have severe consequences in the life of individual members of the subordinate group; (c) divorce law is an open view on the inner workings of halacha including an insight into how much the religious legal system has evolved since biblical times; (d) it reminds us of how much more needs to be done so that Jewish divorce law can serve all individuals bound by it in a non-discriminatory fashion.

The problem, as well as the evolutionary process, begins with biblical law: "A man takes a wife and possesses her. She fails to please him because he finds something unseemly *(ervat davar)* in her and he writes her a writ of divorce, hands it to her, and sends her away from his house" (Deut. 24:1).

A woman who displeased her husband was both physically and psychologically vulnerable. He could divorce her at will, she could not divorce him. It was a man's initiative and right. The logic behind this was — just as he was the one to create the relationship, so must he be the one to sever it. [36]

Nevertheless, biblical law itself begins the process of modifying his absolute rights. First, the fact that he had to write a bill of divorce was in itself a delaying tactic and an improvement over the other alternative widely available in the ancient Near East — irrevocable or oral divorce. Second, elsewhere (Deut. 22:13-21), the Bible teaches that a man had to pay a penalty (alimony) upon divorce, and third, the Torah describes instances in which a man may never divorce his wife (Deut. 22:18-19). These restrictions must be understood in the broader context — the community's prerogative to set limits on a man's absolute private right of divorce.

It must be noted here that biblical narrative portrays a different situation from law. Polygamous marriages were quite rare yet divorce also was extremely rare. The social sanctions against divorce must have been very powerful. It is also of interest to note that while oral divorce was widely practised in the ancient Near East, the parallel Sumerian and Hittite cultures had equivalent divorce laws to those of the Torah. The code of Hamurabi records identical marriage and divorce procedures to those of ancient Judaism. Nevertheless, a contemporary Jew cannot dismiss this problematic law simply as ancient culture-bound mores; it is revelation and is the basis of all halacha that follows.

In subsequent generations, particularly in Talmudic times, the inequity was tempered. A man's right was constricted and a woman's rights expanded. The curb on a man's right took several forms: increasing the number of instances in which the absolute prohibition against divorce applied; encumbering the divorce proceedings which served both to delay action and to require the mediation of the *bet din* (which always tried first to effect a reconciliation); increasing the financial responsibilities of the husband in a manner that greatly discouraged divorce; and enlarging the wife's opportunity to assent or dissent, outlawing forcible divorce, thereby giving her some mastery over her own fate as a married woman. In addition to these practical measures, the Talmud is replete with moral dicta against divorce.[37]

The wife's right to sue for a divorce was also expanded. Many of the conditions which entitled her to divorce had to do with her sexuality. For example, if the husband did not fulfil the prescribed conjugal obligations to her (see below); if she accused him of impotence (the burden of proof was upon him);[38] if she vowed not to have intercourse with him and he did not take pains to annul such a vow;[39] if she wanted to live in the Holy Land or move from one Palestinian city to Jerusalem and he refused to follow her;[40] if he had a serious disease or a continual bad odour from his occupation, such as carrying dung or tanning hides;[41] if he did not support her in the style to which she had been accustomed or, if he was wealthy, in the style proper for his means;[42] or if he failed to live up to anything in the Ketubah, the marriage contract. Given any of these conditions, she was entitled to sue for divorce. Two post-Talmudic grounds for divorce were: if he beat her or if he visited prostitutes.[43]

While much of rabbinic activity whittled away a man's absolute right and increasingly protected and expanded women's rights, a basic problem remains unto today. It is the problem of the *aguna*, the anchored wife, anchored to an absentee husband by reason of the fact that he has given her no gett. In this day and age of female-initiated divorce, there is a growing number of recalcitrant husbands who refuse to give the gett to their wives, for reasons of spite or blackmail. A woman faithful to Jewish law cannot remarry until she has a gett in hand. Some women pay the blackmail, others try to use whatever communal sanctions they can; others just wait it out, their lives in limbo. That there exists a problem in this area for Jewish women today points to the fact that legal manoeuvres on the part of rabbinic authorities throughout the generations to subvert the original inequity were simply not enough.

f) *Menopause*

There is hardly any discussion in the sources of menopause, though it was recognized as a distinct stage of life. Inasmuch as female sexual needs existed independent of generativity, menopause did not indicate a secession of the sexual relationship, nor of the laws of onah (a husband's responsibility to sexually satisfy his wife).

g) *Death*

Death, in all ways, is the great equalizer. It is one of the few times in the tradition that women "go public". Funeral rites are identical for male and female, including a full washing of the body as preparation for burial. This is a symbol of honour to the dead and of the holiness of the body even though life has left it. Every community has a *hevra kadisha*, a holy society, consisting of volunteer members who come together when called to perform this sacred duty of preparing the body for burial. There is a male hevra and a female hevra, for even in death it would be considered unseemly for a group of males to wash a female body and vice versa. After the ritual washing, the body is dressed in white shrouds and buried in a simple pine box. The funeral rites include an eulogy, recitation of the memorial prayers and below-ground burial. For the eleven months following the death of either parent, the daily kaddish, the mourners' prayer, is recited in a minyan — a quorum of ten that constitutes a communal prayer group.[44]

Not so identical are the laws concerning the surviving children. Only sons are obligated to recite the kaddish. This stems from the fact that only males are counted as part of the minyan.[45] Although the daily recitation of kaddish is a demanding responsibility — to organize one's life so as to be at communal prayer morning and evening — it is also a powerful experience of healing grief.

h) *Making amends*

As noted earlier, Judaism is not a static religion. Just as it responded to the cultural mores of ancient Near East, Hellenic Greece, Christian Europe and Muslim Spain, so it has developed during the last two hundred years under the impact of modernity and particularly in response to the feminist affirmation of women's lives and experiences. The differing degrees and tempo of incorporating contemporary values has given rise to a new phenomenon in Judaism — denominationalism. While Judaism is probably no more monolithic now than it was in any other era — such as in the first century with its competing schools of thought and different sects — the denominations have taken on a much more structured differentiation.

In every denomination, some repair is taking place with regard to the celebration of women's life cycles. This process is highly significant in generating new and healthy attitudes towards female sexuality; as is often the case in life, and as is a principle of halacha, values modification is the product of action and not only its precursor. Deeds change attitudes as much as the other way around.

Birth: A new ceremony, first formulated in the 1970s, is that of *simchat bat* or *brit bat*, the rejoicing in the birth of a daughter or the covenanting of a new daughter. Still in the experimental stage, it is a ceremony that is gaining wide acceptance.[46] The basic outlines of the ceremony are: a recitation of various biblical passages; prayers for this baby girl for a life of Torah, marriage and good deeds; an affirmation of her entry into the covenantal community; a formal naming ceremony; sanctification blessings recited over a cup of wine; and the *shehecheyanu* blessing which celebrates a unique and special moment in life. And of course no ritual is complete without speeches and feasting. Within the next century its form will become fixed and Jews living a hundred years from now will likely celebrate the birth of a baby girl as if it had been part of Judaism since the Revelation at Sinai.

Puberty: A formal ceremony for bat mitzvah was introduced by Reconstructionist Judaism in the 1930s. Under the impact of feminism, it has spread to the other denominations — Orthodox, Conservative and Reform. The formal celebration differs in each denomination, some modelling themselves identically on the bar mitzvah rite for boys, with the girl now reading the Torah in the synagogue; others are establishing new forms such as a feast with singing and dancing and the recitation by the girl of a study she has prepared on some aspect of the Torah. All of the ceremonies, in one way or another, are related to the study of the Torah. This increased association of women and Torah is surely one of the factors that opened the way for women's ordination, which is now a feature of all the denominations except Orthodoxy.

Menarche: To date, only one formal quasi-public menarche ceremony has been recorded, and that in the popular literature. I suspect menarche will remain a private moment in a girl's life in the Judaism of Western societies. However, an increasing number of mothers are seeking ways, in a private mother-daughter manner, to ritually affirm the first menses of their daughters. These usually include the recitation of the shehecheyanu blessing in which we thank God for "giving us life, maintaining us and bringing us to this day". Relevant passages from scriptures or liturgy about the generativity of females are also recited on this occasion.

Marriage: No longer the silent partner, many Jewish marriages, particularly in the liberal denominations, incorporate a measure of participation by the bride. In Reformed and Conservative marriages, this tends to be a double ring ceremony and exchange of the marital vows; in the Orthodox ceremony, some brides will recite scriptural verses under the wedding canopy. These passages are usually selected from the Song of Songs (Canticles), a work of love poetry. Where the bride gives the groom a ring, as is often the case among Orthodox couples today, she does so without reciting the marriage formula. According to halacha it is the male who initiates the act of marriage.

It goes without saying that marriages among Jews have changed a great deal under the impact of feminism. Increasingly, women work outside the home. Both breadwinning and parenting roles are shared much more equally between husband and wife. Despite inherited prescriptions in the tradition regarding a woman serving her husband, most Jewish marriages today are based fully on equality of the sexes.

Childbirth: Oddly enough, there has been no formal ritualization of the experience of childbirth. Perhaps that is because there is enough excitement and joy in birth ceremonies focused on the new-borns; perhaps because only recently has there been a fusion of feminist awareness with traditional maternal expression. However, an increasing number of women do recite ritual prayers of thanksgiving, sometimes in private, sometimes in the setting of family and friends. Moreover, the traditional *birkat hagomel* blessing, which in the past was recited only by the husband in the synagogue on the occasion of his wife's safe delivery, is now increasingly being recited in synagogues by the new mother.

Divorce: The different denominations have resolved, in varying degrees, inequities in Jewish divorce law. Understanding the halacha to be indefensible in terms of the ethical and universalist categories central to Reform, that denomination simply dropped Jewish divorce proceedings, in favour of civil divorce. This is not acceptable to the Conservative and Orthodox communities, which require a gett.

The Reconstructionist rabbinate uses the traditional gett and all of the attendant procedures. However, when a woman who was previously divorced (civilly) wishes to remarry but cannot secure a gett from her former husband, the Reconstructionist rabbinic court will give her a document that declares her free to remarry, even though she has no writ of divorce, nor has her marriage been annulled.

A solution newly operative in Conservative Judaism today in problem divorce cases is a broad application of the rabbinic principle of *havka'at* kiddushin — the power of the rabbis to annul marriages *ab initio*. It is based on the Talmudic principle that all who marry within the Jewish community do so with the implied consent and under the conditions laid down by the rabbis. Thus, a man's act of marrying a woman is validated by rabbinic sanctions; the marriage continues to exist only as long as the rabbis agree to its existence. In cases of a recalcitrant husband, the rabbinic court withdraws its sanction of the marriage and the woman is free to remarry.

The Orthodox solution is to resolve cases of recalcitrance in the civil court, not by dropping halachic divorce but rather by making civil divorce dependent on the simultaneous or prior granting of the Jewish gett. The more fundamentalist Orthodox communities that still operate like closed societies manage to use other sanctions against recalcitrant husbands, including on occasion physical force. These, I must admit, sometimes produce the fastest results in releasing a woman from agunah status.

While there has been significant progress in equalizing women in matters of divorce in Judaism, there still is need of unifying legislation that would forever remove imbalances in the law.

Menopause: Given the wide stigma attached to growing old in most contemporary societies, it is not surprising that there has been no religious affirmation of menopause, nor a likelihood that it will happen in the near future. On the other hand, there are two factors that might contribute to such a rite, explicitly celebrating the onset of menopause: (a) women spend a shorter amount of time in their lives in procreative functions; (b) increasingly, women define their lives in terms of other occupations and interests. I can envision some celebration of menopause that would say, in effect, "Relief!"

Death: In the liberal denominations an increasing number of women are taking upon themselves this steady responsibility for reciting the kaddish daily. Women who do so not only have found a nurturing prayer community to be very supportive in their time of sorrow, but also have gained acceptance and respect in what were formerly all-male settings — the daily minyan.

III. Generativity

a) *Procreation*

The law of procreation is the very first law in the Torah: "Be fruitful and multiply and replenish the earth" (Gen. 1:28). Strangely enough, we learn from rabbinic literature that the mitzvah of procreation devolves upon man and not woman.[47] Several interpretations are given: (a) he is the initiator in sex; (b) it is a woman's natural inclination to have children; thus, to command her to bear children is superfluous; (c) as we remember from the curse, childbirth and pain involves a measure of travail. It would be unethical to obligate one to do something that would bring pain. Therefore a woman is technically exempt from the obligation; (d) on the other hand, there is another commandment in the Bible: *"Lashevet* — to settle the earth with human life". That commandment is binding upon women as well as men.[48]

All things are linked to one another. In the sources we learn that the reason that the preferred sexual position is for men to be on top is that he is the one who is obligated.

The commandment of procreation is so significant that "If a man spilled his seed outside of a woman's womb it is as if he spilled blood". Inability of a couple to fulfil the obligation of bearing children within ten years of marriage was ground for divorce. However, in all likelihood it served as ground for a woman to sue in the court for divorce, because a man did not need to establish these grounds for divorce. In fact, it probably never happened. The Talmud relates the story of a married couple, in love with each other yet still childless after ten years. On the eve of their separation/divorce the husband tells the wife that in addition to half of his property she may also take anything that she specially valued from the household. That night she gives him strong wine to drink and as he falls in a sleep she has two men come and carry him to her own house. He was the most precious item that she took with her, and they lived happily ever after.

What constitutes fulfilment of the commandment to procreate? Some say two children — one boy and one girl; others say four children — two males and two females; and yet others that at the very least one must replace himself. "He who has not engaged in procreation, it is as if he has diminished the image of God in the world."

b) *Birth control*

1. Although it would seem to be self-contradictory, the contraceptive laws of Judaism seek to establish the primacy of human regeneration. At the same time, these laws acknowledge that sex drives are healthy, natural, pleasurable — and not for procreation only. In practice, then, Jewish law permits birth control but circumscribes the method and the timing.

One can construct a positive theology of contraception: the basic principle is that the two most sacred human acts are to love and to create life. Both of these should come together in the act of conception, but if a man and a woman were to create life each time they made love this might well lead to a destruction of that love. On the other hand, contraception unlimited might lead to an inner orientation that is selfish, self-centred and dehumanizing. To bridge the gap, then, laws of limited contraception were formulated. It is a practical approach, yet it does not overlook the spark of divinity that inheres in human life's creative process. In other words, the dialectic operates here as well.

Birth control laws themselves are derived from an interplay of three Biblical principles. One, of course, is the commandment to "be fruitful and multiply". This commandment is the most significant one in limiting birth control.

2. The laws of *Onah*, sexual satisfaction of the wife. The broad implications of Onah are that sex is independent of generativity. If this is so, then birth control must be an appropriate condition of married life. Considering the fact that a normal woman ovulates and produces an egg every month for about forty years of her life, and considering that the end period of Niddah, the time of separation of partners during and after a woman's menses, coincides with the peak of fertility, the only alternative would be either to curb sex or to interfere with the generative process. One might say that Onah, the principle of sexual pleasure, served to eliminate rhythm as an option.

3. The third principle is that of *hash'cha'tat Zerah*, the law forbidding proper emission of the semen. One source of this law is the story of Onan, who was destroyed by God because of the sin of "wasting his seed". Every time he would have intercourse with his widowed and childless sister-in-law, whom he had been required to marry in order to carry on the name, he would withdraw before ejaculation (Gen. 38:8-10). From this story, as well as from the commandment "Be fruitful and multiply" the law prohibiting *coitus interruptus* was derived. By extension, so was the prohibition against any other mechanical device that impeded normal intercourse. But hash'cha'tat Zerah was interpreted more broadly than onanism or wasting seed. Indirectly, the second interpretation was linked to the principle of Onah, of marital pleasure. Thus any form of intercourse that impeded the fullest pleasure of the sex act was forbidden. Male and female sex organs were to be in direct and fullest contact.

These three broad factors, plus the ever-present and over-arching considerations of health, were the bases of countless rabbinic decisions regarding birth control throughout the generations. The question was not one of whether or not birth control was permitted; it was, and is. The real question centred on whether a particular type of birth control was permissible or preferable, and under what circumstances was that so. Technically, birth control is not permitted until one has met the minimum requirements of the command "be fruitful and multiply". In times past this was not a problem. Couples immediately centred their lives around the growth of family. It was natural for a woman to begin a family immediately after marriage. In these times, however, that is not the way of many young couples and there are legitimate issues of spacing of children, family planning and so forth. In several of the rabbinic responses we learn that contraception is permitted as long as a couple intends to have children at some point or other in their married life.

The interplay of the three values yielded these rabbinic decisions regarding methods of birth control:[49]

1. No coitus interruptus/no rhythm.
2. Birth control is the responsibility of females — males cannot use artificial methods of birth control because of the commandment upon them to be fruitful and multiply.
3. Sterilization is considered a mutilation and therefore forbidden.
4. There seems to have been some sort of "cup of roots", an oral contraceptive. Some rabbis forbid it on the ground that it is permanent. Others permit it on the ground that it is temporary.
5. Tying the fallopian tubes is permitted by some halachists as it is not considered permanent and does not impede full pleasure in intercourse.
6. The condom is forbidden for the same reason as rhythm and coitus interruptus, because it is not natural and the semen is not deposited in the vagina.
7. The diaphragm is permitted.
8. Spermicides. Some rabbinical authorities say yes and some say no.
9. The I.U.D. is permitted.
10. The pill is permitted. However, some rabbis have forbidden it on the ground that it is injurious to the health of the mother. Other rabbis have forbidden it on the ground that it causes intermittent bleeding throughout the month, rendering the woman in a continuous state of Niddah.

And as is true of any religious community, there are some rabbis who would take a stricter position than the generally accepted ones I have described above.

c) *Abortion*

Abortion is a complex issue. Throughout the centuries, rabbis have recognized it as such. They did not give flat, simplistic rulings, but often made fine distinctions that are so necessary in dealing with the complexities of human life. Many rabbinic opinions regarding abortion have been registered in the vast halachic literature, so that there exist legal precedents that range from very strict to very lenient.

In the opinion of most authorities, abortion is not considered killing. The view is derived, in part, from the law concerning accidental abortion: if a man accidentally injures a pregnant woman and causes her foetus to be aborted, he must pay only damages which are paid to the father of the foetus and not the mother (Exod.21:22). There is no substantial rabbinic discussion of abortion as murder. This can be sharply contrasted to the anti-abortion arguments of today.

The general rule is that abortion is not permitted except under special circumstances:

> If a woman suffers a hard (that is, protracted, life-endangering) childbirth, we are to dissect the child in her womb and bring it out piece by piece, for her life takes precedence over its life. If the greater part of the child has emerged, we may not touch it, for we are not permitted to take one life for another. (*Mishnah Oholot* 7:6)

In case of danger to the mother's life, an abortion can be — must be — performed, even up to the last moment before birth. In consequence of the focus on the life of the mother, there hardly appears in rabbinic literature an explicit debate on the right to life of the foetus. In fact, the rabbinic sources make it clear that foetal life is not the same as newborn life.

What constitutes threat to a mother's life? Here the opinions range from actual, imminent threat to her life at one end, and a threat to her health at the other. The lenient interpretation of threat to health includes psychological stress or other factors significantly affecting her mental health. Interestingly, Jewish law does not require testimony and proof from experts. According to some authorities, her own assessment is sufficient. Thus it can be said that abortion on demand is not permitted, but in cases where carrying to term would aggravate a stressful condition or would place the mother in a situation where she could not cope, some authorities would interpret the law to permit an abortion. Other rabbis forbid abortion even when there is a strong chance of the child being born with serious birth defects, as in the thalidomide cases, and even where parents have tested positively as Tay-Sachs carriers, the rationale being that the law concerns the mother's life and not the life of the child to be born.

In the responses, the interpretation of threat to a mother's health has been broadened to include the health of other family members. For example, an abortion was ruled permissible where the pregnant mother would have been no longer able to continue nursing an older child, endangering its health.

In situations where the mother's actual life is not at stake, timing has something to do with the halachic rulings. Within the first forty days of pregnancy, the foetus is technically considered as water, that is, not fully formed; certain of the rabbinic rulings on abortion reflect that fact. Moreover, some rabbis make a distinction between a foetus in the first three months and the period following.

Timing happens to be one of the complicating factors in the Tay-Sachs controversy. One in thirty Ashkenazi Jews carried Tay-Sachs genes, a very high percentage, which is why Tay-Sachs is often considered a Jewish genetic disease. Therefore, Jewish couples about to be married are routinely encouraged to be tested for Tay-Sachs. If both husband and wife are carriers, there is one chance in 36 that a child will carry the dread disease in which the body begins to decay at birth and the child inexorably dies at age four or five. Amniocentesis, which cannot be performed until the fourth month, can detect the presence of Tay-Sachs genes in the foetus. Certain rabbis discourage Tay-Sachs testing and amniocentesis for fear it might lead to an abortion, at a relatively late stage at that. At the other pole are rabbis who interpret a genetically impaired foetus as valid reason for an abortion, because of the severe mental and emotional stress it can place on the mother.

The traditional position on abortion is such that it gives neither a blanket veto on abortion nor total licence to a woman to decide what to do with her own body.

IV. Sexuality

Again the dialectic! Regarding sexuality the tradition reflects both an inherent earthiness and an ascetic strain. Bodily functions are celebrated and even placed in a spiritual context; yet they are also circumscribed. One example of the earthiness of Judaism vis-à-vis bodily functions is the blessing recited after elimination: "Blessed are you, Lord our God, Ruler of the universe, who has formed the human being in wisdom and created in him (her) a system of orifices and ducts and tubes... If anyone of these opened or closed inappropriately, it would be impossible to exist in thy presence...".. This blessing is recited after leaving the bathroom. (One would imagine in a religion as liturgically oriented as Judaism there would be a blessing either before or after intercourse, but there is none.)

Female sexuality can be understood in two ways — from an examination of the law or from the value statements that one finds throughout the literature. Because it is more relevant and a more accurate reflection of reality, I shall focus primarily on the law rather than on positive or negative statements, which in any event tend to cancel each other out.

Sexual relations between husband and wife — the only sanctioned framework for intercourse — are defined in the law by wide legitimacy of sexual expression and tight control of timeliness. This is achieved through an interplay of two commandments — *Onah* and *Niddah*.

a) *Onah*

The principle of Onah is that a woman has a sexual drive, the satisfaction of which is as basic to her well-being as that of other human needs and drives: "When a man sells his daughter as a slave she shall not be freed as male slaves are. If she proves displeasing to her master, who designated her for himself, he must let her be redeemed. He shall not have the right to sell her to outsiders since he broke faith with her. And if he designates her for his son, he shall deal with her as is the practice with free maidens. If he marries another, he must not withhold from this one her food, her clothing or her conjugal rights. If he fails her in these three ways she shall be freed, without payment" (Exod. 21:7-11). From this passage the basic rights of a bond woman are derived — food, clothing and conjugal rights. If these are the minimal rights of a bond woman, they are surely also the rights of a free woman.

Onah, the word for conjugal rights or sexual satisfaction of the woman, is incumbent upon man (this is also consistent with man and not woman being formally obligated to marry and procreate). There is no corresponding obligation of a woman to satisfy her husband. The Talmud introduces a general concept that she may not consistently and unreasonably refuse sex with her husband; if she does so she is called a *moredet*, a rebellious one. However, in legal fact, attention is focused on her sexual needs, not his.

Given the fact that in many post-biblical cultures in which Jews lived the accepted currency was female serving male in all ways including sex, one wonders why the law of Onah is given its full measure in rabbinic tradition, and not in any way re-interpreted or diminished. I believe there are several reasons: (a) The biblical law of Onah. Some commentators interpret the entire verse as referring to different dimensions of the sex act, not food and clothing and conjugal rights, but rather "in the flesh, in proper surroundings, in proper times". [50] (b) Onah, which is a prohibition (do not deny) is reinforced by a positive precept regarding the female sexuality: "If a man has newly married he shall not go out to join the army, nor is he to be taxed at home. He shall be left free of all obligations for one year in order to bring pleasure to the wife that he has taken" (Deut. 24:5). (c) There was simply a recognition of reality. A woman has sexual needs as much as a man — or perhaps more: "A woman's passion is greater than that of a man". [51] (d) "A man's sexual needs and sexual arousal is obvious through erection, but a woman's impulse is within, no one can recognize her arousal". [52] (e) A woman was considered to be modest and unaggressive. By nature and by cultural conditioning she would be inhibited from taking the initiative. One commentator suggests the meaning of the verse in Genesis "And your desire shall be to your husband's and he shall rule over you" to mean that a wife will feel passion for her husband but that she will be dependent upon him to take the lead. [53] A combination of these factors, plus the desire to protect the social order by confining and controlling man's libidinal drive exclusively within the marriage made the law of Onah a fundamental and persistent definition of sexual relationships.

There are two etymological derivations of the word Onah. One means seasons or proper times; the other "to cause suffering". Thus, rabbinic legislation focused both on quantity (or frequency) and quality of the sex relationship.

Set times: The rabbis were very explicit, linking a husband's frequency of obligation to his profession. For example, a camel driver, who must travel in caravans for some extended period — once every month; sailors — once in six months; an ass-driver (shorter trips) — once a week; common labourers — twice a week; students of the Torah — once a week; men of independent means — every night. [54]

In addition to frequency, there were also special times: before her menses, [55] after her immersion in the *mikrah* (ritual bath); [56] before he departs on a journey. [57] A man was required to observe the laws of Onah during pregnancy and lactation. Some men resist intercourse with their pregnant wives because of the association with their wives as mothers, but the rabbis explicitly state that woman has sexual feelings during pregnancy which must be respected. [58] And finally, beyond the set times and situations, a man was enjoined to respond to his wife when she signalled her desire for him through adorning herself or through modest overtures. He was to be sensitive to her subtle hints at all permissible times. In fact, this latter qualification was the primary one. These special set times established by the rabbis were not carved in stone, they were estimates of what the rabbis thought a woman wanted (or expected according to her husband's occupation). The primary emphasis of Onah was to meet her needs.

A second factor was the quality of a woman's sexual life. While the ascetic, modest and even prudish view does crop up in the literature (particularly during the medieval period) the definitive rabbinic decision is that any type of sexual activity, foreplay or position is permissible. Even the ascetically inclined literature always qualified with reference to female satisfaction. Despite their instinctive fear or diffidence about female sexuality, they had to remain faithful to the principle in Jewish law. For example, the *Schulchan Aruch*, the most authoritative medieval code, gives the following instructions.

> A man should accustom himself to be in a mood of supreme holiness and to have pure thoughts when having intercourse. He should not indulge in levity with his wife nor defile his mouth with indecent jests, even in private conversation with her... He should not converse with her either at copulation or immediately before it, excepting about matters directly needed for the act. However, if he is angry with her, when it is improper for a man to have intercourse with his wife, he may speak kind words to her in order to appease her. The intercourse should be in the most possible modest manner (in a missionary position). He underneath and she above him is considered an impudent act; both at the same level is considered a perverse act... It is forbidden to have intercourse by a direct light... It is also forbidden to have intercourse during the day unless the room is darkened... One is forbidden to look at the genital organ of his wife. Whoever does so is devoid of shame and violates the biblical prescription 'And walk humbly' (in modesty) (Micah 6:8)... It is the duty of every husband to visit his wife on the night she has performed the ritual of immersion; also on the night before he has to set out on a journey, unless he goes out on a sacred mission. When a man sees that his wife is coquetting and primping and trying to please him he is bound to visit her even if it is not the appointed time. From such a union will come worthy children. However, if she demands it openly she is a brazen woman who is considered like a harlot, with whom he must not live altogether.

> When having intercourse his intention should not be to satisfy his personal desire, but to fulfil his obligation to perform his marital duty, like one paying a debt, and to comply to the command of his creator, and that he may have children engaged in the study of Torah and the practice of its precepts. It is also proper to think (during intercourse with a pregnant wife) of improving the embryo; for our rabbis of blessed memory said: 'The first three months of

pregnancy cohabitation is hard on a woman and good for the child; during the last three months it is good for the woman and good for the child for it will cause the child at its birth to be born clean and agile'. If he is overwhelmed by a craving and cohabits with his wife to avert sinful lust, he is likewise destined to receive reward for it, but it is better to conquer his passion.

One should not have intercourse with his wife unless she has a desire for it, but not otherwise and certainly it is forbidden to force her. Nor should one have intercourse with his wife if he hates her or if she hates him and she tells him she does not want his attention although she does consent. If he is determined to divorce her and she is not aware of it, he is not allowed to cohabit with her, even if he does not hate her. Nor should one be with his wife when she is actually asleep nor while he or she is intoxicated. [59]

A more romantically bent medieval sage gives these instructions:

> Therefore you are to engage at first in matters which please her heart and mind and cheer her in order to bring together your thoughts with hers and your intention with hers. You should say such things some of which will urge her to passion and intercourse, to affection, desire and lovemaking, and some which will urge fear of heaven, piety and modesty... And you shall not possess her against her will or force her because in that kind of union there is no divine presence... Rather you should attract her with charming words and seduction and other proper and righteous things as I have explained... Finally, when you are properly ready... do not hasten to arouse your passion until the woman's mind is ready and engage her in words of love so that she will begin to give forth seed first and thus her seed would be like matter and your seed like form as it is said 'When a woman gives forth seed and bears a male child'. [60]

Maimonides, the medieval philosopher and halachist, most succinctly expresses the tension between inherited law and prevalent emotions. "A man's wife is permitted to him, therefore whatever a man wishes to do with his wife he may do. He may have intercourse whenever he pleases, he may kiss any organ he wishes and he may have intercourse in a natural or unnatural manner as long as he does not expend semen to no purpose. And nevertheless the pious way is not to act lightly in this matter and to sanctify himself during intercourse as we have previously explained. And he ought not to deviate from the common practice, for intercourse is really only for procreation."

Thus, while male sexuality is not overlooked, the emphasis is on female sexual satisfaction. Female sexuality, though interior, private and non-initiating, controlled and regulated man's sexual life. We see this most formidably in the laws of Niddah.

b) *Niddah, the menstruant woman and the laws of family purity*

In ancient Judaism, as in most cultures, menstrual blood was assigned a special power, far beyond its simple biological function. This is not surprising in the light of its very real connection to matters of life and death, birth and the destruction of a potential living organism. Menstrual blood was pollution, taboo, impurity, for it represented the ultimate form of pollution — death. The absence of menstrual blood signalled new life; therefore menstrual blood signalled death, as indeed the body issued forth unfertilized or "dead" ova.

Surely that is how it all began. Yet over the span of time, Niddah, the laws of the menstruant woman, were subsumed under a different legal category — family purity. That is the framework in which these laws are operative today. It is fascinating to track the development of the laws of Niddah through history.

The Bible sets forth the initial principles of physical separation during menses.

> When a woman has a discharge and her discharge be blood from her body, she shall remain in her impurity seven days; whoever touches her shall be unclean until evening. Anything that she lies on during her impurity shall be unclean; and anything that she sits on shall be unclean. Anyone who touches her bedding shall wash his clothes, bathe in water and remain unclean until evening and anyone who touches any object on which she has sat shall wash his clothes, bathe in water and remain unclean until evening... and if anyone lies with her, her impurity is communicated to him; he shall be unclean seven days and any bedding on which he lies shall become unclean (Lev. 15:19-24). Do not come near a woman during her period of uncleanness to uncover her nakedness (Lev. 18:19).
>
> If a man lies with a woman in her menses and uncovers her nakedness he has laid bare her flow and she has exposed her blood flow; both of them shall be cut off from all the people (Lev. 20:18).

The law of separation during menses appears in two different contexts: taboos dealing with other forms of defilement, impurity and death (chapter 15); and taboos associated with forbidden sexual relationships (chapter 18). As for the defilements and impurities mentioned in the Bible, these generally are related to death: contact with a dead body, loss of menstrual blood, loss of semen through nocturnal emission, or leprosy — the rampant forces of death taking over as the body's life-giving juices mysteriously cease.

Purification through the living waters symbolizes a renewal, a regeneration of the life forces and such purification was considered a privilege, not a burden. Moreover, there was tangible communal reward: access to the sanctuary and, later, the Temple where one could bring a sacrifice and find oneself in the presence of God who gives life.

The second association concerns the integrity of family relationships. An eternal truth is that society will destroy itself if it lacks ethical sexual relationships. Although no explicit reason is given for forbidding relations during menses, clearly it falls into the category of curbing liaisons that are most open to exploitation or that are most typical of animal rather than human behaviour: incest; sex with individuals not married to each other yet living under the same roof (under the protection of the dominant male members of the household); sex with animals.

After the destruction of the Holy Temple in Jerusalem (70 C.E.) the categories of purity and impurity became almost irrelevant to daily life. A person who came in contact with a dead body, for example, no longer had to undergo ritual immersion, nor did a man who had a bodily discharge. There was no access to Temple and thus no need for purification. The only person still subject to purification rites was the menstruant woman, not for reasons of pollution and taboo but because of proscription of a sexual relationship which had nothing to do with purification for Temple access. Niddah does not apply in an unmarried state or after divorce or widowhood.

Nevertheless, the whole area of Niddah never completely lost its association with impurity and defilement. Indeed, the rabbis strengthened the "fence" around the original prohibition, sometimes building on one base (pollution), sometimes on the other (intimate relations), and most of the time interweaving the two. For example, that which was biblically prohibited for reasons of defilement and included anyone who came in contact with a menstruous woman, such as touching her body, were now prohibited for reasons of sexual arousal and applied only to her husband.[61]

The period of separation was increased during the Talmudic period from 5 to 12 days — 5 for the flow and 7 "clean" days. The Talmud records that it was women themselves who increased the severity of the law.[62] Variations showed up in attitudes as well as practice. We find both pollution and romantic things in the Talmud: "If a menstruous woman passes between two men at the beginning of her menses, she will slay one of them. If she is at the end of her menses she will cause strife between them." "She should be Niddah for seven days following the menses so that she will be as beloved to him (after the period of separation) as on the day of their marriage."[63]

During the medieval period, and in contact with cultures that stressed taboo and the sinfulness of sex, additional prohibitions arose in Jewish law. One was the interdiction against a Niddah entering a synagogue. This taboo is still observed in certain oriental Jewish communities. The purification ritual goes like this: After the minimum 12 days' separation the woman goes to the mikveh, a ritual bath located in the Jewish communities all over the world. The mikveh is a pool, filled with water approximately four feet high. The waters must be "living waters", i.e. gathered from rainfall, lake or sea. Since it is hard to gather a sufficient quantity of natural waters fresh each day, a mixture of tap and natural waters is used. Prior to immersion in the mikveh, the woman bathes herself in a regular bath, shampoos, clips her finger and toe nails, brushes her teeth, and generally cleanses herself thoroughly. This elaborate cleansing ritual indicates that mikveh immersion, which immediately follows the regular bath, is not for hygienic reasons but for purposes of purification and renewal.

A woman enters the mikveh basin, walking down the few steps until she stands in the water at shoulder height. With her arms and legs slightly spread, she dips completely under the water for an instant. A mikveh lady, i.e. attendant, who supervises the immersion, will pronounce it "kosher". Then, whilst still standing in the water, the woman recites the ritual blessing, thanking God for sanctifying us with his commandments and commanding us regarding immersion. Then she dips completely under two more times and is again pronounced kosher by the attendant. She comes up the steps, enters her dressing room, gets dressed and returns home.

Brides come to the mikveh a few days before marriage; converts, male and female, undergo ritual immersion in the mikveh as the final step in their conversions.

Relatively few Jews outside of the Orthodox community observe the laws of Niddah, despite the fact that these laws are considered the essential laws of the Torah and are one of the three primary *mitzvot* (commandments) for women, the other two being the lighting of the candles *(nerot)* and the consecration of a portion of the dough *(hallah)*. Moreover, the building of a mikveh takes precedence in communal life over building a synagogue or buying a Torah scroll.

There are several reasons, I believe, why modern women have rejected these observances: (a) It is an extremely difficult commandment to observe. Sex is as powerful a drive as hunger, yet we have only five fast days a year compared to approximately 150 days of Niddah. (b) Some believe that the laws of Niddah have fallen afoul of brass plumbing. Many people confuse the laws of Niddah with hygiene. This kind of thinking is due in part to an inadequate education on the subject but it is also probably due to the use of words such as "clean" and "unclean" which might not have crept into Jewish tradition had women been part of the process of the unfolding of the law during the last 2000 years. (c) Throughout the medieval period the notion of taboo overpowered the elements of *kedusha*, the holiness of the physical relationship. Taboo and holiness are intimately tied together, that is, setting up of limits so that what happens within them becomes very special. The preponderant focus on taboo left the whole area quite vulnerable. As modern men and women became increasingly disenchanted with taboo, Niddah suffered accordingly.

As a woman who observes this ancient ritual, I believe that Niddah has a significant meaning in a woman's life today and in the shared life of a man and woman who love each other. Niddah serves a broad range of functions in an inter-personal relationship, appropriate to its ebb and flow and to the different stages of growth in a marriage. In the stage when passion and romance dominate, Niddah encourages a man and a woman to develop other techniques of communication as well. In the stage of raising young children and working hard, Niddah is an arbitrarily imposed refresher period. Inasmuch as the law of Niddah regulates the off times, it synchronizes the on times. No law can programme desire, but there is a better chance of the meshing of expectations of couples who observe Niddah. Niddah also can generate a different sense of self for a woman, a feeling of self-autonomy. Some women can generate these feelings out of their own ego strength; for those to whom it is not innate or instinctive, Niddah is a catalyst to this consciousness. And finally like all other mitzvot, the observance of Niddah enables a woman to define herself as a Jew.

Each month, as I immerse myself in the ritual waters, I feel a powerful sense of identity and unity with the generations of Jewish women who lived before me. [64]

It is interesting to note that in the early stages of Jewish feminism, in the late sixties and seventies, the law of Niddah came under strident attack by many Jewish feminists. However, it is a fact that the observance of Niddah is enjoying a revival during the last decade among young women, many of whom undertake it as an expression of their Jewishness and of their femaleness.

c) *Masturbation*

Female masturbation is not mentioned in the sources; by contrast, there are strong sanctions against male masturbation: in the case of a man, "the hand that reaches below the belly-button deserves to be chopped off". [65] This was not law at practice, but strong censure. It seems obvious from other sources on masturbation that while not a punishable offence, it was considered morally wrong. Why then did not female masturbation, which surely also existed, come under rabbinic censure? Because for females there was no transgression involved, whereas male masturbation involved "a spilling of the seed" outside of a woman's body.

d) *Homosexuality*

Homosexuality is considered an abhorrent practice, and is a sexual transgression equal to adultery or incest (Lev. 18 and 20). However, homosexuality is only considered as a sex act between two males. Lesbianism is not mentioned anywhere in the Torah.

The Talmud deals with lesbianism, understanding it as genital contact without penetration. It earns the category in rabbinic literature of "licentiousness" which is a much lesser offense than prostitution and certainly than homosexuality. Lesbianism is viewed as improper, but does not carry any legal significance, not even disqualifying a woman who has engaged in lesbian acts from marrying a priest.

> The father of the sage Samuel did not permit his daughters to sleep together in the same bed. [Was it to prevent lesbianism?] No, rather, his decision was so as not to accustom them to sleep together with a foreign body (outside of marriage). [66]

A third source regarding lesbianism comes from the medieval code compiled by Maimonides:

> Women are forbidden to engage in lesbian practices with one another... as it is said 'You shall not copy the practices of the land of Egypt...' (Lev.18:3)... Although such an act is forbidden, the perpetrators are not liable for flogging since there is no specific negative commandment prohibiting it, nor is actual intercourse involved... It behooves the court, however, to administer the flogging prescribed for rebelliousness, since they (the lesbians) performed a forbidden act.
> A man should be particularly strict with his wife in this matter and should prevent women known to indulge in such practices from visiting her and she from visiting them. [67]

Aside from the fact of no prohibition and no intercourse, one wonders why there are so few references to lesbianism as compared with the extensive treatment in Torah and Talmud of other aspects of sexuality. Three possibilities come to mind: i) female sexuality was so extensively defined in relation to one's husband, that lesbianism simply did not exist; ii) women were understood to be more chaste, pure and restrained than men; iii) men wrote the books and didn't incorporate women's experiences. I believe the first is the most likely explanation.

e) *Rape*

The rape laws in Judaism are most complex. On a personal note: I originally approached this subject with feelings of anger, for it has always seemed to me that the rape laws in the Bible, as in every legal system to date, were patently unfair. By their very leniency in punishment of the rapist, they implied a measure of complicity on the part of the women — the old "She asked for it" slur. These attitudes fall far short of a woman's perception of rape — that a woman is wholly the victim and that a rapist is equal to a murderer and deserving of most severe punishment. After going through the rabbinic sources I came away with a different understanding of the Torah's laws on this subject and a deeper admiration for the rabbinic process. While not every single source is acceptable, nor the punishment severe enough, the bulk of rabbinic sources indicate a full understanding of the trauma and violation that a woman feels, as well as her total victimization.

The biblical laws on rape are as follows:

> In the case of a virgin who is pledged to a man, if another man comes upon her in town and lies with her you shall take the two of them out to the gate of that town and stone them to death: the maiden because she did not cry for help in the town, and the man because he violated his neighbour's betrothed. Thus you will sweep away evil from your midst. But if the man comes upon the engaged woman in the open country and the man seizes her and lies with her by force, only the man who lay with the woman shall die, but you shall do nothing to the woman. The woman is not guilty of a capital offence. For this case is like that of a man attacking another and murdering him. He came upon her in the open: although the engaged maiden cried for help, there was none to save her. If a man comes upon a virgin who is not engaged and he seizes her and lies with her and they are discovered, the man who lay with her shall pay the girl's father 50 shekels of silver and she shall be his wife. Because he has violated her he can never have the right to divorce her (Deut. 22:23-29).

There are several issues at hand here. One is the distinction between a betrothed virgin and an unbetrothed virgin. A betrothed virgin is considered as a married woman and the crime becomes then one of adultery as well as rape, punishable by stoning. A second issue is that of complicity. The barometer of complicity is whether the woman cried out, which means that she should have prevented it and did not. If she did not, then she is considered to be an accomplice. However, if the rape took place in a field where there was no-one around to save her, her crying out for help would have made no difference. In that case, her testimony of whether or not she was raped is sufficient. Third, and most problematic, is the punishment for a man who rapes an unbetrothed maiden: the fine is paid to her father and the rapist is obligated to marry her.

The explanation, or rationalization, is not much better: (a) once she had lost her virginity and was shamed, she was no longer quite as marriageable and the likelihood was that no-one else would have her. So this was a protection for her — that she not go through life unmarried; (b) she did not have to accept the man in marriage, but if she was willing to, then he was compelled to marry her and was responsible for her for the rest of his life; (c) the fine was paid to the father to compensate for his loss of a bride price for a virgin.

The rabbis deal at great length with all of these issues. They introduce several new concepts: (a) The issue of psychological pain for the woman. (b) Compensation for indignity, blemish, pain in addition to the statutory fine. However, these were still paid to the father, who had full responsibility for his dependent daughter. (c) A distinction between a seducer and a violator (both guilty), in the case of an unmarried virgin. (d) Defining rape as any sex act begun under compulsion. Even if a woman consented or liked it towards the end (only a man could think this) she was completely innocent of any degree of complicity. (e) Changing the criteria of complicity from that of location to that of subjective judgment of the woman. If she did not cry out because of fear, that was sufficient to remove the taint of complicity. (f) Extending the concept of rape to the marriage relationship as well. Marital rape is explicitly forbidden in Judaism.[68]

While great compassion for and total exoneration of women can be found in rabbinic sources, insufficient attention is paid to the punishment for a rapist. A great pity, for even though punishment now lies in the hands of civil law, religious tradition could have exerted a strong influence on civil structures in building up protections for women against this heinous crime.

f) *Incest*

Incest and adultery were considered sexual transgressions, the punishment of which was death. Like other sexual prohibitions, which were considered immoral, incest and adultery were perceived as a real and present danger to the social order and to the integrity of that holy institution — marriage. Incest was one of the three transgressions for which one should choose martyrdom rather than commit the act, even under coercion.[69]

The biblical laws regarding incest are addressed to the male; however, they are applied to men and women equally. Thus, though the verses in Leviticus (chap. 20) mention only female relatives of a man — whom the Torah is addressing — the prohibition extends to males in the same relationship to a woman. Moreover, though the prohibition is addressed to the aggressor, both parties in an incestual relationship are punished equally.

Essentially, the prohibition includes all females in a four-generation family: mothers, sisters and daughters; also aunts, sisters, step-sisters, mothers-in-law, step-daughters, daughters of a sister-in law, daughters-in-law and grand-daughters. The one exception is nieces. A man is permitted to marry his brothers' or sisters' daughter. Interestingly, though halacha still does not forbid it, Israeli law does forbid marriage to a niece.

Why is the language addressed to a man? Because it was understood that men were the initiators and aggressors in a sexual relationship. Moreover, in a patriarchal structure, men were heads of households and protectors of the women within them. Thus, the laws of incest were extended broadly beyond the nuclear family, to protect women (whose defences would be down) from their protectors as well as from sexual exploitation outside of the household. As Maimonides writes: "All illicit unions with females have one thing in common: namely, that in most cases these females are constantly in the company of the male in his house and that they are easy of access for him and can be easily controlled by him, there being no difficulty in making them come into his presence; and no judge could blame the male for their being with him."[70]

Although the Bible contains several incidences of incest — Lot's daughters, Judah and Tamar, Amnon and Tamar — the rabbinic literature records no discussion of an actual incestuous relationship. It was probably an extremely rare phenomenon in Jewish life, in part, because the "fences" against forbidden sexual relationships were so strong. Other than with immediate family members, a man was not permitted to be in a room alone with a woman with whom a sexual relationship was forbidden, unless the door remained open the entire time.[71]

g) *Pre-marital sex*

Technically speaking, if a sexual relationship does not fall into the category of adultery, incest, or homosexuality, it is not in violation of an explicit biblical prohibition. If a man and woman have an exclusive sexual relationship, it is considered as a common law marriage. If such a relationship ends, and the woman moves on to another relationship without securing a *gett*, then it is as if she were an adulteress still married to the first man, yet having sex with another.

However, Talmudic law "transformed" this biblical understanding. As mentioned above, cohabitation was ruled out as a proper or legitimate means of constituting a marriage. Therefore, any sex outside of marriage and without the institution of marriage was considered *zenut*, an act of promiscuity and immorality.

While there is no explicit rabbinic law forbidding pre-marital sex, there are many strong statements judging it. Moreover, the "fence" around sexual relations effectively served to limit the possibilities: the rabbis prohibited an unmarried couple to be alone, behind closed doors.

h) *Adultery*

The prohibition against adultery is part of the holiness code, included in the list of forbidden sexual relationships (Lev. 18). It is also the substance of two of the Ten Commandments: "Thou shalt not commit adultery" and "Thou shalt not covet thy neighbour's wife..." which the rabbis explain not only can lead to adultery but is equivalent to adultery of the heart.[72]

Clearly, a double standard exists regarding adultery: if a married man engages in a sexual act with an unmarried woman, it is not considered punishable as adultery, yet if a married woman engages in sex with an unmarried man, the act is considered adulterous and both are punished. The double standard grows out of the fact that a man could have more than one wife or concubines, while a woman's sexuality was considered to be equivalent to a man's exclusive property.[73]

The punishment prescribed in the Torah for adultery is death by stoning. However, in other biblical references, it seems this was not the practice. For an adulterous woman, the penalty was divorce, if her husband so desired. For an adulterous man — again the double standard; it seems he was not required to divorce his wife. If a woman was divorced by her husband, she could not marry her adulterer nor ever remarry her husband.

The biblical law of divorce (Deut. 23:1-4) states that if a man finds *ervat davar* in his wife, he may divorce her. Above, I translated *ervat davar* as something unseemly. That is the majority Talmudic interpretation. However, there was a significant minority opinion that held that *ervat davar* means only adultery (*ervah* is the word used in Lev. 18 with regard to forbidden sexual relationships). Thus, adultery was held by this school of thought to be the only valid reason for divorce. Jewish Christians and subsequently Christianity followed this minority position and thereby forbade divorce.

The Torah records the ordeal, by bitter waters of the Sotah, of the errant woman: if a man suspected his wife of adultery, he would bring her to the priest and make the accusation. The priest would loosen her hair (a sign of prostitution) and say to her: "If you have not gone astray, you will be immune to these waters, but if you are guilty of having carnal relations with a man other than your husband, the Lord will make a curse on you and these waters will induce a spell that will cause your belly to distend and your thighs to sag..."[74] The woman must repeat "Amen, Amen". (Numbers 5:11ff)

Many have pointed out that in comparison to other trials-by-ordeal recorded in history — e.g. burning the tongue, being submerged under water, etc. — this one was relatively mild: loosened hair, taking an oath/ Amen, and drinking waters with a bit of earth mixed in. It was almost a guarantee for a woman to pass the test. Scholars interpret this trial not as one that would convict an adulterer, but rather as one that would exonerate the innocent and clear all suspicion.[75] In a closely-knit community, suspicion of adultery was hard to dispel, and there would always be lingering doubts. The bitter waters ordeal was a simple way to clear her name, with the stamp of divine confirmation and priestly sanction.[76] This understanding of the laws of Sotah grew in part out of the fact that the husband did not gain anything in accusing her publicly; in fact, if he falsely accused her, he forever lost the right to divorce her.

A whole Talmudic tractate is devoted to the issue of Sotah, yet by the time of the Talmud the discussion had become entirely academic. The trial-by-ordeal had long since stopped. "When adulterers increased the bitter waters ceased... the efficacy of the bitter waters depended on a husband's guiltlessness..."

The real punishment in cases of adultery is carried by the children of such an illicit union. They are considered *mamzerim*, unmarriageable to any other Jew.[77] Oftentimes, the rabbis tried to look the other way, by considering the children as legitimate children of the husband and not of the lover. The discussion of mamzerim, which is a greater problem today than at any other time in Jewish history because of Reform Judaism's stance on divorce law, is highly complex and beyond the purview of this paper.[78]

i) *Polygamy*
Polygamy was permitted; polyandry forbidden. This was a general feature of patriarchal cultures, probably a reflection of the biological fact that maternity was always self-evident but paternity of a child was not.

However, beyond the lives of the patriarchs, and throughout all of scriptures, there is only one other recorded instance of a polygynous marriage — other than for kings — and the narrative highlights the friction and disharmony (2 Sam.). In rabbinic literature, only monogamous marriages are referred to — both among rabbis and the general population. Still, the principle of polygyny is not formally revoked: "If a man says to a woman: 'Become betrothed to half of me' (and she accepts), then she is betrothed. If he says to her, 'Half of you is betrothed to me', she is not betrothed."[79]

The rabbis also tightened the conditions so as to make polygynous marriages untenable — a man had to perform the obligation of Onah equally for each wife and had to treat all of them equally in all respects, an impossible feat!

In the medieval period, under the influence of Christianity, which forbade polygyny, Jewish law was formally revised. Though polygyny had not been practised amongst Jews for several thousand years, in the 10th century C.E. the halacha incorporated a *takkanah*, a rabbinic ruling that placed a ban of excommunication on anyone entering into a polygynous marriage.[80] (One could not rewrite biblical law; one could subvert its intention by different legal means.)

Interestingly, the ban was operative only for European Jewry, in Christian countries. Jews who resided in Islamic countries, where polygyny was permitted, continued the practice of multiple wives. In 1948, with the creation of the state of Israel, the Chief Rabbinate extended the ban/prohibition to Jews of all nationalities.

j) *Celibacy*
In Judaism, celibacy is not a popular or even highly valued model, either for men or for women. Given the primacy of procreation, this is

quite understandable. History records few celibates, called Nazirites, who take upon themselves a vow to abstain from worldly pleasures such as wine and sex.

k) *Virginity, chastity, modesty*

Virginity: A very high value was placed on female virginity. We noted this above, in connection with the rape laws; virgins were compensated differently from non-virgins. Similarly, in the standard *ketubah* (marriage contract), a virgin is eligible for alimony payment twice as large as that for a non-virgin.

A priest was not permitted to marry a widow, a divorcee, or a prostitute. What did these three types of women have in common? The loss of virginity. In ancient Israel, the bedsheets were examined after the wedding night for signs of virginity. A man could divorce his wife and be free of alimony if she came to the marriage as a non-virgin.

Why was virginity so important? Because it was a tangible measure of fidelity. Throughout scriptures, virginity is the paradigm for the faithfulness of the Jewish people to God. [81]

Chastity: Over and above the double standard that existed in the laws of adultery and polygamy, chastity was an optimal value for men and women alike. Chastity was not limited to relationships outside of marriage, nor, for that matter, to behaviour alone; one must be chaste even in marriage and must also have chaste thoughts. "Do not have your mind on another when you are making love to this one", enjoined the Talmud. This proscription also meant that a man should not arouse himself by artificial means, including fantasy of a third party. The sages of the Talmud were not only teachers, they were also models of behaviour. Thus, "Scholars should not go to their wives like roosters." [82]

Modesty: While generally considered a virtue for all human beings, modesty was more highly emphasized in relation to women — modesty of dress, of demeanour, of behaviour. The following midrashic commentary on the creation of woman from a rib sums it up well: "And God said, I will not create her from the head, lest she hold her head up too proudly; nor from the eye, lest she become a coquette, nor from the ear, lest she become an eavesdropper; nor from the mouth, lest she become too talkative; nor from the heart, lest she become jealous; nor from the hand, lest she become acquisitive; nor from the foot, lest she be a gadabout; but from a part of the body that is hidden, that she be modest." [83]

l) *A woman's body*

Now that I have described some of the laws pertaining to female sexuality — which is more positive than negative — I feel perfectly unconstrained to cite the misogynist statements concerning a woman's body. These had limited impact on the unfolding of the law. Nevertheless, they cannot be dismissed altogether, for they reflect two fundamental biases: that men wrote the sources; that women were often viewed primarily in terms of their sexuality. "When a daughter is born, a man gains worries for the rest of his life. He cannot sleep at night out of fear for her. When she is small, he worries that she might be seduced; when she grows to be a maiden, he worries that she will become promiscuous; when mature — that she will not marry; when married — that she will not have children; when old — that she will produce witchcraft."[84]

"A woman's body (...ankle...toe) is a source of temptation."[85] "A man should not walk behind a woman."[86] "To gaze on the toe of a woman is as if one were to gaze on her private place."[87] The Bible tells us that Jewish males were admonished by Moses not to have sex with their wives for three days prior to receiving the Torah (Exodus 13:1).

Tradition records many more positive value statements about women than negative or sexist ones. Moreover, as I indicated a moment ago, these statements hardly affected women's lives or freedom of movement. Thus, it has always seemed to me to be largely irrelevant, and to make capital of negative value statements in tradition is simply to flail a dead horse.

Suddenly, however, I have come to a different realization: that a domino effect operates here, too, that perhaps a connection does exist between these negative judgements about female sexuality and other areas of Jewish law and life.

A significant principle obtains in Judaism regarding women and the performance of *mitzvot* (commandments). Women are exempt from time-bound positive commandments — i.e. those rituals and obligations that must be performed within a specific period of time, such as morning, afternoon, and evening prayers recited only in the appropriate spans of time. No reason is given for this exemption in the Talmud, where the principle is laid down, but post-Talmudic sources suggest that the open-ended nature of tasks of nurture and family construction would pose a conflict with time-bound ritual obligations.[88]

In 1973, an important piece of scholarship was published by an American rabbi on the issue of women's exemption.[89] Goaded by the feminist critique of sexism in Jewish ritual life, Saul Berman analyzed the exemption/exclusion of women from certain obligations, and came up with a novel understanding: that the exemptions had less to do with time than with space — or place. Women were exempt from certain (though not all) rituals that would take them into the public sector — from communal prayer (in the synagogue), from daily study of Torah (the *beit midrash*, or house of study), from serving as witnesses (in courts of law). As in most pre-feminist cultures, females were distanced from roles in culture and society.

Perhaps the relatively few and "harmless" misogynous statements regarding female sexuality that had crept into the sources provide a subtle yet significant key of a deep-seated suspicion and fear of female sexuality that found expression in other seemingly unrelated measures defining women's role in Judaism.

V. The transmission of values

Where does the solution lie? Certainly, we cannot re-write the sources, nor would we want to, for that is part of our history and our tradition. The solution does not lie, therefore, in direct confrontation with the sources, for that would use up enormous time and energy and would lead nowhere.

How, then, do we overcome thousands of years of ambivalence regarding female sexuality and bodily functions — fear, power, respect, temptation, infatuation, disgust, admiration, defilement, glorification, subordination, appreciation?

Judaism has built up remarkable and multiple structures for transmission of values. Primary among them is the family and the home. One of the central commandments is a pedagogic one: "And you shall teach them (tradition, laws, and values) to your children. And you shall speak of them when you are sitting at home, when you go out into the streets, when you lie down, and when you rise up" (Deut. 4:7). The intergenerational responsibility has always featured prominently in Jewish life.

Second, the synagogue was not only the place of prayer, but also of study. The Torah is read in entirety each year in the synagogue, Sabbath by Sabbath. It is interpreted through rabbinical sources of all previous generations.

Third, because of the primary emphasis on education of the young, an elaborate educational system has been built up through the ages. Jews have had a system equivalent to universal public education for several thousands of years.

But family and institutions are also a sieve for values of contemporary culture. A strength of Judaism is that it has always incorporated, gradually and in varying degrees, the values of contemporary culture so as to be part of history and not outside of it.

Which brings us to the question of process. There are two elements to process. One is the continuous explication and interpretation of inherited tradition. "Gradual and varying degrees" are particularly valuable components, enabling Judaism of the twentieth century to remain connected to the past, yet refreshed and renewed by the present. Thus, hermeneutics made it possible for halacha to remain continuous with revelation, yet adapt itself to the needs of a living community. While it will not be achieved overnight, the new understanding of women in this generation will become an integral part of Jewish values and not at odds with them.

A second dimension to process is the action orientation of Judaism. Mitzvot — observances, commandments, deeds, performance, ritual, obligations, restraints — these are the measures of a life. One cannot simply express values — one must live them, religious and ethical values alike. In Judaism, what you say is less important than how you act. The premise is that deeds as often bring about change in values as grow out of them. The examined life is a life not only of sentiments and emotions, but of actions.

That is why the new gains achieved during the last decade in areas of women and ritual, women and religious leadership, women and liturgy, women and public roles, are of such significance in relation to female sexuality and bodily functions. As the new religious and ritual celebration of women will find its full halachic expressions, so, too, will the underlying attitudes towards female sexuality undergo change. Any lingering stigma will be rooted out in the process of reinterpreting law, practice, and custom.

Conclusions

Female sexuality in Judaism can be characterized as a dialectic. It runs through the sources from earliest times until our own. Within a certain range, this dialectic allowed for majority and minority opinions; for human input in selecting inherited values by which to model human behaviour; for the influence of other cultures which were either integrated or rejected.

Someone else could have written this paper in an entirely different manner — wholly critical, selecting only misogynist sources; or wholly positive, selecting only those that glorified and apologized. I have tried to select moderate sources of each type, rather than extreme ones, because I believe they are a more accurate reflection of where we stand today in

Judaism, closer now than at any time in history to bridging the gaps that exist between male perception and the reality of female sexuality.

Having said that, I want to say a final word about role distinctiveness, which I have indicated above, as a prominent feature of Judaism.

I believe we have to walk a fine line regarding role distinctiveness. Role distinctiveness can spill over into sexism, and we must be vigilant that this not happen. Still, there should be left a bit of mystery about female sexuality. It is something quite mysterious, if not magical, what a woman's body can do. To obliterate all distinctions is to blur the lines of human sexuality, which might lead to more chaos and confusion than would be healthy for male or female. It would also make life more dull. We should take care to preserve the mystery and majesty of human sexuality.

Moreover, role distinctiveness need not in every single instance signify inequity. Ultimately, sexual equality means not sameness or identicality but human dignity, value, and appreciation of the godliness in male and female, body and soul alike.

We must take the dialectic in a new direction — distinctive yet equal, mysterious yet not hierarchical. "And God created humankind in His image, male and female He created them." Sexually distinctive, but of equal value in the eys of God. There it is, at the very source, waiting to be renewed. As women and men work towards equality and elimination of hierarchy, we understand that we are bringing our traditions closer to their own best values.

NOTES

[1] There is a range of belief as to what constituted revelation at Sinai. Most traditional Jews believe that, in addition to the Pentateuch, some of the interpretations and future applications were made known at Sinai; most liberal Jews believe that Sinai was but the beginning of a process that took root over the course of many centuries. In either case, there is an ongoing dynamic of interpretation in which both tradition and present values continuously interact and thereby bring all aspects of life within a religious framework.

[2] This is the traditional dating of the Talmud. Contemporary scholarship has shown that the Talmud contains insertions from the 6th and 7th centuries as well.

[3] This theme underlies much of rabbinic tradition, so any one citation does not quite do it justice. The following sampling of sources, however, will give the reader some idea of the pervasiveness of the "image of God" concept in Jewish tradition; Jerusalem Talmud (J.T.) Nederam 30b, (ch. 9, Halacha 4); Babylonian Talmud (B.T.) Sanhedrin 37a; B.T. Shabbat 133b; Vayikra Rabbah ch. 34, para. 3. See also Maimonides, Mishnah Torah (M.), Hilchot Deot, ch. 1, para. 5-6; for a modern commentary, see also S.R. Hirsch, *The Law Relating to Moral Dispositions and Ethical Conduct, Genesis*, New York, Jewish Press, 1971, p.33.

42   Women, Religion and Sexuality

[4] For a fuller discussion of this biblical concept as the basis for women's equality, see Blu Greenberg, *On Women and Judaism: A View From Tradition*, Jewish Publication Society, 1981, pp.39-56.

[5] B.T. Yevamot 61a.

[6] See Anne McGraw Bennet, "Overcoming the Biblical and Traditional Subordination of Women," in *Biblical Religion*, Vol. 1, Spring 1974, p.28.

[7] See Phyllis Tribble, "Depatriarchalizing in Biblical Interpretation", *Journal of American Academy of Religion*, Vol. 41, No.1, March 1973, p.40.

[8] Some have suggested that the prelapsarian tradition was a positive one towards women and the postlapsarian tradition a misogynist one. See Leonard Swidler, *Women in Judaism*, Scarecrow Press, 1976, ch. 1. I disagree with Swidler; I believe the two attitudes coexisted all the way through.

[9] B.T. Niddarim 31b.

[10] B.T. Sanhedrin 43a.

[11] B.T. Baba Mezia 59a.

[12] B.T. Shabbat 33b.

[13] B.T. Nedarin 45b.

[14] B.T. Kiddushin 82b.

[15] See P. Birnbaum, Daily Prayer Book, p.761.

[16] B.T. Berachot 45a.

[17] B.T. Berachot 45b.

[18] This is certainly true of post Talmudic law, but even in the Talmud we find ways for a woman to inherit directly from her father's estates. See B.T. Baba Batra 131b. For a fuller discussion, see Judith Hauptman, *Images of Women in the Talmud*, p.195; Rosemary Radford-Ruether, *Religion and Sexism*, New York, Simon and Schuster, 1984.

[19] (Mishnah) Baba Batra, 9:1.

[20] For example, B.T. Shavout 30a.

[21] B.T. Yevamot 63-65.

[22] B.T. Yevamot 113a.

[23] B.T. Sotah 20a.

[24] *Ethics of the Fathers*, 5:21.

[25] B.T. Kiddushin 21:30.

[26] B.T. Sanhedrin 76a.

[27] B.T. Yevamot 62b.

[28] B.T. Kiddushin 41a.

[29] See B.T. Kiddushin 2a on the use of the phrase "is acquired."

[30] M. Ketubot 7:8.

[31] Numbers 30:9, 13, 14.

[32] For example, he was obliged to provide her with food, clothing, shelter, sexual satisfaction, medical and dental care, ransom if necessary, guarantees of support in event of death or divorce; she was required to grind flour, bake bread, wash clothes, cook food, nurse the children, make his bed, work in wool, fill his cup and wash his face, hands and feet.

[33] B.T. Baba Mezia 59a.

[34] B.T. Yevamot 62b.

[35] Swidler, *op. cit.*, p.79.

[36] B.T. Kedushin 24b; 9b.

[37] For a fuller discussion, Greenberg, *op. cit.*, pp.125 ff.

[38] B.T. Yevamot 651a-b.

[39] M. Ketubot 5:8-9.

[40] B.T. Ketubot 110b.

[41] M. Ketubot 7:9.

[42] *Ibid.*, 5:8.

[43] Shulkhan Arukh, Even Ha'ezer 154:3.

[44] For a more comprehensive discussion of Jewish laws of death and mourning, see Maurice Lamm, *The Jewish Way in Death and Mourning*, New York, Jonathan David Publishers, 1969.

[45] B.T. Sanhedrin 74b, Berachot 21b.

[46] The Jewish Women's Resource Center, 9 East 65 Street, New York City, is a central repository for many different forms of this and other rituals for women that are being newly created in our times.

[47] B.T. Yevamot 65b.

[48] Genesis 1:28.

[49] The definitive scholarly work on this subject as well as on abortion is David Feldman, *Material Relations, Birth Control, and Abortion in Jewish Law*, New York, Schocken Books, 1968.

[50] Nachmanides, *Commentary on the Torah*, Ex. 21:11.

[51] B.T. Bava Mezia 84a.

[52] B.T. Sanhedrin 7a.

[53] See commentary of Rashi and also Nachmanides on Genesis 3:26.

[54] B.T. Ketubot 62b.

[55] B.T. Pesachim 72b.

[56] B.T. Ta'anit 1:6.

[57] B.T. Yevamot 62b.

[58] B.T. Niddah 31b.

[59] Schulchan Aruch, Even Ha'ezer, *The Laws of Chastity*.

[60] Iggeret Hakodesh, attributed to Nachmanides ch. 6, The Fifth Way Concerning the Quality of Intercourse.

[61] B.T. Shabbat 12a-b.

[62] B.T. Niddah 31b.

[63] Pesachim IIIa.

[64] Niddah 31b.

[65] For a more extended analysis of the laws and a fuller discussion of the interpersonal themes, see my chapter, in defense of the daughters of Israel, *On Women and Judaism*, pp.105-123.

[66] B.T. Niddah 13a.

[67] B.T. Shabbat 65a-b.

[68] Maimonides, *Guide to the Perplexed*, BK, III:49.

[69] For a full discussion on rape laws, see Louis Epstein, *Sex Laws in Judaism*.

[70] Maimonides, *Mishneh Torah*, Hilchot Issurei Biah 21:8.

[71] See Epstein, *op. cit.*, for a full discussion of the laws of chaperonage, pp. 119-131.

[72] There is some indication in rabbinic literature that an adulterer could pay a fine to the husband as punishment for his act and as settlement of the claim. I say "almost" because a man could not "sell" his wife's sexuality.

[73] B.T. Sotah 17b.

[74] See Rachel Biale, *Women and Jewish Law*, New York, Schocken, 1984, p.187 and footnote 10.

[75] B.T. Sotah 17b.

[76] B.T. Josephta Sotah 14:41ff.

[77] Actually, they are marriageable only to other "mamzerim".

[78] B.T. Kiddushin 7a.

[79] Many individual communities instituted this procedure; in the 10th century a takkanah was promulgated by Rabbenu Gershom which formally prohibited polygyny. It was widely accepted by European Jewry, which had not ever practiced polygyny, but was not accepted as binding by Sephardic Jewry (Jews of oriental countries) where the practice of multiple wives was quite common, in fact a sign of status.

[80] See Ezekiel 23 and Hosea 2:14.

[81] B.T. Nedarim 20.

[82] Midrash Rabbah Genesis 18:2.

[83] B.T. Sanhedrin 100b.

[84] B.T. Berachot 24a.

[85] B.T. Berachot 61a.

[86] B.T. Shabbat 64b.

[87] B.T. Kiddushin 29a-b.

[88] For example, Sefer Abudraham ha-Shalem (Jerusalem, 1959) Order of the Weekday Prayers — Mourning Blessings.

[89] Saul Berman, "The Status of Women in Halakhic Judaism," *Tradition* 14, Winter 1973, pp.5-28.

Women and Sexuality: Traditions and Progress

Pnina Navè Levinson

This article attempts to give an overview of beliefs and practices pertaining to women as these have developed in reformed and liberal Jewish congregations in a number of countries, contrasting them to beliefs and practices of Orthodox Judaism. It seeks to complement the preceding paper.

A. Preliminaries

1. When describing Judaism we have to note that the vast majority of religious Jews belong to streams and organized movements outside those of Orthodoxy. Within the many orthodoxies — Eastern European, Western, Asian, African — mystical and anti-mystical groups foster their own special views and customs, often claiming to be the only true way. Thus, in some Orthodox communities the use of wigs to cover the shorn hair demanded by some authorities has become a sign of the married woman, presumably signalling special chastity or modesty. Others regard wigs as singularly immodest and prefer a kerchief or cap. Non-Westerns draw the line between unmarried and married modesty differently: open hair for the former, and braids worn as long as they grow for the latter. This is just one example of literally thousands of different customs concerning the central Orthodox concept of chastity.

2. To be as objective as possible, we need to seek out and compare traditions concerning men when considering those about women. Indeed, we find negative and positive statements in the Bible about men and about women, as well as in the *Mishnah*, the *Gemara*, and the vast body of *Agadah*, the narrative theology of the ancient and medieval rabbis. Today, Jewish men and women of all movements add their specific

Agadah, also called *Midrash*, "hermeneutics", to the ever-growing treasure of ongoing revelation.

3. Also, we have to differentiate between fundamentalist positions and other open-ended Jewish positions. For fundamentalists, Torah and Tradition are static values insofar as everything is contained in *Halakhah*, religious law, seen as immutable legislation. Thus, when changes are considered necessary by feminist men and women, the answer usually given is that Halakhah is against the idea of change; or, that Halakhah is divine and therefore non-democratic. Every non-fundamentalist concept of Judaism sees religious law as man-made, often inspired, always striving to assure a continuation of Jewish life, and therefore always having been open to change. The tragedy of Orthodoxy today is that in reaction to nineteenth century religious modernization, the usual halakhic processes of change and adaptation to life conditions have been curtailed in many areas. This is true in relation to religious laws concerning women. Most ultra-Orthodox movements have introduced Torah studies for girls, since the home and neighbourhood no longer impart the knowledge necessary to pursue the prescribed life-style. However, they frown on co-education as practised by moderate Orthodoxy. There seems to be no limit to the dangers inherent in contact with female teachers, whatever their age.

Thus, the octogenarian professor of Bible, Nehama Leibowitz of Tel Aviv University, who is strictly Orthodox and always wears a cap, was asked to lecture from behind a curtain to male Talmud students, according to an ancient custom for female teachers.[1]

It is both a weakness and a strength of tradition that *custom is equal to law*.[2] While assuring in some cases that practice is just as important as theory, thereby recognizing *de facto* the authority of the community, it nevertheless prevents adaptations which are possible by law. Interestingly, new practices of Reform and Conservative communities crept into Orthodox ones and became customary and are not seen as undermining chastity. Thus men and women mingle in synagogues at weddings, embrace and kiss. The same is true of family members after services, although men and women still sit in separate sections. With the growing trend towards fundamentalism, new young rabbis are disturbed by this. Recently, the second largest Orthodox congregation in London was required by their young rabbi to refrain from kissing, as kisses are immodest and meaningless, and because Christians do not kiss in church.[3]

4. What about customs, habits, and fears of sexual taboos? Anxieties about these matters must be brought to light and examined to find out whether such traditions help or hinder the achievement of a meaningful Jewish life. After all, this is the main interest of religious Jews. If people abstain from practising their religion, as about half of American Jews do, (the percentage is higher in France and England), Judaism will inevitably disappear. So it is important that the various Jewish religious movements recognize the validity of each others' efforts. In revitalizing Jewish life, one might use the method of the British theologian, Rabbi Louis Jacobs. A non-fundamentalist traditionalist, he looks for the spiritual values in laws and customs. Some will have to be discarded or changed. His three categories are: a) the significant; b) the meaningless; c) the harmful. In the last category there are "very few, and largely in the area of women's rights". While fundamentalists are convinced that these are only seeming injustices, since they stem from God who is just, Jacobs joins us in declaring that unjust laws cannot claim the allegiance of Jews.[4] One of the scholars analysing this category of harmful laws concerning women, especially in the area of Orthodox divorce procedures, is Rabbi Professor Emanuel Rackman, Chancellor of the Orthodox Bar-Ilan University in Israel.[5]

B. Theology

Jewish understanding of biblical anthropomorphy, human form of the Godhead — like the voice, hand, emotions, of the Creator — says that these are ways of expressing functions, or actions, in metaphors, word pictures. God has no physical aspects, yet the parallel to ha-Adam, humankind (not "the Male"!), exists: being in "the Divine image" means freedom of will — which constitutes the difference between angels, who are all-good, and animals, who have no free choice.[6] "Walking in God's ways", "imitating Divinity" means compassionate and just reaching out to other human beings. Being made male and female points to emotional and ethical complementary elements in our make-up, both being symbols or metaphors, for Divine aspects. Thus, in the so-called second creation story it does not say that man needs a female helpmate, but the Hebrew male noun *ezer* is used (Gen. 2:18) meaning help. The same word is used of God (Psalms 121:1,2). It is an expression of strength rather than of second-class existence. Therefore ancient rabbis stressed that the male should *not* "rule", subdue, the female. Gen. 3:16 has for them the ethical implication that the man should ask for his wife's preferences in sexual pleasure.[7] As for the rib story, their advice was to see the Creator as a sculptor, allowing us to look at the process of forming humankind: the word translated *rib, tzela*, also means "side". The first couple, ha-Adam, were formed as one unit, they could only move together, but could not face each other. Thus the second stage of their making was to split this unit so that two backs were formed, making it also necessary to first anaesthetize the not-yet-two beings.[8] Thus "the side" was taken. It is told that a Roman lady asked a Galilean rabbi (such discourses were part of ancient life): Why did God steal in order to make woman? His answer: If someone deposits with you an ounce of silver in secret and you return him a pound (=12 ounces) of silver openly, is that theft?[9] Here we have an ancient tradition also found in Plato. It should be pondered upon in addition to the dialectical explanation which stems from Rabbi Soloveitchik.[10]

Where do we find the Divine example for humanity? Let a few biblical quotations suffice. In Isaiah 66:13 God is heard saying: "As a mother comforts her son so will I comfort you."[11] God's mercy is really mothering in Hebrew. Mercy, *rahameem*, is derived from *raheem*, which actually means love in Aramaic and Arabic, while the root word is *rehem*, uterus. Thus, Divine love and mercy are bound up with the deep feeling of womb and birth. The biblical *rahoom*, as one of God's attributes (Ex. 34:6) thus conveys the happiness of being embraced, safe and saved.

If dialectical tension exists in us, its archetype is found within the Godhead. Thus, God is "far" and "near". The nearness is indicated by his female aspect, the Shekhinah, "indwelling". This post-biblical word is derived from the biblical verb *shakhan*, dwell, as in Exodus 29:45: "I will abide among the Israelites, and I will be their God."[12] First understood without any special stress on femininity, Shekhinah in the course of the millennia was charged with this content, especially in the mystical movements and their literature. Thus, in women's prayers in the old Judaeo-German language one finds the pious term "Oh you dear and holy Shekhinah" side by side with "dear God". In kabbalistic theory, the Sabbath is a bride and as such, identical with the Shekhinah. Making love on Friday night, the first half of the Sabbath, always has been a special aspect of Judaism. For the mystics it is the loving human response to the divine harmony of the hidden God and his Shekhinah.[13] Many Jews shy away from Shekhinah piety, while for others it is an important emotive and cognitive core of their belief. The line runs across the different movements. Recently, some Jewish theologians have begun to refer to God as he/she, or just she. All are of the opinion that the Godhead has no physical body. This should allay fears of paganism, or idolatry, or a too great nearness of expression to Catholic Christianity.*

C. Liberal Judaism and traditions about women

1. PLURAL JUDAISM

Reforms in Judaism began in the 19th century in Germany. The reformers saw themselves as continuing an ongoing process at a time when for many, Judaism had become so out-dated that it seemed impossible to bridge everyday Jewish life with much of tradition. Scholars and laity alike developed the adaptations in theology and practice which became known as Reform, Liberal or Progressive Judaism. After some generations this movement became widespread in the Western world.[14] In reaction to this, another one grew, the Historical School, which in America took the name Conservative Judaism.[15] Together they account for well over two thirds of religious Jewry. Both have important educational systems and colleges. As an answer to them, Modern Orthodoxy also arose in the 19th century and spread from Europe to America. Many changes and innovations which first occurred in Reform or Conservative groups were later taken up in Modern Orthodoxy.

Other streams of Orthodoxy try to preserve their traditions as best as they can. They decline to recognize all other movements, with few exceptions. In Israel, old-style types of Orthodoxy rule those areas of law which touch on personal status. Therefore the other streams, including Modern Orthodoxy, need to win ground step by step.[16] Despite frequent denials by many Orthodox believers, Jewish life is a plural entity — if not always as pluralistic, meaning mutually tolerant, as many of us would like it to be.

2. WHOSE AUTHORITY?

Jewish religious groups exist by the consent of their members. There is no institution of hierarchy. A revered or respected rabbi is accepted as authority. Rabbis are ordained by institutions which in their turn are set up by congregations belonging to particular groups.[17] Each ordained rabbi who is accepted by consent of colleagues and congregants is largely independent. The presupposition is that he will strive for Jewish continuity out of Jewish traditions. These, however, have always been

---

* As the central theme of the relation of God and humankind is part of any discussion of Jewish traditions, I chose to give this short overview to our specific theme.

changing. Thus, many of the biblical commandments are not practicable because they concern institutions which have not existed for thousands of years, such as commandments relating to kings, temple priesthood, animal and other sacrifices.

Some 150 years ago Jews decided to express their traditions in a liberal way. Rabbis and congregants went the way of trial and error out of the courage of their convictions. Since then, Reform Halakha is being formulated. Reform rabbis by definition are not authoritarian. They know as well as their Orthodox colleagues that people have to come to accept changes in behaviour and concepts. Some changes occur more quickly than others.

3. STATEMENTS

The integration of women was one of the first tasks Reform set itself, since equality was part of the gains of Enlightenment and Emancipation. As early as 1837, reformer Abraham Geiger declared that there should be "no distinction between duties for men and women, unless flowing from the natural laws governing the sexes", introducing equality in the synagogue, in the marriage ceremony, and abolishing "fetters which may destroy woman's happiness".[18] In 1846, a pace-setting rabbinical conference at Breslau resulted in demands for achieving the necessary changes in the halakhic position of women. The comparison is made between Jews as a minority, suffering injustice despite nominal emancipation, and the even less complete emancipation of women. Therefore, "it is a sacred duty to express more emphatically the complete religious equality of the female sex,... thus supplying our religious community with a strength of which it has been deprived for all too long". As an expression of all necessary changes, the man's blessing God for not having been made a woman, in the morning prayer, should — and did — disappear from Reform prayer books. Girls should come of age religiously at thirteen, as boys, and not at twelve, and from then on should be counted in the *minyan* (the minimum of ten persons for public service).[19]

The acceptance of some or all of these Reform halakhic changes took time. Sometimes, congregations had to compromise with members who could not adapt themselves. In other cases, new congregations were founded by those whose conscience and theology differed from traditionalists. As each congregation is an autonomous body, no ecclesiastical rule could prevent this development. However, an instance is found of a much earlier development in the Spanish and Portuguese

Synagogue in London: here membership was — and is — granted by recommendation and vote of the Council. In 1784, the statutes were changed to include the membership of single or widowed women — but not married ones. [20] The refusal of this congregation to introduce reforms led in 1842 to the founding of the West London Synagogue.

In America, the European developments were fostered by immigrants who left Germany because of the political reaction which followed the unsuccessful bourgeois revolution of 1848. The separation of church and state as a constitutional principle allowed American groups to establish congregations according to their own wish and conscience. Thus, one impediment found in Europe disappeared, namely the decree by the state that membership in one local community was prescribed for all Jews. European liberal groups had to go to court, or to Parliament, as in England, in order to get equal rights with orthodoxy. Therefore, in autocratic countries like Tzarist Russia no Reform development was possible. Rabbis from many countries studied at the first modern Jewish theological schools in Germany, and went to serve congregations in America. The halakhic decisions of Reform were adapted to local necessities. The conferences which had been interrupted in Germany because of reactionary trends in state and society were renewed, partly by the same rabbis, in Philadelphia in 1869. The Pittsburgh Platform of 1885 set forth the essence of Reform convictions. [21]

Looking back on the advances registered, the foremost Reform leader, Rabbi Isaac M. Wise, wrote about the change in the role of women: first, women were admitted to the choir (which Orthodoxy sees as immodest since "the voice of woman is seductive"); then, confirmation of boys and girls together was introduced (in Reform, confirmation requires an extent of study not always present at the 13-year stage of Bar- and Bat-Mityvah. Again, the togetherness is deemed "unseemly" by the Orthodox, to this day); girls were allowed to read the Torah. He states that the regular presence of women improved order and decorum which often had been lacking. Wise asked the congregations to give women the right of vote. They should be eligible for boards, for the sake of principle. When women were members as "part" of their husbands, they were not independant, voting members. Wise set the programme: "The principle or justice, and the Law of God inherent in every human being, demand that women be admitted to membership in the congregation and given equal rights with man... We will debate the question with anyone who will show us in what woman is less entitled to the privileges of the synagogue than man, or where her faith is less important to her salvation (sic!) than man's is to him. Till then, we maintain that women must become active members of the congregation for their own sake, and for the benefit of Israel's sacred cause."[22]

After 40 years of American Reform, the women members of the congregations set up the Federation of Temple Sisterhoods which in the course of time has become one of the most active groups fostering Jewish studies by men and women alike.

4. ABOLISHING CASTES

Reform has declared as meaningless and harmful two ancient caste systems deriving from the Bible which are part of Orthodox concepts:

a) The so-called offspring of Temple priesthood whose lineage in any case is rather doubtful. Since Reform does not wish to re-introduce sacrificial rituals in the future, they have no function. This solves the problem of a Cohen, priest, who is not allowed to marry a divorcee or a proselyte. Many tragedies occur when a bride finds out she cannot marry because her beloved is a Cohen. Solutions can be found in some of these cases, but at best they are under-the-table compromises. This applies especially to the State of Israel where no civil marriage exists, in spite of many attempts to provide for it. Most people who have a Cohen lineage are completely secular but cannot change this born-into class, or rather caste. (For case histories, see Abramov, note 16.)

b) The other biblically decreed caste is the *Mamzer*, fem. *Mamzeret*. Usually translated as "bastard", it does not mean, however, a person born out of wedlock as such — because, in that case, the child is not illegitimate by Jewish law. Rather, it is the child of a mother by a man whom she may not marry by traditional law — either because she was still religiously married at the time, or because of close kinship. If one parent is non-Jewish this does not make the child a *Mamzer*. While being part of the Jewish people, *Mamzerim/ot* and their offspring may marry only among themselves, or among proselytes. Moreover, the suspicion of *Mamzerut* is cast on whole Jewish communities whose *Halakha* differs from the mainstream of tradition, making marriage with one of their members difficult or impossible in the eyes of orthodoxy. Such groups are the Karaites from Russia and Egypt; the Benai Israel from India, the Falashas from Ethiopia; and all non-orthodox groups where after a civil divorce no religious *gett*, or bill of divorce, was obtained by the wife from her husband before a new marriage. Such groups are secular Jews in all countries, and of course all Reform Jews, since they do not require the *gett.* Most orthodox rabbis preferred to remain ignorant about cases of *Mamzerut,* but where whole sectors of Jewry are involved they, and people depending on them, remain with the problem in spite of many urgings within their own fold to show courage in changing laws, just as has been done all through the millennia, and even now — as long as areas other than personal status are concerned. Accusations that "Reform divides Jewish unity" will not change matters. Only changes in Orthodox Halakha will solve things which are within Orthodox responsibility, just as Liberal and Conservative rabbis solve such problems according to their reading of traditions, laws and customs. [23]

5. RELEASING THE "ANCHORED" WIFE, AGUNA

Reform and Conservative Judaism have found ways of unbinding a wife from the "anchor" of a dissolved marriage in case the husband refuses or is unable to do so. Traditional law states that in order to remarry in an Orthodox ceremony, a woman needs a bill of divorce, *gett,* from her husband, if he is still alive. Otherwise, she would commit bigamy (a civil divorce changes nothing in this case). If the husband has disappeared, proof of death is necessary to release her from the marriage bond. Rabbis always did all they could to work out solutions to such problems, short of abolishing the law. The husband is not thus affected should the same happen to him, since he may be given a rabbinical licence to remarry. In cases of disappearance due to persecution or war, a conditional divorce was customarily granted. [24] The Hebrew author Sh.Y. Agnon derived his pen-name from "Aguna", the theme of the first story he published in Palestine, 1908.

Reform follows the secular law in case of divorce or disappearance.

6. NO BONDAGE FOR THE CHILDLESS WIDOW

By orthodox Halakha, a childless widow is bound by biblical commandment to be married by a brother of her husband, called in Hebrew *Jabam* and in Latin *Levir,* hence: levirate marriage. The original idea was to provide for her and, should she have a son, to consider him as the deceased's and thus to continue his memory. When these laws were made, there still was no Jewish belief in a personal life beyond the grave. This was introduced only later by the Pharisees, thus providing Jews, Christians and Muslims alike with the concept of eternal life, other-worldly bliss, and the resurrection of the dead. Therefore it was especially hard to be "cut off from the living" without sons to continue one's life. In both respects the biblical law generally was a boon (Deut. 25:5-6). When a brother of the deceased did not marry the widow, she applied to the court of justice and was freed to marry someone else. This was accompanied by a ceremony which was ignominous to the man, the loosening of his shoe and spitting out (Deut. 25:7-10). The procedure is called *Halitzah*, "loosening of shoe". A special ceremonial right shoe is used for it. In Talmudic times, the requirement was cut down to cases when the deceased did not leave a child, including a daughter, by any marriage, including a child born after his death, even if it subsequently dies (Babylonian Talmud, Yebamot, Mishnah 2,5;22b; Niddah, Mishnah 5,3; codes of Jewish Law). The law was interpreted as applying only to his paternal brothers. However, if a brother was born even one day before he died, the widow has to wait 13 years for him to release her on attaining legal fitness to either marry her or release her (see Ruth 1:11). The setting-free is required even where a levirate marriage is forbidden because the woman is a divorcee and the men are priests, where the marriage is valid once it has taken place (Mishnah Yebamot 2:3 and Rashi). The discussion about the priority of marriage or *Halitzah* fills volumes of Jewish Law over the millennia. Mystics advise marriage because of the "benefit to the deceased's soul". In Oriental and Sefardic (=of Spanish origin) communities, levirate marriage is the custom, especially where Islamic law allows polygamy. The brother is obliged by rabbinic law and by the state of Israel to pay for the widow's upkeep till he gives her Halitzah. [25] In Israel, thousands of childless widows wait for the procedure. Blackmail is widespread, extortion money paid to brothers-in-law. Some get answers, as on the Radio Programme "Ask the Rabbi", when some years ago, the Sefardic Chief Rabbi of Tel Aviv replied to a question by a young widow that "deep mysteries are involved and therefore one should not rush". Needless to say, I was shocked when hearing this answer with my own ears.

For secular Israelis, the solution lies in either having a civil marriage in any other country or a marriage contract with one of the women's rights' lawyers such as MP Shulamit Aloni. In both cases their marriage will be registered by the Ministry of the Interior. This might change if Orthodox pressure to repeal the procedure succeeds. Others choose to be married religiously in a Reform ceremony in countries where Reform rabbis have the power of registrar. In Israel, the state recognizes as valid any marriage which is valid in the state where it took place.

The principles of Reform implied from the very beginning that modern ethics and sensibilities override archaic rites which cause unhappiness and include undignified procedures like spitting out in front of a person in order to be free to marry. Codification for Liberal rabbis in German-speaking countries stated at the Augsburg Synod, 1871: "The rule of the Tora in regard to Halitza has lost its significance, since the circumstances which brought about levirate marriages and Halitza no longer exist and since the basic thought underlying this precept has become foreign to our religious and social consciousness. The omission of Halitza is no impediment to a widow's remarriage. However, for the sake of the freedom of conscience, no rabbi will refuse to perform a Halitza in appropriate form if the participants so desire."[26]

In Western countries, persons who wish to solve the above-mentioned problems come to non-orthodox groups. Thus, since the Reform Beth Din, rabbinical court, was set up in 1948 in London, members of orthodox congregations often turn here. They agree to sign that the procedures are not recognized by Orthodox authorities. While accepting most traditional marriage laws, the ritual of Halitza is disregarded: "We do not believe that, in this age, the peculiar ceremony... bears any relevance to a widow's potential remarriage."[27]

7. NO SILENT BRIDES

In the traditional marriage ceremony, the bridegroom puts the ring on the bride's finger with the ancient formula: "Behold, you are sanctified unto me with this ring according to the law of Moses and Israel." Reform codification of a major change was set down at the Augsburg Synod, 1871: "It is permissible that during the marriage ceremony... the bride in her turn also gives the bridegroom a ring with a few appropriate words."[28] This became the rule all over the world, wherever Liberal and Reform congregations exist. They cannot visualize the much-praised honour of the Jewish wife starting with silence at the outset of their lives as partners.

It will be noted that many Jewish husbands do not wear a marriage band. In Israel, they simply are not given one, except in the few Reform and Conservative synagogues where the ceremony follows the enforced Orthodox one. The majority of Israelis, being secular, never even heard of marriage rings for men.

Orthodoxy insists on having an unadorned ring since one tradition asks for the exact value of precious stones in order to avoid a deception. Others think this is not justified. The leading halakhic scholar of Reform, Rabbi Solomon B. Freehof, states: "This custom no longer has any meaning in Reform Jewish congregations."[29] Thus, Reform Jewish couples may choose the kind of rings they wish, and use them at the ceremony and ever after.

8. THANKSGIVING AFTER BIRTH

Jewish traditions always have fostered private and semi-private prayers of women. Sometimes they are found in older printed collections. They are a treasury of piety, of women relating to their sex. Especially important are the very rare prints of Judaeo-German women's prayers in Hebrew letters. In the 19th century, teachers of Jewish girls in Germany and Austria supplanted these by newer prayers, written by men. They contain the standard prayers, plus private ones, including thanksgiving after birth, the mother's prayer at her child's confirmation, etc. Especially in religious education of girls as required mainly by Reform, such books might be given to a daughter at her confirmation in the Temple and be her companion for life.[30] In 1854, Fanny Neuda, recent widow of a rabbi, brought out her own prayers which she often taught girls. The book was meant to serve as "a memorial of loving recollection" to her husband. In spite of "many excellent books by men,... I hope that mine will find a readier echo in women's hearts, being the outpouring of a female heart." The book contains German meditations to accompany all prayers and all private situations, such as before and after birth, at circumcision of a son, namesgiving of a girl, etc.[31] The many editions testify that this book was widely used and formed the consciousness of generations of Jewish women.

In England, we find that a mother publicly gives thanks after birth in Orthodox as well as Reform synagogues. The Orthodox Authorised Daily Prayer Book follows the Polish rite and it has been in use since 1890. Containing an English translation, it went through scores of editions and is now a treasured tradition in "the British Commonwealth of Nations". It contains the "Prayer of Thanksgiving for Women after Recovery from Childbirth" (pp.412-414), in the following order: Psalm verses on entering the Synagogue; the Gomel blessing (thanking God for safeguarding in danger), with the response given by the Minister (=Rabbi); a beautiful prayer containing the words: "Bestow thy blessing upon thy handmaid; strengthen and uphold me together with my husband... Keep the tender babe in all his (her) ways. Favour him (her) with knowledge, understanding and discernment, and let his (her) portion be in thy Law...". If the infant is brought into the synagogue, the Minister is to pronounce the (priestly) benediction over it.[32]

The Liberal prayerbooks have similar services of "Thanksgiving after Childbirth and Naming of a Child". The parents come together to the synagogue, and it is the mother who offers the words of thanks.[33]

The new American Reform prayerbooks contain moving prayers, i.e. in the volume "Gates of the House", by the husband during the childbirth (p.108), by the parents on the birth or adoption of a child (p.109), and on the birth or adoption of a grandchild (110). [34]

Many new rituals are being tried. It is to be hoped that some Orthodox congregations too will overcome their fears of so-called innovation and let the mothers come into the men's section of the synagogue in order to give thanks together.

9. WELCOMING A DAUGHTER

In the above rituals, the baby girl is welcomed into the Household of Israel and given her name(s). Long before the rise of Reform, home and/or synagogue rituals were widespread to celebrate the occasion. Wherever such customs declined or were unknown, girls got the message of being less important than sons. Two such customs are known to me. Others may exist and need to be described and preserved.

a. Zebed ha Bat — the gift of a daughter

In the Spanish and Portuguese ritual this is the Hebrew title for the English "For the naming of a daughter". The verses used are taken from the Song of Songs, and the child is given a blessing containing the names of the four Mothers of Israel, the prophetess Miriam, the beautiful Abigail, and Queen Esther. [35]

b. Hollekreisch, Haut-la-crèche

This is the ceremony for naming a girl, and previously also a boy's non-Hebrew name, in Southern Germany, parts of Switzerland and Eastern France. The custom stems from medieval times. Probably it was adapted from Christian neighbours who gave it up since all children were given their names in church at baptism. It seems to stem from casting out Holle, who is the pagan German equivalent of Lilith. In its Jewish form, the order is as follows: the mother goes to morning service in her best clothes, accompanied by the rabbi's wife and a group of important women. The father is called to the Torah. The mother sends him a wrapper for the Torah scroll embroidered with the child's name. Later, at home, the guests stand in a circle around the cradle. Haut-la-crèche means in French "Raise the cradle" — this is the way many Jews, to this day, understand the custom. The cradle is lifted, and the girls (boys if it is a boy) call out three times: "Hollekreisch, Hollekreisch, wie soll das Kindlein heissen?" Each time the regular, non-Hebrew name is called out to them. Gifts and a party make it a joyous occasion to remember. Recently, young couples have taken up the custom so that their new-born daughters may be fêted — just as boys are.[36]

10. COMING OF AGE: BAT-MITZVAH

Even for Reform, a sound barrier had to be overcome in order to bring girls into the *active* liturgy of the synagogue. At first, the custom of Confirmation was introduced, marking the conclusion of religious instruction. The age might be 14 or 15, depending on the school system in different countries. The time is *Shavuot*, Pentecost, celebrating the giving of the Torah at Sinai. All the girls appear together in front of the Holy Ark and promise to be faithful Jews. They are not called individually to the reading of the Torah to say the benedictions, since in most Reform congregations it is the rabbi who reads a portion, and boys are not called up either. Wherever this tradition has been re-introduced over the last generation girls, as well as boys, learn the difficult art of chanting the portion from Torah and/or Prophets, on the Sabbath after their thirteenth birthday.

Once obligatory for boys, the Reform principle of equality demanded the same active and individual part from girls as well. However, the first to have Bat-Mitzvah for girls was the Reconstructionist movement, founded in the 1930s by Rabbi Mordecai M. Kaplan and his pupils. As rabbis from several streams of Judaism joined this mainly educational movement, its influence was being felt in many synagogues. Girls and women who did not have this education in their youth often study for Bat-Mitzvah at any age when they feel ready for it and continue taking their place at the Torah readings.

11. MENSTRUATION IS A PRIVATE THING

In the Reform tradition, no differences are observed with regard to synagogue activities based on the bodily functions of men and women. Long ago the biblical rules for men were removed. Reform Halakha did the same for women. It is assumed that everybody has the good sense to decide when they wish to take an active part in public services, as is the case in any other activity. Therefore the development towards more study and active participation in services by Reform women progressed once the role consciousness was changed. This took time, and even in America Jews only took steps in this direction after Christian society, the majority group, did so. Thus, the changing role of women was in part a response to community needs, and in part a result of general changes in society. At any rate, the time-consuming debate which is taking place in other religious trends of Judaism was not necessary in Reform. Except for Orthodoxy, the private dates of women are not pried into when setting the wedding date. The *Mikveh*, or ritual bath, likewise is no more practised. Instead, sexual ethics are taught and discussed.[37] Besides, as "unobservant Orthodox" are the majority users of the Mikveh, the new "cult of the Mikveh" is sometimes criticized.[38]

12. THE ORDINATION OF WOMEN AS RABBIS

Despite the blood taboo of *Niddah*, women were recognized as teachers of Torah and community leaders in all ages.[39] Thus, with a change in social climate, they could become preachers, leaders of synagogue services (=cantors), and rabbis. In England, Lilian Helen Montagu (1874-1963) was one of the founders and lay preachers of the Liberal Synagogue as far back as 1902. In American Reform, a resolution was passed on the principle of accepting women as rabbis in 1922.[40] However, the first woman to be ordained as rabbi was my teacher Regina Jonas in Berlin, Germany, in the thirties. She perished in Auschwitz.[41] It took another forty years until the first American woman was ordained as rabbi (1972). When the Reconstructionist Rabbinical College was founded in Philadelphia in 1968, its egalitarian principles admitted women to rabbinic studies and ordination. Meanwhile, women also studied and were ordained at Leo Baeck College, London. Conservative women were still being denied equal rights; they went over to study either at the Reform schools in New York and Cincinnati, or in Philadelphia, in order to serve their own congregations.

Meanwhile, women studied at the School of Sacred Music in New York and were invested as cantors. They serve in Reform and Conservative congregations. By 1988 more than one hundred women had been ordained and invested. They are a sorely needed professional force. In 1985, Conservatives too began ordaining women. As their experts include Orthodox scholars, it was a difficult battle to win. However, it is important that male scholars showed the way in removing the ancient fears and the "terror of Orthodoxy", as it was called. By their not-so-liberal rules they had to show why ancient limitations placed on women as judges, witnesses, Torah readers, etc., were not applicable to the present function of rabbis. But most important, members of Conservative congregations were not willing to put up with limitations in the choice of a profession. Without women rabbis many of them would simply join the Reform movement. Once again it was the requirements of Jewish life that won the argument, rather than the fine points of sophistry.[42]

Ten years after the ordination of Rabbi Sally Priesand, the American Jewish Committee "brought together some of those who have succeeded in achieving the hitherto male roles of rabbi, synagogue president, cantor and professor at a theological institution to share their experiences with us".[43] Since then, progress can be seen year after year. Ingrained emotional reactions of men and women are often much harder to overcome than religious law itself. The momentum produced by the part played by self-assured girls and women within their synagogues and homes certainly is a more important factor than showing why Deborah could be a judge in ancient Israel, or whether she only taught men how to be judges, as a medieval French tradition posed the dilemma.[44]

D. Inroads into Orthodox enclaves

In Israel, over the past several years rigid Orthodox standpoints have led to impasses in the functioning of municipal bodies. The two matters in question were membership of observant, Orthodox women deputies in local religious councils and in the electoral college which designates the Ashkenazic Chief Rabbi of Tel Aviv. In public statements one could hear and read about the dangers to the venerable rabbis' personal morality if forced to sit in the same room as and discuss things at the same table with females who are not their wives. Some declared they would resign if they lost. As debates continued, not-so-subtle changes were heard: that electing a Chief Rabbi is a once-only matter and not as dangerous as regular meetings. Finally, the election of the only candidate took place without anybody becoming religiously or morally tainted. It was pointed out that in the past local rabbis in Israel were elected by councils which included women. However, the argument was won by necessity and not by precedence.

Several cases of various women who serve on local Religious Councils are pending at the High Court of Justice. The male members, some of them rabbis, will have to explain what prevents them from sitting together with women. Of course, even ultra-Orthodox delegates sit in the Knesset, Israel's Parliament, where there are women members, female staff, etc. Hopefully, here too emotional barriers will be overcome by facts and the necessity to share responsibilities and privileges. Modesty and chastity have nothing to do with the real issues.[45]

The equality of women and men is probably the most important achievement of the Reform movement. Even if nothing more were achieved than bringing about other progressive movements as well, it would certainly be a major contribution to Jewish existence. [46]

NOTES

[1] For her approach to the sources, see her 5 vols. on the Pentateuch. Nehama Leibowitz: *Studies in the Book of (Genesis, etc.) in the Context of Ancient and Modern Jewish Bible Commentary*, Dept. for Torah Education, World Zionist Organization, Jerusalem 1972-78.

[2] See Menahem Elon: "Minhag (custom and usage)", *Encyclopaedia Judaica* (EJ) 12 (Macmillan, Jerusalem 1971), 4-26. Reprint in M. Elon ed., *Principles of Jewish Law*, Jerusalem, Keter, 1974, 91-110.

[3] J. Finkelstone (London) in *Ma'ariv* (Tel Aviv, 16 September 1988), Hebres.

[4] Louis Jacobs: *A Jewish Theology*, London, Darton, Longman & Todd, London 1973, 225-230.

[5] He explains delays as clashes of culture and consciousness between Rabbi Soloveitchik, see note 10, and the master's disciples like himself. See Rackman on Soloveitchik's meta-historical approach, *Sh'ma* 15/... (New York, 1985). For his critique of the establishment, see "Ferment in Orthodoxy" in his: *One Man's Judaism*, Tel Aviv, Greenfield, 1973, 373-78.

[6] A short survey is Louis & Rebecca Barish: *Varieties of Jewish Belief: Questions and Answers about Basic Concepts of Judaism*, New York, Jonathan David, 1979. It seems to be the first book by a rabbi and his wife as co-authors, rather than the usual procedure of thanking the wife for her work.

[7] Babylon. Talmud, Yevamot 62b, and Codes; see discussion in David M. Feldman: *Marital Relations, Birth Control and Abortion in Jewish Law*, New York, Schocken, 1974, 2nd ed., 63-4.

[8] Midrash Genesis Rabba 8,1; 17,6. The English translation in 10 vols. (Soncino, London 1939, reprints) is useful for general readers.

[9] Mid. Genesis Rabba 17,7 — Soncino version. Another version says: One ounce of silver, one pound of gold. See Hebrew edition by N.A. Mirkin (Yavneh, Tel Aviv, 1956).

[10] Rabbi Joseph B. Soloveitchik is the leading scholar of Modern Orthodoxy in America. He introduced the dialectical and tragic view of mankind, see "The Lonely Man of Faith", *Tradition* (New York, Summer, 1965). On his influence and way of thinking, Eugene B. Borowitz: *Choices in Modern Jewish Thought* (Behrman, New York 1983), ch. 10, dealing also with the avoidance of solving problems of women's status, 241-2.

[11] *The Holy Scriptures: A New Translation. Part 2: The Prophets*, Philadelphia, Jewish Publication Society of America, 1978.

[12] Part 1, The Torah (1962; slightly changed 1967).

[13] See Gershom Scholem: *Major Trends in Jewish Mysticism*, New York, Schocken, 1946, rev. ed.), 229-35; 275. *Von der mystischen Gestalt der Gottheit*, Frankfurt a.M., Suhrkamp, 1962), 135-91. Yosef Dan, "Shekhinah", EJ 14, 53-4.

[14] W. Gunther Plaut: *The Rise of Reform Judaism*, New York, World Union for Progressive Judaism, 1963, vol. 1; The Growth of Ref. Jud. (1965), vol. 2.

[15] Arthur Hertzberg: "Conservative Judaism", EJ 5, 901-6. Seymour Siegel: *Conservative Judaism and Jewish Law*, New York, Ktav, 1979.

[16] See S.Z. Abramov: *Perpetual Dilemma. Jewish Religion in the Jewish State*, Jerusalem-New York, World Union for Progressive Judaism, 1976.

[17] Elliot L. Stevens ed.: *Rabbinic Authority*, New York, Central Conference of American Rabbis, 1982). Reform.

[18] Plaut 1 (see note 14), 253.

[19] Plaut 1, 253-5.

[20] Albert M. Hyamson: *The Sephardim of England*, London, Methuen, 1951, 190.

[21] Plaut 2,33-34.

[22] Plaut 2, 339-40.

[23] For traditional sources, see Judge B.Z. Schereschewsky: "Mamzer", EJ 11, 840-2 = Elon: Principles, 435-8, see note 2. Contains a legal solution for such cases by declaring that non-Orthodox marriage is not recognized by Orthodoxy and therefore may be disregarded, voiding the suspicion of bigamy and hence, of Mamzerut. Case histories in Abramov, note 16. On group conflicts in Judaism, see Pnina Navè Levinson: *Einführung in die rabbinische Theologie*, Darmstadt, Wissenschaftliche Buchgesellschaft, 1982, 11-18. The designation as *castes* is mine.

[24] See B.Z. Schereschewsky: "Agunah", EJ 2,429-33 = Elon: Principles, 409-14; "Divorce", EJ 6,122-37 = Elon, Principles, 414-24.

[25] See M. Elon: "Levirate Marriage and Halizah", EJ 11, 122-31; = Elon: Principles, 403-9. In EJ, also description of the revolting ceremony (here called "solemn"), and illustrations. Author: Louis Rabinowitz.

[26] Plaut 1,219.

[27] Michael Curtis: "The Beth Din of the Reform Synagogues of Great Britain", Dow Marmur, ed.: Reform Judaism (Reform Synagogues of Great Britain, London 1973). Rabbi Curtis was for 25 years the Convener of the Reform Beth Din.

[28] Plaut 1,219.

[29] Solomon B. Freehof: *Reform Jewish Practice and its Rabbinic Background*, New York, 2 vols. Union of American Hebrew Congregations, 1944, 1952, vol. 1,91. Rabbi Freehof's fame mainly rests on his: Reform Responsa, 7 vols. (Hebrew Union College Press, 1960-1980). Because of their easily attainable wealth of halakhic material, they are also used by Orthodox colleagues. More materials on questions of Jewish life may be found in books by Freehof's successor as chairman of the Responsa Committee, Walter Jacob: ed. American Reform Responsa 1889-1983 (172 responsa; 1982), and as author: Contemporary Reform Responsa (1987; both Central Conference of American Rabbis, New York.)

[30] Examples are, Jacob Freund (teacher of religion at the Breslau community): Hanna. Gebets- und Andachtsbuch für israelitische Mädchen und Frauen (Koebner, Breslau 1867); Rabbiner Dr. Max Grunwald: Beruria. Gebete und Andachten für jüdische Frauen und Mädchen (Schlesinger, Wien 1913; separate edition for girls, as the congregation's gift at Confirmation).

[31] Fanny Neuda: *Stunden der Andacht. Ein Gebets- und Erbauungsbuch für Israels Frauen und Jungfrauen*, Prag/Breslau, Brandeis, 1854, 24th ed. 1916.

[32] S. Singer ed.: *The Authorized Daily Prayer Book*, London, 1890; new edition under the Direction of Israel Brodie, Chief Rabbi (1962).

[33] Service of the Heart (Union of Liberal and Progressive Synagogues, London 1967), 432-5. Forms of Prayer of Jewish Worship (The Reform Synagogues of Great Britain, London, 7th ed. 1977), 284-6, in the order: Psalm by father; Prayer by mother for child or adopted child; blessing by Rabbi.

[34] Gates of the House. The New Union Home Prayer Book (Central Conference of American Rabbis, New York 1977).

[35] Book of Prayer of the Spanish and Portuguese Jews' Congregation, London (Oxford University Press, 1901; 2nd. ed. 1958), vol. 1, 180. With English translation instead of the ancient Spanish of the Sefardim who fled from the Inquisition: ed. Ferrara, 1552, sponsored by Donna Gracia Nasi, the rescuer of thousands of persecuted fellow-Jews. Cecil Roth: *Doña Gracia of the House of Nasi*, Philadelphia, Jewish Publication Society, 1948, 2nd ed. 1977.

[36] Description and literature in Hayyim Schauss: *The Lifetime of a Jew*, New York, Union of American Hebrew Congregations, 1950, 44-47, 310.

[37] For example, Richard L. Rubenstein: "The New Morality and College Religious Counselling", in Earl Grollman, ed.: *Rabbinic Counselling*, New York, Bloch, 1966; Rubenstein: *Morality and Eros*, McGraw Hill, 1970. Eugene B. Borowitz: *Choosing a Sex Ethic: a Jewish Inquiry*, New York, Schocken, 1969 — delves into traditional source material. See also his "Reading the Jewish Tradition on Marital Sexuality", *Journal of Reform Judaism*, 33 No. 3, 1982.

[38] William Wolff, ed.: *Manna* 20, London, The Sternberg Center for Judaism, 1988, 25.

[39] Bernadette Y. Brooten: *Women Leaders in the Ancient Synagogue. Inscriptional Evidence and Background Issues*, Brown Judaic Studies 36. Scholars Press, Chico, California 1982). Sondra Henry, Emily Taitz: *Written Out of History. Our Jewish Foremothers*, Fresh Meadows, New York, Biblio. rev. ed. 1983.

[40] Central Conference of American Rabbis, Yearbook, vol. 32 (New York 1922). Reprinted in Walter Jacobs, ed., see note 29.

[41] Wolfgang Hamburger: "Die Stellung des Reformjudentums zur Frau". *Emuna* 10, Supplementheft 1, Frau im Judentum (Frankfurt/Main, 1976), 19.

[42] The Jewish Theological Seminary of America, the Faculty, Position Papers: On the Ordination of Women as Rabbis ("for information only", New York 1979). As meanwhile they were printed, some examples: "... the synagogue must be an arena for women to assume leadership positions. To channel this energy into the pulpit rabbinate is not to subvert Judaism but to Judaize Feminism", David G. Roskies. "We have demonstrated that there are no insurmountable halachic objections to the granting of ordination, *per se*, to women", Joel Roth. "Why start with the rabbinate? There are other religious functions in which women do not participate at the present, like *Milah* (=circumcision) and *Shechitah* (=ritual slaughtering) ... they are religiously more important. Why not start with them?", David Weiss Halivni. "Commission Report", with Resolutions and Minority Opinion, *Conservation Judaism* 32,3 (Summer 1979). For an exhaustive discussion, see issue: Women as Rabbis. *Judaism* 33,1 (New York, Winter 1984). Pay attention to — Blu Greenberg: "Will there be Orthodox women rabbis?", 23-33. B. See also Pnina Navè Levinson: "Die Ordination von Frauen als Rabbiner". *Zeitschrift für Religions- und Geistesgeschichte*, 38,4, 1986, 289-310.

[43] Consultation, The Role of Women in Jewish Religious Life: A Decade of Change 1972-1982. Papers (The American Jewish Committee, New York, 1982).

[44] Tosafah (=French commentary, 13-14.c.) on women as witnesses or judges in Babylon. Talmud, Niddah 50a, caption *kol*.

[45] For documentation, files are obtainable at the *Jerusalem Post* archives.

[46] See also Pnina Navè Levinson: "Sexualität im Judentum", — Michael Klöcker, Udo Tworuschka, ed.: *Ethik der Religionen — Lehre und Leben, Band 1. Sexualität*, Göttingen, Vandenhoeck & Ruprecht, München, 1984.

Hindu Perceptions of Auspiciousness and Sexuality

Vasudha Narayanan

The Hindu tradition does not recognize a centralized religious leadership or one holy book as its authority. There is a fluid scriptural canon, supplemented by oral tradition and ritual practices. Generalizations made in this paper ought to be taken with some caution; there are always exceptions to the rule. To a large extent, my essay is based on evidence in written sources, both scriptural and modern, and on rituals that I have observed and participated in over several years. While a lot of material is drawn from sources in the Tamil language, and some of it reflects the viewpoints from the Brahmin class of Hindu society, pan-Indian generalizations have been made where warranted.

This paper is divided into two parts. I shall first deal with attitudes towards women in the Hindu tradition, trying to draw in large strokes common themes and continuity in the perception of women in sacred writings and modern fiction. I shall briefly discuss the notion of "auspiciousness", a fundamental category in the Hindu tradition; a category which will be vital in understanding the link between the social status of women and their sexuality. In the second part of the paper, I shall focus on perceptions of the female body and its functions, and discuss the religious rituals and attitudes connected with menstruation, marriage and childbirth.

Perceptions of three types of women

Dharma and auspiciousness

Tulsidas, an influential 17th-century poet, grouped women with cattle, morons, servants and drums — objects best fit to be beaten.[1] Manu, centuries earlier, had said: "Though destitute of virtue, or seeking pleasure elsewhere, or devoid of good qualities, a husband must be constantly worshipped as a god by a faithful wife" (Manu 5.154). The same author, however, went on to say that a wife is verily the goddess of fortune and auspiciousness (Manu 9.26) and that, only if women are honoured, the gods are pleased and the religious rituals beneficial (Manu 3.56). Hindu literature has, on the whole, maintained discordant views on women. A woman is portrayed — and often by the same author — as a servant and a goddess, a strumpet and a saint, a protected daughter and a powerful matriarch, a shunned widow and a worshipped wife. There is, however, a rationale in these conflicting views, and we shall survey some of the criteria used in the perception of women in Hindu society.

Images of the widow and the prostitute can only be understood in the context of the Hindu female ideal: a wife whose husband is alive and who is therefore considered to be "the auspicious married one" *(sumangali)*. This paper examines these three categories of women from current images that are continuous with written and practised traditon: auspicious wives (sumangali), wanton women (including the distinct sub-categories of "sacred" prostitutes, the various kinds of commercial harlots and adulterous women) and, finally, widows. Underlying the understanding of this tripartite typology are notions of "auspiciousness" and "inauspiciousness" (which are distinct from purity and pollution)[2] as well as the idea of dharma, (duty, righteousness) that is incumbent upon a person by virtue of her caste and station in life.

There is a rather wide category in Hindu life that includes certain kinds of people, animals, rituals, smells, sounds and foods; a category that has been referred to by the Sanskrit words *kalyana, mangala, subha* and *sri*. The English word "auspiciousness" has been used as a shorthand term for these words to indicate the power and tendency to bring about good fortune and a good quality of existence *(su asti)*.[3] This good quality of existence frequently refers to prosperity in this life; thus at this level, the understanding of auspiciousness is seen in terms of wealth, progeny, along with the symbols and rituals connected with these. Cattle, elephants, kings, married women with a potential for bearing children, rituals connected with birth and marriage were auspicious. These are connected with the promotion of this-worldly existence and the three human goals — duty/righteousness *(dharma)*; wealth and prosperity, *(artha)*; sensual pleasure *(kama)* — that are recognized therein.

There is also a second level of auspiciousness: one that is connected with the ultimate goal of liberation *(moksa)* and the path leading to it. The two levels of auspiciousness have been implicit in Hindu religious literature and rituals. Parasara Bhattar, a Srivaisnava theologian, articulated it clearly in the 13th century when he said: "There are two kinds of auspiciousness: one, pertaining to this life; the other, leading to the spiritual way" (Narayanan, 1985). In some ways, the two levels were perceived to contradict each other; auspiciousness of this life was life-promoting, and usually considered death to be negative. In the "higher" level, death is considered to be the point at which the soul is liberated from life and auspiciously united with the deity, thus leading to complete, eternal and the best form of happiness.

This section of the paper focuses on the connection between a woman and this-worldly auspiciousness, the variety that is life-promoting and that is in the rightness of things. Auspiciousness at this level is always within the realm of dharma and is frequently perceived to be feminine. One of the most ideal carriers and bestowers of this auspiciousness is the married wife whose husband is alive (sumangali). It is the thesis of this paper that she is the ideal woman, with high auspiciousness, because she alone is able to participate with her husband in activities to get and maintain the goals of dharma, artha and kama. The prostitute, by virtue of her continuing relationships, is perceived to be continually auspicious *(nitya sumangali)*. But such excessive auspiciousness is ridiculed, and adulterous women, because they slip from their dharma, are definitely not auspicious, despite their relationship to a man and potential for child-bearing. A widow because of her lack of auspiciousness, arising from her non-participation in a man's pursuit of dharma, artha and kama, has traditionally been looked down upon by Hindu society; an aspect that is perhaps one of the uglier chapters in the history of the religion. Many of these perceptions find their way into Indian fiction, drama and movies. Almost all such works destined for public consumption reinforce stereotypes while ostensibly attempting to challenge them. The audience for vernacular fiction — which is serialized in popular weekly or monthly magazines with very wide circulation — is considerable, and loyal as the soap-opera fans of some western countries. India is also the largest producer of commercial entertainment movies. The success of the stories and plots depends on not offending the viewer, who will not tolerate certain kinds of behaviour in the hero or heroine. Lindholm notes:

...It is a common occurrence for Tamil readers to chide an author if something in the development of the narrative is discordant to their conception of how such an event should proceed. Jayakantan reports in the preface to his novel *Certain People at Certain Times* that at the conclusion of its serialization in *Tinamani Katir* numerous letters urged him to change the ending such that Ganga (the heroine who was raped at a young age and who becomes an alcoholic when she is unable to marry her repentant rapist) either marry the man or, preferably, die. Such episodes seem to reveal an implicit apprehension that the writers of fiction are involved in the creation of a fabric of cultural statement, a mythology, of their times and that as such fiction belongs not just to the author but to the culture as a whole. (Lindholm, 2)

In this paper, as we note traditional images and paradigms that are remembered and quoted in everyday life, we shall also keep an eye on 20th century fiction to see how they reflect traditional values, sometimes while claiming to defy them.[4]

The Sumangali: an auspicious married woman

Perceptions of the sumangali have not changed radically in the last two thousand years in certain aspects. The ideal virtuous women are still held to be Sati, who sacrificed herself to save the honour of her husband; Sita, who complied with Rama in every aspect; and Savitri, who, by her wit and virtue, brought her husband back to life.

When a girl is given away to a man in marriage by her father, the bridegroom is told that she is to be his partner in the performance of dharma, in the attainment of prosperity (artha) and pleasure; he is not to prove false to his bride on these points.[5] The epic *Mahabharata* quotes the elderly Bhisma as telling the new king Yuddisthira that a wife is a man's partner in dharma, artha and kama.[6] Significantly enough, the marriage ceremony by which a girl is given away to the bridegroom is called kalyanam or "auspiciousness" in Tamil. Vatsyayana writes in the *Kama Sutra*:

> When a girl of the same caste, and a virgin, is married in accordance with the... Dharma Shastras, the results of such a union are: the acquisition of Dharma and Artha, offspring, affinity, increase of friends, and untarnished love ... (*Kama Sutra*, 135).

The word used frequently for "wedding" in the Tamil language is *kalyana* (from Sanskrit, meaning "auspicious"); in some cases the word *subha* (auspicious) precedes the word marriage *(vivaha)*. The auspicious marriage was the way to fulfill man's obligations to society. According to classical scriptures, a man was born with three debts: to the sages, the gods and to the ancestors. A wife helped repay these debts; with the performance of correct domestic and social rituals *with his wife*, a man paid his debt to the gods; by having children, the debt to the ancestors was discharged (Kane, II, 1: 560). The wife is called *sahadharmacarini*; a partner in the fulfilment of dharma; even Lord Visnu's wife *Sri* is called his sahadharmacarini. A man could not perform his religious obligations without his wife; in the last section of the epic *Ramayana*, when Rama exiles his faithful wife Sita, he has a golden image made of her to keep by his side while performing religious rites.[7] This perception is still a dominant one in society. A Tamil manual for sumangalis called "May you be a sumangali always" published in 1979 (henceforth referred to as *The Sumangali Manual*) articulates popular opinions and stereotypes with admiration: "In household matters, the wife has the upper hand in dharma rituals. Only women can maintain dharma; if they are unwilling, a man cannot perform dharma. That is why we call her a partner in dharma *(dharma patni)*; we never say 'dharma husband'... Our scriptures say that a wife is a husband's life companion, his accomplice in the performing of dharma. A woman is a man's friend." *(Sumangali Manual:* ch. 1,4).[8] This is consistent with Varahamihira, a sixth century compiler of religious law; he says that dharma and artha depend on a woman; from her, a man derives sensual pleasures (kama) and the blessing of sons (Kane, II, 1:579). A woman's death may create a temporary vacuum in the performance of dharma; but her husband can always remarry to fill the gap, or have his son and his wife officiate at religious rites. Thus, in a south Indian Brahmin wedding, if a widower cannot give away his daughter as a bride, he asks his son and daughter-in-law to fulfill his obligations for him. A rightful duty of the wife was also to help fulfill a man's quest for prosperity (artha). She is exhorted to be thrifty, manage a man's worldly possessions and be economical in expenditure (Manu 5.510). Such a woman *(stri)* was not different from the goddess of fortune and auspiciousness *(Sri)* (Manu 9.26). The woman was also a man's partner in love; *rati* (sexual pleasure) was one of the principal purposes of marriage (Kane, II, 1:4429). To be his sexual partner, she was to render herself attractive to him; and *only* to him. "For if the wife is not radiant with beauty, she will not attract her husband; and if she has no attraction for him, no children will be born" (Manu 3.61). The *Sumangali Manual* repeats this and adds a qualification: "A woman is celebrated by many characteristics... One of these is feeling irritated if a man other than her husband touches her. When Karaikkal Ammaiyar (a Tamil poetess, circa 5th-6th century A.D.) heard that her husband had left her, she asked God to change her beautiful appearance to that of a ghoul. When it was established that her beauty was of no use to her husband she made up her mind, her beauty would be destroyed. This indeed is virtue" (*Sumangali Manual*, 17-18). It is in being a rightful and righteous wife, bearing children in wedlock, helping a man achieve the goals approved by society, that a woman attained her auspiciousness; she was now fulfilling her dharma and being a partner in her husband's fulfillment of dharma. These two characteristics, i.e., doing one's own duty *(svadharma)*, and being a partner in her husband's quest for dharma *(sahadharmacarini)* characterize the ideal woman in the *Mahabharata*.[9]

The dharma of a sumangali was based on complete, unconditional fidelity to her husband. Hook (p. 40) is quite accurate in his demonstration that the stories of "Sita and Savitri provide an exhaustive archetypal structure for stories of India-wide appeal that involve women" and that "marriage and fidelity characterize that fate of the Indian heroine." The myth of Savitri and its enactment in ritual, both daily and annually, reinforces this point.

> The princess Savitri chooses to marry Satyavan despite the prediction that he has just one more year to live. She repeats a prayer taught to her by Narada, a divine minstrel, for the longevity of her husband. A year later, Yama, the god of death comes to claim Satyavan. Savitri follows them to the end of the earth; touched by her devotion, Yama grants her three wishes, except the life of her husband. The third wish is for a hundred sons and since no Indian wife can correctly have sons out of wedlock, Yama is eventually made to relinquish Satyavan's life.[10]

The *Sumangali Manual*, in a chapter called "Prayers to remain in sumangali," repeats the prayer that Savitri was taught by Narada and asks every wife to say it, morning and evening: "O goddess... bless me to have the fortune of having children, grandchildren, and all auspiciousness." The manual also describes the *nompu (vrata)*, a ritual conducted by women annually. Every sumangali prays then for her husband's prosperity and longevity and that she should die before her husband does. Young girls pray to find a good husband. The manual concludes: "We pray that, following Savitri, that jewel among faithful wives, we say this mantra every day and get all the auspiciousness. We should thus live as sumangalis for a long time" (*Sumangali Manual*, 45).

The absolute necessity for a girl to marry is emphazied in Hindu society. In reductionist and somewhat circular terms, this is seen as the consequence of the absolute dependence of women on men. Manu says:

"By a girl, by a young woman or even by an aged one, nothing must be done independently, even in her own house. In childhood a female must be subject to her father, in youth to her husband, when her lord is dead, to her sons; a woman must never be independent" (Manu 5.147-148). Sometimes, the ritual of marriage is seen as a passport for women to enter heaven. This is seen in a story from the *Mahabharata:*

> Subhru was the daughter of the sage Kuni. Her father wanted to give her in marriage but she would not consent. She remained unmarried all her life, practising severe penance. At the time of her death, however, she learnt to her great surprise that she could not go to heaven because her body was not consecrated by the ritual of marriage. With great difficulty she then induced the sage Sringavat to marry her, stayed with him for one night and was then enabled to go to heaven... (Altekar, 39).

The sumangali's dharma involved sexual fidelity as well as total obedience. The Hindu wife — at least in all the so-called "upper" castes, by tradition, and in the "lower" castes, by emulation — is monogamous and quite faithful to her husband in life and to his memory if he dies. The wife may occasionally be abandoned, but social pressures would make it difficult if not almost impossible for her to leave her husband. Hook quotes an instructive example. Ibsen's play *A Doll's House* was adapted in the regional language of Marathi. An integral component of the English version is that the heroine Nora becomes convinced that her husband is not worthy of her love, leaves him and builds an independent life in her hometown. The Marathi play *Kulawadhu* did not retain this element of Ibsen's plot. Hook comments: "Rangnekar, the adapter, does not allow the least possibility of unchaste behaviour to Bhanumati, the heroine. She does leave her husband, but leaves him to go off and live with *his* parents!" (Hook, 40). Several comparable examples in which the authors are extremely anxious to preserve the virtue of their heroines can be cited to confirm this (*Manual*, 36-37; Lindholm, 13).

The dharma of a faithful wife *(pativrata)* was to worship and serve her husband as god. A pativrata is one who is true to her husband. Her dharma is summed up in a line from the *Padma Purana*: she should ideally be like a slave in service, a harlot in love, a mother in offering food and nourishment to the husband and like a counsellor in times of need.[11] The *Sumangali Manual* repeats this with approval. In a recent anthropological study on women in Karnataka *(Hindu Women and the Power of Ideology)*, the author devotes three chapters to the topic of pativratya, the notion of a faithful, chaste wife, because it was considered to be extremely important for the women she studied. [12]

A pativrata woman, however, conversely, but consistent with the Hindu value system, had almost limitless powers. This was the power of the pativrata, a true and faithful wife, acquired because she was a wife. Let me summarize a story to make this point:

> A crane disturbs Kausika, a sage meditating in the forest. Kausika is angered; he opens his eyes and the glance is enough to burn the bird to ashes. Later the sage goes to beg his daily meal. The housewife's duty is to take care of such holy men; however, this time the lady is intent on serving her husband and does not come out immediately. The sage, predictably, is angry at being made to wait. The virtuous wife merely glances at the sage and asks: "Did you think I was a silly crane to be burnt?" The sage is dumbfounded at the powers of clairvoyance that a mere wife has acquired just by doing her dharma.

In this story, the wife's obedience and sense of service to her husband are overstated to make the point. While the texts harp on a woman's service, through the service, she is granted almost limitless powers. The *Skanda Purana* says: "Just as a snake charmer forcibly draws out from a hole a snake, so a pativrata snatches away her husband's life from the messengers of death, and reaches heaven with her husband, and the messengers of death, on seeing the pativrata, beat a hasty retreat" (Kane, II, 1:568). A pativrata could, through her power, "burn the world, stop the motions of the sun and the moon" (Kane, II, 1:568). This power was acknowledged; and perversely enough, men demanded a display of it as a proof of their wives' chastity, for the power was concomitant with their fidelity. Thus we have the story of Vasistha and Arundhati:

> Vasistha is meditating at dawn. His wife Arundhati has just milked the cow and has brought some fresh milk to her husband. Vasistha suddenly doubts her fidelity; he says: If you are true to me, the milk in your pot should boil over now. Arundhati looks at the milk and wills it; the milk boils over and her husband is convinced (*Sumangali Manual*, 37)

Arundhati continues to be a symbol of fidelity on a pan-Indian level. She is identified as a companion star to one of the seven that form the Great Bear constellation. In Indian astrology, the seven stars are seven sages and Vasistha is one of them. After every Hindu wedding there is a ritual called "Arundhati darsana" ("The sighting of Arundhati") and the stars of Vasistha and Arundhati are pointed out to the couple. The bride is urged to be as faithful as Arundhati.

A woman's virtue is an important part of her dharma; in traditional Hindu literature, a woman does not tolerate any slur on it. Sita, in the epic *Ramayana*, upset that her husband Rama has questioned her chastity, enters fire; and of course the fire returns her unharmed to this world. This intolerance of suspicions about one's sexual fidelity marks even 20th century fiction.

> The wife of a man handicapped by a bus accident is forced to take a job while he stays at home. One evening she returns home very late due to an office party for a new manager. He is offended and insinuates that she may be headed for an extra-marital relationship ... she is stunned by his suspicions and renounces all interest in being anywhere but by his side ... In the morning she is dead, having left a note saying she takes this course to prove her faithfulness. Before breathing her last, she has considerately left for him on the table his morning idlis and coffee. He is convinced. (Lindholm, 10)

Lindholm pertinently remarks that this story is different from the epic *Ramayana* in that there is an avoidance of supernatural intervention in the 20th century story and consequently the heroine dies. However, her sexual fidelity is convincingly portrayed; her virtue is vindicated.

The earlier notions of the powers of a faithful wife have not been entirely discarded. About 2000 years ago, Manu said:

> Where women are honoured, there the gods are pleased; but where they are not honoured, no sacred rite yields rewards. Where the female relations live in grief, the family soon perishes; but that family where they are not unhappy ever prospers. The houses in which female relations, not being duly honoured, pronounce a curse, perish completely, as if destroyed by magic (Manu 3.56 to 58).

The *Sumangali Manual* repeats the sentiment: "... a family that makes a sumangali suffer will be ruined for generations. Mantresvara says in his book on astrology that these people will forever lose their peace of mind" (30). "This attribution of power to chaste and virtuous wives is also implicit in a ritual prayer done by sumangalis in honour of dead sumangali to seek blessings" (Narayanan: 1985). A virtuous sumangali, dead or alive, is still a carrier of power; perhaps not as dramatic as the Nalayini or Sita variety, but still rather potent in terms of the well-being of the family. When honoured, she radiates auspiciousness; when offended, she has the power to curse. It is in this context that she is morally almost *more* powerful than the man; that she is as worthy of worship as her husband.

Wanton women

Any discussion of traditional Hindu perceptions of women's sexuality should include the attitudes to prostitutes and adultery. Vatsayana's *Kama Sutra* or the *Manual of Love*, (circa 1st to 3rd century A.D.) clearly distinguishes between wives and prostitutes and their respective duties. A wife was to:

> ... act in conformity with her husband's wishes as if he were a divine being and with his consent should take upon herself the whole care of his family. She should keep the whole house well cleaned... make the floor smooth and polished... surpass all women in her cleverness, her knowledge of cookery,... and her manner of serving her husband. The milk that remains after the meals should be turned to ghee or clarified butter. Oil and sugar should be prepared at home: spinning and weaving should also be done here... She should also attend to the pounding and cleaning of rice, using its small grain and chaff in some way or another. She should pay the salaries of the servants, look after the tilling of the fields, the keeping of the flocks and herds, superintend the making of vehicles, etc. (*Kama Sutra*, 158-161).

On the other hand, a prostitute

> ... should be possessed of beauty and amiability, with auspicious body marks. She should have a liking for good qualities in other people, as well as a liking for wealth. She should take delight in sexual unions resulting from love, and should be... of the same class as the man with regard to sexual enjoyment.
>
> She should always be anxious to acquire and obtain experience and knowledge, be free from avarice and always have a liking for social gatherings and for the arts...(*Kama Sutra*, 207-208).

The distinction is clear as well as to their respective dharmas.

Extra-marital sex can, for our discussion, be simplified into two major categories: that which is the dharma of certain groups of people; and that which is non-dharmic and therefore, frowned upon. Issues of auspicious/ inauspicious as well as morality are dependent on this classification. In the first category, one may perceive in traditional scripture a standard classification: a royal courtesan *(rajavesya)*, a city prostitute *(nagari)*, a clandestine prostitute from a good family *(guptavesya)*, a temple dancer or servant of god *(devavesya)* and a harlot who frequented holy places to seduce pilgrims *(tirthaga or brahmavesya)*. For simplicity, one may reduce these to three major categories: a "temple" prostitute, a "city" prostitute (ranging in quality from a royal courtesan to a street harlot), and finally the clandestine woman of the streets, usually an adultress. The first two categories are within the lines of dharma; the last is strictly unethical.

Dancers associated with temples, the so-called "servants of god" *(devadasi)*[13] have traditionally been sexual-companions of human beings.[14] Socially, certain communities have traditionally offered their daughters to this profession, often as fulfilment of a vow, without any social stigma, and the dedication ceremonies themselves were fairly elaborate and resembled weddings, whereby an "auspicious thread" (*mangala sutra* or the wedding necklace) was tied by proxy on behalf of the deity on the young girl (Trivedi, 77-79). Since devadasis belonged to and were united with a deathless deity, they could never technically be "widowed". They were continuously auspicious (nitya sumangalis); a perception that continues till today. Trivedi reports: "As a 'Devadasi' is symbolically married to a god... she is immune from widowhood as gods are immortal. Her presence anywhere, at any time, is supposed to be auspicious" (Trivedi, 81). The auspiciousness of the sacred prostitute is acknowledged because she cannot be a widow; Trivedi concludes his discussion, saying "... a Devadasi attains immunity from the state of traditional inauspiciousness of widowhood. She is called *akhandasobhagyavati*, i.e., a woman whose marriage is intact forever" (Trivedi, 81-83).

In 1927 Mrs Muthulakshmi Reddi's Bill for prohibition of keeping devadasis paid through endowments was passed by the Madras Legislative Council; in 1947 a Bill against the dedication of children to temples was passed,[15] but instances are reported in many places still.[16] Trivedi (133-139) gives eleven case studies of young girls from scheduled castes in the Bijapur district who were offered to temples. Since "sacred" prostitution is illegal, they moved into commercial prostitution. The reasons for the dedication were poverty and/or propitiation of the deity.

There was a distinction, even if theoretical, between the sacred prostitutes and the "public" prostitutes. The latter category was probably much older; it is certainly established by the time of Canakya's *Arthsastra* in the fourth century B.C. This manual of statecraft has a chapter called "The superintendent of prostitutes" and clearly gives the duties of and taxation procedures for the prostitutes. Later, the *Kama Sutra* also describes the intricacies of the art of being a woman about town. In these books, as well as the *Mahabharata*, and some puranas (especially *Matsya*, ch. 70) we find a list of their duties to a king, his guests and retinue; their salary (1000 panas annually for the chief prostitute in a court; Arthasastra, 139); the fines that a prostitute must pay (two days' wages per month; (*Arthasastra*, 141); the punishment for a prostitute who kills her lover (thrown to dogs); what a king must pay to retired court prostitutes (monthly stipend for maintenance); those eligible to get a stipend from the government (including those who train the prostitutes in their art; *Arthasastra*, 141), the sixty-four arts of a refined prostitute (the list includes, alphabetically, art, arithmetic, carpentry, logic, magic, mimicry, music, poetry, sword play, etc.; *Kama Sutra* 69-72); the ways in which a king could use a prostitute (spying, extracting information from other spies) etc. (*Arthasastra*, 142). These prostitutes had a definite place and role in society. The prostitute had her own dharma and, as is true of all Hinduism, if she performed her dharma scrupulously, she acquired untold powers. Thus we have the rather unusual story of the old courtesan Bindumati; when King Asoka (3rd century B.C.) in an idle moment asks if anyone can make the river Ganga flow upstream, the courtesan meets the challenge and succeeds. The king asks the old prostitute: "...You, a thief, a cheat, corrupt, ...vicious, wicked old sinner who have broken the bounds of morality and live on the plunder of fools... what is this act of truth (by which you succeeded)?" (Zimmer, 161-162).

The prostitute's answer is simple; she says whoever courted her services, whatever his caste, she treats them all equally; she does not fawn or insult; she simply serves them, truthfully; that is her act of truth, of dharma, and she is powerful because of that.

While the prostitute had her own dharma she could not be a partner in a man's pursuit of dharma, like his wife. Even if her lover eventually married her, she could not be accepted as a full partner, because prostitutes were only from the "lower" castes by definition. Women from the upper three classes of society were not allowed technically to be prostitutes. The *Kama Sutra* (208) also clearly says that a prostitute does not consort with a man for dharma. She also definitely did not help in the pursuit of artha or worldly wealth; rather, prostitutes were rich because they took that money away from men and were sometimes said to procure from a man wealth that had taken his family generations to accumulate. The fifth century Tamil epic *Cilappatikaram* talks of the rich hero Kovalan being reduced to poverty after squandering all his wealth on the dancer/courtesan, Matavi, while his faithful wife Kannaki waits patiently at home. When the husband finally returns home after several years, Kannaki offers him the only jewels left on her body to help him start a new business. The *Kama Sutra* (1964:216-218) in fact goes on to even list the various wiles and ruses that a prostitute may use to get a man to spend money on her, for jewelry, trinkets, entertaining, payment of bills and support on a more permanent basis.

A prostitute does (and excessively) satisfy a man's quest for kama or sensual pleasure; and it is because of this, along with the Hindu concept of "marriage", that a prostitute has earned the name for being continuously auspicious, like the devadasi. When a prostitute becomes a man's partner in love and the association continues to resemble anything more permanent, she becomes a concubine and perhaps (as in early dramas), even a wife. When the relationship becomes anything more than casual, the prostitute is urged (by the *Kama Sutra*) to start acting like a wife to assume a wife's dharma. "When a courtesan is living as a wife with her lover, she should behave like a 'chaste' woman, and do everything to his satisfaction" (*Kama Sutra*, 211-213).

The prostitute's association with a man, even if not formalized by the ritual of marriage, acquires the colouring of one in popular perception because of the several meanings of the word "marriage" in Hindu culture. These are *Brahma*, *Daiva*, *Prajapatya* and *Arsa* (approved forms of marriage, for they maintain traditional ritual, including the giving away of the bride by her father, and sometimes financial transactions of an acceptable nature are involved). The last three in the list of "marriages" are *gandharva* (where lovers unite without any formal wedding ritual preceding the union), *raksasa* (the abduction of the bride after killing some of her kin) and *paisaca*, the seduction of a woman when she is intoxicated or asleep. The last three were always more questionable than others and, later in history, the term "marriage" was not applied to them. But the fact that they were considered "marriage" for several centuries is significant; by implication, practically any kind of liaison, whether premarital sex or forcible abduction, was "legal". The question of whether a gandharva or raksasa marriage should be followed by a regular wedding ritual of *saptapadi* (the taking of seven steps around the fire) is left open.[17] There is generally no evidence in earlier literature that the gandharva and other marriages had to be followed by the trappings of a regular approved marriage. Kanva specifically mentions to Sakuntala that the gandharva marriage is one in which sacred words (mantra) are said.[18]

A prostitute, then, at least in popular perception, was continually "wedded" even if it was just physically; she was continuously being rendered a sumangali, without danger of being widowed. The presence of both temple dancers and city prostitutes endowed any occasion with auspiciousness; the sight of a prostitute was always a good omen and she accompanied kings to meet royal guests.

While devadasis and "city" prostitutes were auspicious, adultresses were not. Prostitutes performed their dharma but adultresses *(asati)* had definitely strayed from their paths. Manu says twice: "But for disloyalty to her husband, a wife is censured among men, and (in her next life) is born in the womb of a jackal and tormented by diseases, the punishment of her sin" (9.30 and 5.164).

Hindu society itself has never come to terms with the acceptance of adultresses after Manu. The position of the fallen wife was not always bad in Hindu society. Prior to Manu, in the epics and in the Arthasastra, the woman's error was considered regrettable, but not absolutely condemnable. She was allowed to resume a reasonably normal life after undergoing prescribed penances and rituals of purification; her menstrual cycle was supposed to purify her (Kane, 571, Altekar, 376-377). It is interesting — and certainly significant as a reminder of past leniency — that of the five women *(panca kanya)* remembered by Hindus in their daily prayer (Mukherjee, 37) four (both dharmically and non-dharmically) consorted with more than one man. The five are Ahalya (Gautama's wife, who had a liaison with Indra), Tara (the wife of Vali who marries Sugriva without absolute proof of her husband's death), Draupadi (married in dharma to five men), Kunti (who had a pre-marital union with Surya, and after marriage to Pandu, consorts, albeit with his permission, with Dharma, Vayu and Indra) and finally, Mandodari, the wife of the *raksasa* Ravana, who of all the women mentioned above is the only person faithful to just one man. (In South Indian versions, Kunti is replaced by Sita: *Sumangali Manual*, 64-66). Whatever the extenuating circumstances were in these cases — and certainly there were, for none of the women are referred to as "adultresses" — the fact remains that they were venerated along with the pativrata women in earlier times. After approximately the time of Manu, however, the emphasis on fidelity to one man increased steadily. Hook quite correctly says:

> ...in a number of stories in the *Vetalapancavimsati* we find married women who are not faithful to their husbands. Collections such as this and the *Kathasaritasagara* at one time enjoyed immense popularity in India. Nevertheless, the heroines in these stories seem to have left little trace on the collective consciousness. They are not known by name to the ordinary person. They are not alluded to in ordinary conversation. In short, they have not received ratification as cultural archetypes.

The one difficult and oft-quoted counter-example in this issue is Radha's relationship with Krishna. Radha was a married woman, but also the friend and lover of Lord Krishna. Hook (41) discusses the figure of Radha and shows that her position is unique; and the paradigm is seen as spiritually applicable, rather than serving as a social example in Hinduism.

Indian fiction and cinema do not tolerate an adultress as a heroine. In a Tamil "realistic" story — later made into a movie that was not accepted by the public — called "Parvati, without a direction" (based on a story "Tikkarra Parvati" by the eminent statesman, C. Rajagoplalchari), the heroine is unfaithful to her alcoholic husband in one desperate moment; the story ends in the only way that it can in an Indian situation — the heroine commits suicide. The adultress's sexual adventure definitely renders her inauspicious, for they are not within the boundaries of wifely dharma.[19] The prostitute, however, in fulfilment of her dharma, achieves the opposite effect.

The auspiciousness of a prostitute and her role in social functions did not mean that she was accepted wholeheartedly by all society. We saw the emperor Asoka reviling prostitutes. Women of higher classes and status were asked definitely to avoid the prostitutes, except for the occasional association between royal ladies and their dancing or music teachers. Sanka definitely forbids any wife from associating with a prostitute (Kane, II-1:564). The *Kama Sutra* (160) itself says that a virtuous wife must not associate with "unchaste and roguish women". Manu classes prostitutes with gamblers, cruel men and thieves, and rogues (Basham, 186). The word *tevar atiyar*, Tamil for devadasi, was and is still used as a pejorative term. Later manuals suggested that the murderer of a prostitute does not have to be punished (Basham, 186). The auspiciousness of a prostitute was selectively needed on certain occasions; in any other situation, she was morally inferior, at least in the last two thousand years.

A widow

Lillian Brown, a traveller in India in 1950, writes about a wedding that she witnessed, and says:

> Hastily I pressed some flowers into the little bride's hand. "May you have many sons, and may your husband outlive you," I whispered. In India, these are the things a wife prays for above all...

Later she muses that perhaps the old husband of the bride may soon die and the bride may know some freedom; but her servant tells her: "That's where you are mistaken, Memsahib. When he dies, her troubles begin. Life holds nothing for the Hindu widow. She must spend the rest of her life in mourning. She can never remarry" (Brown, 78-79). Brown was merely reporting something that has been more or less in practice — with a few exceptions that we shall note later — for at least two thousand years. A widow has been considered inauspicious, a bad omen to anyone who encounters her; and in Tamil, the word for "widow" is used as a word of abuse in everyday situations. A widow's appearance distinguished her from society and even in educated, reform-oriented circles vestiges of this attitude remain. In a front-page article in the newspapers (May 19, 1983), the then Prime Minister of India, Indira Gandhi, was quoted as objecting to her widowed daughter-in-law wearing the clothes of a *suhagin* (a woman whose husband is alive) within ten days of her husband's death. The next day, in a box-item, the daughter-in-law is reported as "resenting" these remarks and adding that the statement by the Prime Minister "left not only me, but the entire country aghast."[20]

Traditionally, the higher the social caste of the widow, the greater was the differentiation, and Brahmin widows underwent tonsure (complete shaving of the head) till the middle of this century. This was a plight worse than it appears for the Brahmin lady; for in India women are not usually touched by men other than close relatives, and a barber, being of a low caste, could not associate normally with any high class men, let alone women. For a Brahmin woman's head to be shaved by such a person was the ultimate disgrace, the ultimate personal and social disfigurement. Even stories that pleaded for a removal of this grotesque custom toed the line with the ending of the story subtly reinforcing the practice though the ostensible intent was, through pathos, to rebuke society. The story of Kethariyin Tai (The Mother of Kethari) is a case in point:

> Kethari's father deserts his mother to live with another woman. Later, Kethari marries. About 18 years later, while he is studying in England, he hears that his father had died. When Kethari returns home, he does not recognize the mother whose head has been shaved though she had not seen her husband for several years. Kethari is shocked and falls ill, vowing that he will fight for social reform to end this ugly practice if he gets well. Kethari dies; his wife's head is now shaved because of tradition. (*Manuel*, 28)

The status of a widow in recent years is summed up in *Toward Equality: Report of the Committee on the Status of Women in India*, an official publication of the government's Minsitry of Education and Social Welfare (1974):

> ... the converse of (the) notion of marriage as women's destiny and the married state as more desirable, is the idea of inauspiciousness and loss of the

right to full participation in socio-religious life associated with widowhood. In contrast, a Hindu male has no fasts to observe for the wife's long life and welfare. The husband wears no distinctive marks signifying the married state and does not incur any inauspiciousness at the death of his wife... The common blessing for a woman, "May your husband live long", is self-explanatory. Although the strict code of conduct prescribed for widows is no longer operative in its most restrictive and oppressive aspects, there are certain disabilities associated with widowhood. A widow is barred from active participation in auspicious occasions. Besides the items of decoration associated with the married state, she is expected to discard colourful clothes, glass bangles, wearing of flowers, and attractive jewellery. Plain white colour is associated with widowhood, and by implication is forbidden traditionally for Sumangali, i.e., one whose husband is alive. The widows of Bengal, who abstain from fish, and the Kammas and Reddy widows of Andhra/Pradesh who give up meat, are not yet extinct. Among the Brahmin and also among such non-Brahmin communities which do not have the custom of widow remarriage, there are a number of ways of restricting the life of a widow so that she gets little pleasure out of life and her natural desires are suppressed.

The report goes on to say, significantly: "A distinct contrast between the status of a widow and a Sumangali is characteristic of India as a whole."[21]

The 20th century social reforms to improve the lot of widows to keep pace with legal reforms that were enacted in the 19th century (Proscription of suttee, legalization of widow remarriage etc.) were largely due to the efforts of (among others) Pandita Ramabai, Mrs (Sister) Subbulakshmi and the exhortations of several editorials in leading newspapers. Pandita Ramabai's letters and books were acknowledged and quoted by leading Indologists like Max Mueller, who wrote to the London *Times* in September 1887, proposing a number of reforms for "these waifs and strays of womanhood". The reforms were slowly and painfully accomplished to some degree, primarily by raising the legal age of marriage (to lessen the number of child widows), the acceptance of widow re-marriage and by encouraging education of all women, especially of young widows. The story of Mrs Subbulakshmi, (told in "A Child Widow's Story" by Monica Felton) with her father refusing to allow the shaving of her head and, sin of all sins, actually enrolling her in a co-educational institution, where she could be seen by men, caused a social scandal initially, but was only one of the pioneering cases in the trail of improving the lot of widows.

Prior to the beginning of the Christian era the status of widows (as was true of adultresses) was not too bad in India. By the time of the Vedas

(1500 B.C.) the old Indo-European custom of burning a wife with her husband was only a distant memory. At best,[22] she was sometimes allowed to remarry, or if childless, and she so agreed, a brother-in-law might be appointed by the family to consort with her till a son was born. The *Arthasastra* outlines a number of courses that a widow could take, with special financial bonuses if she remained true to her husband's memory (*Arthasastra*, 175). Gradually, inheritance rights were denied to sons born of levirate marriages; by the time of Manu, absolute chastity was recommended for the widow and the practice of levirate marriage barely sanctioned. The status deteriorated with time.

In southern India, the picture from the earliest literature is different, and definitely more dismal. Hart notes the do's and don'ts of a widow:

> ...Widows did not wear ornaments (*Purananuru* 223, 253 and 261), they caked their shaven heads with mud (*Pur.* 280) and slept on beds of stone (*Pur.* 246)...it is not surprising perhaps that with such empty lives to look forward to many widows committed suicide upon the death of their husband... (Hart, 1, 102).

Both tonsure of the head and a form of suttee is referred to in these poems. The first is clear in *Purananuru* 280; and if these poems were composed between the 1st and 3rd century A.D., the custom is much earlier than the suggestion of Kane who feels that "the practice was gradually evolved after the 10th and 11th century... by rendering them ugly it might have been intended to keep them chaste" (Kane, II, 1). The Sanskrit works that come down really hard on the status of a widow were not written till much later,[23] suggestive of the fact that the more stringent behaviour expected of these unfortunate women on a pan-Indian level was perhaps due to the interaction with the culture of southern India.

In many ways, a woman was seen as responsible for her husband's death. Virtuous women had good karma and their husbands prospered; we have already noted that the pativrata had the power to snatch her husband from the hands of death. Thus Savitri, by her wit and virtue, saved Satyavan; Atimanti saved her husband.

> Atimanti and her husband are swimming in a river, when the current drags him to his death; Atimanti piously follows the river till it reaches the sea, begging for her husband's life; the river goddess, touched by her devotion, hands back her husband, alive and well (*Sumangali Manual*, 56).

This story was mentioned as early as the first Tamil poems that have survived.[24] The pativrata women, if pure, could save their husbands; it was their bad karma that was perceived to draw them to the state of widowhood. [25] The fact that they lived was in itself an accusation, at least in oral tradition, that they were not absolutely true to their husbands. Brhaspati (c. A.D. 300-500) is credited with the statement that a true wife dies on the death of the husband (Kane, II, 1:567). Most women did not die on hearing about their husband's death. Child widows frequently had not even seen their husbands after the wedding day. For several centuries at least one way that a woman ostensibly retained her honour and died a sumangali was to immolate herself with the body of her husband; an act referred to as "suttee" by Western writers. [26] This was prohibited by law in 1829 by the British, though public cases occurred (and still continue to occur) from time to time. The sati of Roop Kanwar that took place only a few years ago in front of hundreds of witnesses has received the notoriety it deserves. [27]   In the middle ages one hears not just of widows, but occasionally even betrothed girls who commit sati. The status of an engaged girl whose fiancé died had been frequently discussed in Hindu sastra. Some believe that she should be treated as a widow (Altekar, 181-183), but others (including Manu) hold that until the saptapadi and the wedding rituals are performed the girl is not considered married and, therefore, the death of a fiancé does not render a betrothed girl a widow. It must also be pointed out that the incidence of sati was probably not very high. However, while complete statistics are unavailable, limited figures show the spread of sati all over India. In northern India, it seems to have been prevalent only after the eleventh century, gradually increasing after A.D. 1400 (Altekar, 153). It seems to have been most approved for the warrior/royal families. There were many conditions and sometimes even prohibitions about a Brahmin widow committing sati (Altekar, 1511, quoting *Padma Purana*, Srstikhanda, 49, 72-73). The final consensus seems to have been that she was allowed *sahamarana* (immolating herself with the corpse), but not *anumarana* (immolating herself with a piece of her husband's clothing or other article on hearing of his death in a distant land) (Kane, II, 1:633).

It is, however, important to remember that both in the practice of sati and overall attitude to the widow, the higher castes were considered to be trend-setters. So, while there were no injunctions for women in the "lower" castes to commit sati, or any practice of disfiguring the widow, they did it in imitation of the higher classes. Thus, Pandita Ramabai notes that "some of our lower castes too have adopted the custom of shaving widows' heads and have much pride in imitating their high caste brethren" (Ramabai, 46). Trivedi (31) also confirms this self-conscious imitation of the higher classes by the lower caste groups: "It is interesting to note here i.e. in marriage customs etc., that while emulating the higher caste traditions and practices... the untouchables are not always raising the status of their women." Thus, to a large extent the traditional freedom (and generally more humane attitudes) granted to women in the "lower" castes did not always work in practice, in their eagerness to imitate the higher castes, their women were also subject to negative treatment. In a predictable way, this has resulted in "fossilization" of attitudes in the lower castes today. Traditionally, the higher castes have not allowed ritual participation in certain dharmic activities for widows; but, with better education today, it seems that they may look upon it favourably. On the other hand, the narrow outlook discriminating against widows had filtered down into the "lower" classes which traditionally had been more lax. Many communities which traditionally allowed widow remarriages (like the Virasaivas) do not automatically approve of them.

Widows were banned from participation in social dharma and could not be partners to anyone in its performance. They could not participate in the pursuit of artha with a male partner other than a husband and now were an added encumbrance to many families. With the increasing value on virtue and fidelity to a husband, even if he was dead, a widow had no place in fulfilling a person's quest for kama. Therefore, she did not have the potential to help a male repay his debts to gods and the ancestors by participating in rituals of dharma and by producing sons. In terms of the three goals of this life, she had no role to play, no purpose in life. She was — and is — still perceived in many circles to be inauspicious. Social and economic handicaps faced by widows led to their escaping, when convenient, into a life of prostitution. Even now it is held that "... social discouragement of remarriage of young widows has helped in the recruitment of prostitutes from village India. Caste inequality and sex exploitation by the economically well-off castes are other factors" (*Toward Equality*, 92). Lannoy confirms this, but with a qualification: "Many Hindu widows escaped from a life of servitude, frequent fasts, shaven hair and absence of legal protection by becoming prostitutes. Only rarely did widows have a chance to gain fulfilment as matriarchs in the joint family, though in some cases they actually became its head" (Lannoy, 104).

The qualifying line at the end is significant. Mothers, especially those with sons, were an important exception to the ill-treatment meted out to widows and this was reflected by scripture. The *Skanda Purana* callously says: "The widow is more inauspicious than all other inauspicious things;

at the sight of a widow no success can be had in any undertaking", but adds a rider: "excepting one's widowed mother, all widows are void of auspiciousness" (*Skanda Purana* III, Brahamaranya ch. 7, 50-51, quoted in Kane, II, 1:585). A mother, whatever her faults and even if an outcaste, should never be abandoned by the son. She is considered to be the highest teacher and superior to the father. Even Manu who has so many negative things to say about women says: "The teacher is ten times more venerable than a sub-teacher, the father a hundred times more than the teacher, but the mother a thousand times more than the father" (Manu II.145).

Auspiciousness rests in the state of being married and fulfilling one's dharmic obligations. Since a prostitute is either wedded to a deathless deity or is continually "wedded" through sexual liaisons, she is perceived as continually, eternally, auspicious. A widow has no partner and cannot fulfil man's kama within the boundaries of dharma defined by post-Manu sastras. She is inauspicious. Since neither the satisfaction of kama in an excessive manner or the lack of ability to fulfil it constitutes the ideal amount of auspiciousness in Hindu perceptions, we have to look for the other two goals: dharma and artha. Neither the prostitute nor the widow is a partner in dharma or artha. The ideal woman, with the ideal amount of auspiciousness is still the sumangali, a full partner in dharma, artha and kama, through whom children are born and wealth and religious merit accumulated. It is only the married woman who bears the prefix *Srimati*: the one with *Sri* or auspiciousness; she has been traditionally the most honoured woman in Hindu society, especially if she bears children; it is she who is adorned "auspiciously" even in death and in funeral rites.

On the whole, perceptions of the sumangali have changed least through the years. Our discussion has spanned roughly three ages: pre-Manu where restrictions were not too stringent; post-Manu to the early 20th century, and the 20th century, after 1930. In all these ages, perceptions of the sumangali and her dharma have remained more or less constant; traditional values are still reflected in the *Sumangali Manual*, fiction and drama. While we have dealt primarily with women from the "upper" castes, the tendencies of the "lower" castes to emulate the higher ones have been noted by so many studies, and mass media today reinforce the images so well that conceptions of the ideal have to a large extent been made uniform.

Perceptions of the prostitute have perhaps changed most in the last thirty years. She is now an object of contempt, or at best a symbol of romantic pathos in fiction and movies (Manuel, 29, 36; movies such as the Hindi and Tamil *Aranketram* exemplify this trend). Some reasons for the further decline in their status are obvious. Poverty and exploitation among the "lower" castes have driven women into cheap prostitution with or without the veneer of "sacredness" attached to the profession. Ideas of western morality have wrought more changes than previous Hindu consciousness of Buddhist or Muslim disapproval. Another reason is that the arts of classical dance and music which had been preserved by devadasis and royal courtesans (so exclusively that Monica Felton in her biography of Mrs Subbulakshmi reports the family's horror when the young girl was given a violin by her father; even in the late 19th century, everyone knew that only women of ill-repute learnt to play musical instruments!) have now passed on into the secular world.

Perceptions of the widow have changed considerably, though she is still regarded in some circles as "inauspicious." She is no longer rendered "ugly" by the shaving of her hair, though she is expected to shun most forms of adornment. Some earlier practices still remain. Kane reported that an untonsured Brahmin widow was not allowed a vision of the deity in the Pandharpur temple (Kane, 593). In certain south Indian communities even today, widows whose heads are not shaved are not allowed in the presence of religious leaders and the special *sathari* (a symbol of the Lord's grace) is not placed on their heads: an instance where social customs have not kept pace with the philosophy of the community. Remarriages of young widows is increasingly taking place, especially among the uneducated classes; however, widows who are about 36 or more do not usually remarry.

Attitudes to body and bodily functions

From our discussion above, it seems clear that traditional attitudes towards women are based on their ability to share a man's life — in a dharmic manner — and procreate. Scriptural sources are almost entirely androcentric and a perpetuation of these images has taken place over the centuries, filtering down today to images presented in mass media. Virginity is important before marriage and sexual fidelity to one's husband after marriage.

While a mother is worshipped and her procreative ability celebrated, the very body that procreates is not held in high esteem. Both scriptural sources and ritual practices reflect attitudes towards female bodily functions which project them as "polluted" and "unclean" during menstruation and childbirth. We shall consider some of these rites of passage to understand some Hindu notions of the female body.

A young girl is protected by the family against unnecessary "touch" by other male members of the family. Frequently, it is only brothers, a father or grandfather, who can hug a young girl. In some south Indian communities they do not touch the girl, even in affection, unless moved by emotion. This is to protect the girl's "purity" or the notion of virginity, which extends even to physical embraces.

Menstruation

This protection intensifies after the young girl has her first menstrual period. She has now come of age; in the Tamil sayings, she is considered to have "blossomed". The first menstrual period is celebrated by the female members of the family, for now the girl is ready for procreation. The intensity of celebrations varies from community to community; some still put on a big show (this is to indicate to potential bridegrooms that they are a family of "means"), but in many other families, only some basic rituals are conducted.[28] Many communities used to celebrate this rite of passage in a grand way till the nineteen fifties; with increasing westernization, these rituals are considered "shameful" and "vulgar" by young girls. However, in many villages, the celebrations still take the form of a mini-wedding; and the young girl is showered with presents from the family. Usually the presents are in the form of money or clothing.

Hindu mothers generally do not discuss menstruation or sex with their daughters. Girls get their information from cousins, friends, aunts and other women they may know, in a fragmented way, and fraught with superstition. What is known — and observed — is that a menstruating woman is considered "polluted" during the time of her periods. This attitude, which was observed in almost all communities (with the notable exception of the Virasaiva and some other traditions) in the past, involved a total segregation of the woman from everyday life. In many households, especially the higher castes, the woman could not even be in the same room, or sometimes the same house as the others. She was kept separate in a little room, with her own plate and mug to eat from. She could not cook, go out, or participate in daily prayers. The Tamil words for menstruation most commonly used are *turam* (far — referring to the physical segregation of the girl) or *tittu* (pollution). After the fourth day, she had a "ritual bath", washing her hair and herself thoroughly, and was then incorporated into the family. Dhruvarajan (1989, 67) reports from her study of Brahmin women in the village of Musale:

Among Brahmins, customs like seclusion of a woman during menstruation and her ceremonious purification afterwards dramatically point out to her that her body is susceptible to ritual pollution and that she should be careful with regard to her conduct during this time. A woman can have evil effects on growing things at this time and therefore should be careful not to plant any seeds or seedlings or to go near any young plants. Since she is polluting, she should not go near anyone doing a religious ritual nor should she show her face or let her voice be heard. She is secluded and eats alone in a segregated place which is purified after her period is over. She is believed to have evil magical powers, therefore, she should keep away from auspicious occasions such as weddings, otherwise there will be disaster. [29]

However, this strict segregation is not observed in many communities today. During the fifties and sixties, I knew of many women who went to school or college while menstruating, but once they came home, they observed the segregation from the rest of the family. While these barriers within households — especially, urban — have broken down to a large extent, vestiges remain in many families. Frequently, the menstruating woman (even in Virasaiva households) is prohibited from cooking,[30] but in almost all cases, she still will not go to the household shrine, participate in any religious ritual, or go to a place of worship during her periods. Whether this Hindu woman is in India or overseas, she almost invariably has the purifying ritual bath on the fourth day, and in fact, counts her cycle from the day of the "bath". "Bathing" becomes the euphemism for having periods in many parts of India; Jacobson and Wadley report that when a young (north Indian) girl started menstruating, her sister-in-law reported to her mother "Your little girl has begun to bathe" (42). In several south Indian communities, pregnancy is announced with the statement, "She is not bathing."

This sense of pollution extends to childbirth. The occasion of a childbirth is happy and "auspicious"; nevertheless, it is ritually defiling and polluting, in some communities, to the entire family. For a certain number of days after a child is born, the family cannot go to a temple. However, in many areas, it is only the mother who is in this defiled state, sometimes for 40 days, but the negative attitude associated with monthly menstruation is not present at childbirth.

Because sexual functions are not discussed directly with young girls, the consummation of a marriage could be somewhat traumatic in some communities. This ceremony is called by various names (*shanti kalynam* in Tamil — peaceful/propitiating and auspicious ceremony; *gauna*[31]; "Flower-bed" in Bengal[32]). Traditionally, in most communities, very little is spoken about the sexual functions and needs of a woman. She was considered to be a passive partner and her wishes do not seem to have counted for much.

Recent studies on non-literate audiences indicate that it is the woman who takes responsibility for contraception and family planning, because any measure taken by a man is considered as threatening to his sexual functions. [33]

Rapid changes in Hindu society are visible in urban areas. The media have heralded in some of these changes; in movies like the Hindi *Arth* [34], and the Tamil *Cirai*, the heroine shows independence and anger, and a refusal to conform to the traditional norms. A recent issue of *India Today* (September 1989) which caters to a modern, educated Indian audience, discussed the growing sexual demands articulated by women. While this may reflect only a small percentage of the larger population, the trend-setting media may both be commenting on on-going changes and catalyzing more [35], and one may see a tangible break from Manu, two thousand years after he wrote his views on women.

NOTES

This paper is a revised version of earlier talks given at Harvard University, Center for the Study of World Religions (April 1982), the University of Florida (December 1982) and the American Academy of Religion, National Meeting (December 1983). I am grateful to Professors John Carman, Bill Harman and Austin Creel for their comments and suggestions.

[1] Tulsidas, in *Ramacaritamanas*, and quoted in *Toward Equality*, p.40.

[2] On this issue, see works of Frederique Marglin listed in the bibliography.

[3] For a discussion of "auspiciousness", see Marglin and Carman (1985), Marglin (1985) and Kersenboom-Story (1987).

[4] Studies which include discussions on fiction and movies in reflections of traditional values include Madan (1976) and Ziffren (1988).

[5] This is in the rite of *kanyadana*. A girl's father says that the bridegroom should not prove false in dharma, artha, and kama and he responds with the words: "naticarami." On textual variations of this ritual, see Kane, p.533.

[6] *Mahabharata*, Santiparva, ch. 142-142, quoted in Mukherjhee, 1978, p.15.

[7] Kane, 1978, p.558, quoting Ramayana VII,9,25.

[8] The book referred to as "The Sumangali Manual" is written by one Najan. Its full title is *Dirgha Sumangali Bhava*, a common blessing uttered by older people when young girls or married women bow to them. The book is written from the Brahminical standpoint and reflects views popularly held by the Brahmin community of Tamil Nadu, South India. Because this book repeats several stereotypes and proclaims very traditional views on women, I have found it a useful volume to quote from, to depict the perpetuation of typical "Hindu" generalizations on "ideal women."

[9] *Mahabharata, Anusasana parva* 134-32 to 55; quoted in Mukherjee, p.15.

[10] The story of Savitri is found in *Mahabharata, Vana parva*, pp.293-299.

[11] *Padma Purana Srstikhanda*, 47, v.55 quoted in Kane, p.565 and in the *Sumangali Manual*, 51. The *Sumangali Manual* quotes it from a work called *Niti venpa*.

[12] The chapters are entitled "Pativratya: The ideology," "Pativratya and Women's Personality" and "Pativratya and the Hindu Women's Destiny". Vanaja Dhruvarajan, *Hindu Women and the Power of Ideology*, 1989.

[13] Jordan says that the "[a]lthough the term 'devadasi', which literally means female servant of god, originally referred to women who came from the upper castes and served in south Indian temples, under British rule, the term was indiscriminately applied to any woman of any caste dedicated to serve a deity." Jordan, 1989 a 5.

[14] One of the most sophisticated and informative studies on devadasis is Frederique Marglin's *Wives of the God King: The Rituals of the Devadasis of Puri*. See also the recent work of Saskia C. Kersenboom-Story, *Nitysumangali: Devadasi Tradition in South India*.

[15] For devadasis and the legal system, see Jordan 1989a and 1989b.

[16] See "Devadasis 'still there'" in *Deccan Herald* (Bangalore), 4 April, 1983. In this article, the Deputy Inspector General of Police from Bangalore is said to have witnessed 14 such cases.

[17] Kane, after some discussion, concludes (primarily from selected literature on svayamvaras) that these "marriages" were followed by saptapadi (Kane, II, 1:521), but Altekar is of the oppostive view. (Altekar, 51).

[18] *Abhijnanasakuntalam* 4-94-60; quoted also by Altekar, 51.

[19] There is a story that I have heard which seems to be an exception to this general rule. A certain husband wanted his wife to take care of a guest. The guest wanted to go to bed with his hostess; with great reluctance she complied and her husband lauded her obedience. Here two dharmas clash: duty to one's husband and duty to one's guest. It is solved by obedience to husband which also causes happiness to the guest.

[20] *Deccan Herald*, Bangalore, 19 and 20 May, 1982.

[21] The report (p.79) also includes statistics to show that nearly 60% of Hindus approved of changes in mode of dress for even young widows and adds: "even in educated circles, deviation from this norm on the part of a widow is commented upon".

[22] Kane cites several earlier discussions (625); see also Altekar, chapter 4 passim.

[23] Altekar, pp 183, 188, 192 195; Kane ch. 12.

[24] See A.K. Ramanujan, 120.

[25] Pandita Ramabai wrote in 1882. "... Throughout India, widowhood is regarded as the punishment for a horrible crime or crimes committed by the woman in her former existence upon earth... disobedience and disloyalty to the husband, or murdering him in an earlier existence, are the chief crimes punished in the present birth with widowhood" (Ramabai 1976:39).

[26] For earlier discussions, see Altekar, ch. 4; Kane ch. 12. Recent books on sati include Arvind Sharma, *Sati: Historical and Phenomenological Essays*, 1988.

[27] Campbell, the Time-Life bureau chief in New Delhi between 1952-1954, reports about a wife who committed sati in the city of Jodhpur and of the thousands of sumangalis who came to the cremation ground to venerate and pray to the dead wife. By this time the sati was accredited with all the supernatural powers that go with the trappings of a pativrata:

"Mr. Bhatkal shouted explanations at me. 'This is where the sati took place. The fire has been kept going ever since. The coconuts are offerings to the sati, who has passed through the fire to become a goddess.'

"The background to the scene was a large marble tomb... luridly hung with coloured electric light bulbs... that reduced it to the level of a gaudy exhibit at a fair.

"Mr. Bhatkal pointed to this monstrosity and shouted: 'That is the tomb of the sati's grandfather. It has been decorated in her honour by the Jodhpur Electricians' Union, entirely at their own expense.'

"Presently, after Mrs. Bhatkal had cast her coconut, smeared her head with ashes, and finished praying, we left the cemetery. At the gate a coloured print was thrust into my hand by a street vendor.. who tried to sell me, in addition, a garland and a poem specially written for the occasion. The print showed a woman, seated amid decorative flames and cradling a dead man's head in her lap. Hovering over the flames was a viman or mythological Hindu airplane, heavy with gilt and shaped like a balloon's gondola. In the gondola, smiling happily, sat the same woman and man, both transfigured into deities. Brahma, Krishan, and Sita looked on approvingly, ... other Hindu gods and goddessses rode lions, played lutes, held tridents and showered down flowers" (Campbell 1958: 75-76).

[28] For an example of a community which does *not* celebrate the first menstruation, see Jacobson and Wadley, *Women in India*, 42.

[29] Dhruvarajan, 1989, 67-68; for north Indian example see Jacobson and Wadley.

[30] Dhruvarajan, 68. Jacobson and Wadley report about a Thakur household in northern India: "Rambai's mother-in-law, Hirabai, suspected the girl might be pregnant when she continued to cook every night for three months straight. When a woman menstruates, she does not cook or enter the kitchen or touch others, since she is considered ritually unclean for five days. But Rambai had failed to ask anyone to take over her cooking tasks for three months, and finally the older woman asked her, 'Is something there?'"

[31] Jacobson and Wadley, p.54.

[32] Manisha Roy, *Bengali Women*, pp.89-94.

[33] See Vasundhara Varadhan's "The impact of the Indian Government's family planning films on non-literate rural audiences: a case study, 1983-1984", New York University, 1985.

[34] This movie depicts a young woman who refuses to accept her husband's infidelity. The movie, with this surprising ending, was astonishingly successful and may mark a transition in traditional depictions of women. See "India's film dandies delight the masses and relieve hard lives" by Mary Anne Weaver, in *The Christian Science Monitor*, 28 November, 1983, pp.1 and 36.

[35] For perceptions of media on women, see the articles in Rehana Ghadially, *Women in Indian Society*.

BIBLIOGRAPHY

Altekar. *The Position of Women in Hindu Civilisation*. Benares: Publication House, 1938.

Arthasastra. (Chanakya). Translated by R. Shamasastry. Mysore: Mysore Printing & Publishing House, 1967.

Basham, A.L. *The Wonder that was India*. New York: Macmillan, 1953.

Brown, Lillian. *I married a Dinosaur*. New York: Dodd Mead & Co., 1950.

Buhler, G. tr. *The Laws of Manu*. Delhi: Motilal Banarsidass, 1964.

Campbell, Alexander. *The Heart of India. New York: Alfred Knopf*, 1958.

Druvarajan, Vanaja. *Hindu Women and the Power of Ideology*. Granby: Bergin & Garvey, 1989.

Everett, Jana Matson. *Women and Social Change in India*. New York: St Martin's Press, 1979.

Falk, Nancy Ellen Auer. "Women In-between: Conflicting Values in Delhi". *The Journal of Religion*, 1987, pp.257-274.

Felton, Monica. *A Child Widow's Story*. Madras: 1963.

Ghadially, Rehana ed. *Women in Indian Society: A Reader*. New Delhi: Sage Publications, 1988.

Hart, George. *The Poems of Ancient Tamil*. Berkeley: University of California Press, 1975.

Hook, Peter. "Marriage of Heroines." In *Aryan and Non-Aryan*, ed. Madhav Deshpande. Ann Arbor: Center for South and South East Asian Studies, 1979.

Jacobson, Doranne and Susan Wadley, *Women in India*. Columbia: South Asia Books, 1977.

Jordan, Kay K. "The Devadasis and the Courts: Traditional and Modern Values in Conflict?" Paper presented at the National Meeting of the American Academy of Religion, Anaheim, November 1989. (1989a)

Jordan, Kay K. "From Sacred Servant to Profane Prostitute: A Study of the Changing Legal Status of the Devadasis, 1857-1947." Ph.D. dissertation, University of Iowa, 1989. (1989b)

Kakar, Sudhir. *The Inner World: A Psycho-analytic Study of Childhood and Society in India*. Delhi: Oxford University Press, 1982.

Kama Sutra of Vatsyayana, tr. R.F. Burton, New York: E.P. Dutton, 1964.

Kane. *History of Dharmasastra*, vol. II, pt. 1. Poona: Bhandarkar Oriental Research Institute, 1978. Kersenboon-Story, Saskia C. *Nitysumangali: Devadasi Tradition in South India*. Delhi: Motilal Banarsidass, 1987.

Khanna and Varghese. *Indian Women Today*. New Delhi: Vikas, 1978.

Kishwar, Madhu and Ruth Vanita eds. *In Search of Answers: Indian Women's Voices from Manushi*. London: Zed Books, 1984.

Lannoy, Richard. *The Speaking Tree*. London: Oxford University Press, 1971.

Lindholm, James. "Power and Pathos: Woman in Tamil Fiction." Paper presented at the National Meeting of the Association for Asian Studies, Chicago, 1978.

Madan, T.N. "The Hindu Woman at Home". In *Indian Women: From Purdah to Modernity*. Delhi: Vikas Publishing House, 1976, pp.67-86.

Manu. See Buhler.

Manuel, Vimala. *Man in Modern Tamil Fiction*. Madras: The Christian Literature Series, 1973.

Marglin, Frederique and John Carman eds. *Purity and Auspiciousness in Indian Society* Leiden: Brill, 1985.

Marglin, Frederique. *Wives of the God King: The Rituals of the Devadasis of Puri*. Oxford: Oxford University Press, 1985.

Marglin, Frederique. "Menstruation: 'Woman' Deconstructed." Paper presented at the National Meeting of the American Academy of Religion, Chicago, 21 November, 1988.

Mukherjee, Prabhati. *Hindu Women.* New Delhi: Orient Longman, 1978.

Najan. *Dirgha Sumangali Bhava.* Madras: Pratibha Press, 1979.

Nanda, B.R. ed. *Indian Women: From Purdah to Modernity.* New Delhi: Vikas Publishing House Pvt. Ltd., 1976.

Narayanan, Vasudha. "Two Levels of Auspiciousness in Sriviasnava Literature and Ritual." In Marglin and Carman, eds. *Purity and Auspiciousness in Indian Society.* Leiden: Brill, 1985.

Ramabai Sarasvati, Pundita. *The High Caste Hindu Woman.* Connecticut: Hyperion Press, 1976.

Ramanujan, A.K. *The Interior Landscape.* Bloomington: Indiana University Press, 1975.

Richman, Paula. *Women, Branch Stories, and Religious Rhetoric in a Tamil Buddhist Text.* Syracuse: Syracuse University, Maxwell School of Citizenship and Comparative Affairs, 1988.

Robinson, Sandra. "Hindu Paradigms of Women. Images and Values." In *Women, Religion and Social Change*, ed. Y.Y. Haddad and E.B. Findly. Albany: State University of New York Press, 1987.

Roy, Manisha. *Bengali Women.* Chicago: University of Chicago Press, 1975.

Sharma, Arvind. *Sati: Historical and Phenomenological Essays.* Delhi: Motilal Banarsidass, 1988.

The Sumangali Manual. See Najan.

Thomas, P. *Kama Kalpa.* Bombay: Taraporevala and Sons, 1959.

Towards Equality: Report of the Committee on the Status of Women in India. New Delhi: Government of India, Ministry of Education and Social Welfare.

Trivedi, H.R. *Scheduled Caste Women: Studies in Exploitation.* Delhi: Concept Publishing Co., 1977.

Varadhan, Vasundhara. "The impact of the Indian Government's family planning films on non-literate, rural audiences: A case study, 1983-1984." Ph.D. dissertation, New York University, 1985.

Ziffren, Abbie. "What is Lost when Feminism is Found: Treatment of Women in Tamil Fiction." Paper presented at the National Meeting of the American Academy of Religion, Chicago, 21 November, 1988.

Zimmer, Heinrich. *Philosophies of India.* New York: Pantheon Books.

An Islamic Perspective

Riffat Hassan

The Islamic tradition: primary sources and their interpretation
It is necessary to clarify at the outset what one means by "the Islamic tradition". This tradition — like other major religious traditions — does not consist of, or derive from, a single source. Most Muslims, if questioned about its sources, are likely to refer to more than one of the following: The Qur'an (the book of Revelation believed by Muslims to be the Word of God), the Sunnah and Hadith (the practice and sayings ascribed to Muhammad, the Prophet of Islam), Fiqh (jurisprudence) or Madahib (schools of law), and Shari'ah (the code of life which regulates all aspects of Muslim life). While all of the above "sources" have contributed to what is cumulatively referred to as "the Islamic tradition", it is important to note that they do not form a coherent or consistent body of teachings or precepts from which a universally-agreed-upon set of Islamic "norms" can be derived. Many examples can be cited of inconsistency between various sources of the Islamic tradition as well as of inconsistency between various sources of the Islamic tradition and the Hadith literature. In view of this fact, it is inappropriate, particularly in a scholarly work, to speak of "the Islamic tradition" as if it were monolithic. Its various components need to be identified and examined separately before one can attempt to make any sort of generalization on the Islamic tradition.

Since it is not possible, within the scope of this paper, to discuss the complex subject of women's sexuality and bodily functions comprehensively in the light of all of the sources of the Islamic tradition, I will focus, for the most part, on the Qur'an which is *the* primary source of *normative* Islam. Reference will also be made to some *ahadith* (plural of hadith: a tradition ascribed to the Prophet Muhammad) which have had a formative impact on Muslim ideas and attitudes pertaining to women's sexuality. Here it may be useful to mention that, according to Islamic theory, the Qur'an has *absolute* authority since it is believed to be God's unadulterated message conveyed through the agency of Archangel Gabriel to the Prophet Muhammad, who then transmitted it to others without change or error. However, since the early days of Islam, the Hadith literature has been the lens through which the words of the Qur'an have been seen and interpreted.

It must however be pointed out that every aspect of the Hadith literature is surrounded by controversies. In particular, the question of the authenticity of particular *ahidith* as well as of the Hadith literature as a whole has occupied the attention of many scholars of Islam since the time of Ash-Shaft'i (died in A.D. 809). As stated by Fazlur Rahman in his book *Islam*, "a very large proportion of the Hadiths were judged to be spurious and forged by classical Muslim scholars themselves."[1] This has generated much scepticism regarding the Hadith literature in general amongst "moderate" Muslims. Though few of them are willing to go as far as Ghulam Ahmad Parwez (leader of the "Tulu' e Islam" or "the Dawn of Islam" movement in Pakistan) who rejects the Hadith literature virtually *in toto*, many of them are likely to be in agreement with the following observations of Moulvi Cheragh Ali, an important Indian Muslim scholar who wrote in the nineteenth century:

> The vast flood of tradition soon formed a chaotic sea. Truth, error, fact and fable mingled together in an undistinguishable confusion. Every religious, social, and political system was defended when necessary, to please a Khalif or an Ameer to serve his purpose, by an appeal to some oral traditions. The name of Mohammad was abused to support all manner of lies and absurdities or to satisfy the passion, caprice, or arbitrary will of the despots, leaving out of consideration the creation of any standards of test... I am seldom inclined to quote traditions having little or no belief in their genuineness, as generally they are inauthentic, unsupported and one-sided.[2]

Though valid ground exists for regarding the Hadith literature with caution, if not scepticism, Fazlur Rahman is right in saying that "if the Hadith literature as a whole is cast away, the basis for the historicity of the Qur'an is removed with one stroke."[3] Furthermore, as pointed out by Alfred Guillaume in his book, *The Traditions of Islam*:

The hadith literature as we now have it provides us with apostolic precept and example covering the whole duty of man: it is *the basis* of that developed system of law, theology, and custom which is Islam...[4] However sceptical we are with regard to the ultimate historical value of the traditions, it is hard to overrate their importance in the formation of the life of the Islamic races throughout the centuries. If we cannot accept them at their face value, they are of inestimable value as a mirror of the events which preceded the consolidation of Islam into a system.[5]

Not only does the Hadith literature have its own autonomous character in point of law and even of doctrine,[6] it also has an emotive aspect whose importance is hard to overstate since it relates to the conscious as well as to the sub-conscious patterns of thought and feeling of Muslims individually and collectively. As H.A.R. Gibb has observed perceptively:

It would be difficult to exaggerate the strength and the effects of the Muslim attitude toward Muhammad. Veneration for the Prophet was a natural and inevitable feeling, both in his own day and later, but this is more than veneration. The personal relationships of admiration and love which he inspired in his associates have echoed down the centuries, thanks to the instruments which the community created in order to evoke them afresh in each generation. The earliest of these instruments was the narration of hadith. So much has been written about the legal and theological functions of the hadith that its more personal and religious aspects have been almost overlooked. It is true, to be sure, that the necessity of finding an authoritative source which would supplement the legal and ethical prescriptions contained in the Koran led to a search for examples set by Muhammad in his daily life and practice. One could be certain that if he had said this or that, done this or that, approved this or that action, one had an absolutely reliable guide to the right course to adopt in any similar situation. And it is equally true that this search went far beyond the limits of credibility or simple rectitude, and that it was in due course theologically rationalized by the doctrine of implicit inspiration.[7]

Having underscored the importance of the Qur'an and the Hadith literature as primary sources of the Islamic tradition, it is necessary to point out that through the centuries of Muslim history, these sources have been interpreted only by Muslim men who have abrogated to themselves the task of defining the ontological, theological, sociological and eschatological status of Muslim women. While it is encouraging that women such as Khadijah and A'ishah (wives of the Prophet Muhammad) and Rabi'a al-Basri (the outstanding woman Sufi) figure significantly in early Islam, the fact remains that the Islamic tradition has, by and large, remained rigidly patriarchal till the present time, prohibiting the growth of scholarship among women particularly in the realm of religious thought. In view of this it is hardly surprising that until now the overwhelming majority of Muslim women have remained almost totally unaware of the extent to which their "Islamic" (in an ideal sense) rights have been violated by their male-centred and male-dominated societies which have continued to assert, glibly and tirelessly, that Islam has given women more rights than any other religious tradition. Kept for centuries in physical, mental and emotional confinement and deprived of the opportunity to actualize their human potential, even the exercise of analyzing their personal life-experiences as Muslim women is beyond the capability of most Muslim women. Here it is pertinent to mention that while the rate of literacy is low in many Muslim countries, the rate of literacy of Muslim women — especially those who live in rural areas where the majority of the population lives — is among the lowest in the world.

In recent times, largely due to the pressure of anti-women laws which are being promulgated under the cover of "Islamisation" in some parts of the Muslim world, women with some degree of education and awareness are beginning to realize that religion is being used as an instrument of oppression rather than as a means of liberation. For instance, in the face both of military dictatorship and religious autocracy, valiant efforts have been made by women's groups in Pakistan to protest against the enactment of manifestly anti-women laws and to highlight cases of gross injustice and brutality towards women. However, it it still not clearly and fully understood even by many women activists in Pakistan and other Muslim countries, that the negative attitudes pertaining to women which prevail in Muslim societies, in general, are in general rooted in theology. Unless and until the theological foundations of the misogynistic and androcentric tendencies in the Islamic tradition are demolished, Muslim women will continue to be brutalized and discriminated against despite improvement in statistics relating to women's education, employment, social and political rights, etc.

Sexuality and the Islamic tradition

Underlying the discussion on almost any women-related issue which is of importance in Muslim communities or societies are some widely prevalent notions concerning sexuality in general, and women's sexuality in particular. The Muslim attitude towards the former generally tends to be highly positive. The Muslim attitude towards the latter, however, is far more complex, as will become evident in this paper.

Sexuality, which in its broadest sense refers to "the quality of being sexual"[8] is affirmed by the Islamic tradition (much as it is by the Jewish tradition) because the creation of human beings as sexual as well as sexually-differentiated creatures is believed to be an integral part of God's plan for humankind. Unlike dualistic traditions, whether religious or philosophical, the Islamic tradition does not see sexuality as the opposite of spirituality, but describes it as a "sign" of God's mercy and bounty to humanity, as the following Qur'anic passage shows:

> And among His (God's) signs
> Is this, that He created
> For you mates from among
> Yourselves, that ye may
> Dwell in tranquillity with them,
> And He has put love
> And mercy between your (hearts)
> Verily in that are signs
> For those who reflect (Surah 30:Ar-Rum:21).[9]

It is noteworthy that in the above passage, sexuality is not associated with animality or corporeality (as it is in some religious and philosophical traditions), but is regarded as the divine instrument for creating man-woman relationships characterized by togetherness, tranquillity, love and mercy.

It is important to note that, in the context of human creation, the Qur'an describes man and woman as each other's *zauj* or "mate". The term "zauj" is generally used to refer to one of two in a pair when reference is made, for instance to "a pair of shoes" or "night and day". Not only are both parts necessary to complete a pair but also the proper functioning of each requires the presence of the other.[10] While the Qur'anic usage of *azwaj* (plural form of "zauj") to refer to husbands and wives is well known in Muslim societies, it is not generally known that the Qur'an uses the term *zaujain* (dual form of "zauj") for man and woman in describing the process of creation itself, as can be seen from the following passages:

> He (God) did create
> In pairs ("zaujain") — male and female,
> From a seed when lodged
> In its place [11] Surah 53: *An-Najm*: 45-46).
> Does Man[12] think

That he will be left
Uncontrolled, (without purpose)?
Was he not a drop
Of sperm emitted
(In lowly form)?
Then did he become
A leech-like clot;
Then did (God) make
And fashion (him)
in due proportion.
And of him He made
Two sexes ("zaujain"), male
And female[13] (Surah 75: *Al-Qiyamat*: 36-39).

In other words, man and woman — two sexually-differentiated human beings — created by God from a unitary source (*nafs in wahidatin*[14]) are related to each other ontologically, not merely sociologically. The creation and sexuality of one is, thus, inseparable from the creation and sexuality of the other. That man and woman, or men and women, are bound together not only by virtue of their common source but also by virtue of their interdependent (though different) sexualities seems to be implicit in a number of Qur'anic statements about human creation. These statements warrant the inference that sexual differentiation between man and woman was intended by God to create closeness, not opposition, between them. It is interesting to see how, in a sense, Muslim societies honour this intent, for besides the relationship between husbands and wives (in which "sexuality" becomes associated with "sexual intercourse") they also promote a variety of other relationships between men and women (which are not characterized by "sexual intercourse"). A strong sense of the interdependence of men and women generally pervades Islamic societies which, despite their frequently blatant patriarchalism, acknowledge the pivotal role of women in maintaining the physical, emotional, moral and spiritual well-being of the *ummah* (community).

With regards to sexuality in the context of a heterosexual marriage, a highly affirming attitude is to be found both in sources of normative Islam as well as in actual Islamic societies. The Qur'an encourages Muslims who are able to marry a "single" or "virtuous" man or woman to do so regardless of the differences in status or wealth between them:

Marry those among you
Who are single, or
The virtuous ones among

Your slaves, male or female:
If they are in poverty
God will give them
Means out of His Grace:
For God encompasseth all,
And He knoweth all things[15] (Surah 24: *An-Nur*: 32).

Recognizing that marriage to a slave woman might put less economic strain on a man than marrying a free woman,[16] the Qur'an says:

If any of you have not
The means wherewith
To wed free believing women,
They may wed believing
Girls from among those
Whom your right hands possess:
And God hath full knowledge
About your Faith.
Ye are one from another:
Wed them with the leave
Of their owners, and give them
Their dowers, according to what
Is reasonable[17] (Surah 4: *An-Nisa'*: 25).

A major reason why Muslims are encouraged, even urged, to marry is because the human need for sexual satisfaction and intimacy is considered "natural" by the Islamic tradition which regards Islam as the "Din" (religion) of Nature. According to the Qur'an, monasticism, which followers of Jesus had imposed upon themselves, was not prescribed by God.[18] In other words, from the Qur'anic perspective, neither renunciation of the world nor celibacy is required of those who wish to dedicate their lives to the service of God or to spiritual (as opposed to material) pursuits. Marriage is seen by Muslims generally not as an obstacle to attaining the "higher" goals of life, but rather, as an aid to the creation of a just and moral society. It protects human beings (particularly men) from immorality and lewdness[19], providing them with a religious framework in which their sexual and other energies can be channelled constructively.

It is of interest to note here that there are many Qur'anic prescriptions relating to the regulation of man-woman relationship in marriage. The assumption underlying these prescriptions is that if men and women can attain justice in their marital relationship which is the basis of the family — the basic unit of society — then they can also attain justice in the ummah and the world at large. The larger ramifications of marital relationships for the Muslim ummah have generally been recognized by the Islamic tradition which would appear to endorse the popular Hadith in which the prophet of Islam is reported to have said that by marrying Muslims they had fulfilled half of their "Din". [20]

That is to say, sexuality in general, particularly in the context of marital relationship, is viewed as normal and wholesome both by the primary sources of Islam and by Muslims generally. However, when one considers issues relating to women (as sexually differentiated from men) one discovers many instances when divergence is found not only between normative Islam and popular Islam but also between Qur'anic teachings and individual ahadith. There are also many cases of one Hadith contradicting another. In view of these discrepancies or inconsistencies it is not possible to give a simple answer to the question: What is Islam's view of women's sexuality and bodily functions? Even as the question is complex, so also the answer must include reference to a number of interrelated issues pertaining to significant stages and aspects of women's lives. In the account which follows, an attempt is made to answer the above-stated question in the light both of normative Islam (which represents Islamic ideals) and of Muslim practice (which represents Islamic realities), for both are part of the Islamic tradition which spans a period of over thirteen centuries.

Women and normative Islam: three fundamental theological issues

Much of what has happened to Muslim women through the ages becomes comprehensible if one keeps one fact in mind: Muslims, in general, consider it a self-evident truth that women are not equal to men. Men are "above" women or have "a degree of advantage" over them. There is hardly anything in a Muslim woman's life which is not affected by this belief, hence it is vitally important, not only for theological reasons but also pragmatic ones, to subject it to rigorous scholarly scrutiny and attempt to identify its roots.

The roots of the belief that men are superior to women lie — in my judgment — in three theological assumptions: a) that God's primary creation is man, not woman, since woman is believed to have been created from man's rib, hence is derivative and ontologically secondary; b) that woman, not man, was the primary agent of what is customarily described as "Man's Fall" or Man's expulsion from the Garden of Eden, hence "all daughters of Eve" are to be regarded with hatred, suspicion and contempt; and c) that woman was created not only *from* man, but also *for* man, which makes her existence merely instrumental and not of fundamental importance. The three theological questions to which the above assumptions may appropriately be regarded as answers are: i) How was woman created? ii) Was woman responsible for the "Fall" of man? and iii) Why was woman created? While all three questions have had profound significance in the history of ideas and attitudes pertaining to women in the Islamic, as well as the Jewish and Christian tradition, I consider the first one, which relates to the issue of woman's creation, to be more basic and important, philosophically and theologically, than any other in the context of man-woman equality. This is so because if man and woman have been created equal by Allah who is the ultimate arbiter of value, then they cannot become unequal, essentially, at a subsequent time. On the other hand, if man and woman have been created unequal by Allah, then they cannot become equal, essentially, at a subsequent time.

It is not possible, within the scope of this paper, to deal exhaustively with any of the three questions. However, in the brief discussion of each question which follows, an attempt is made to highlight the way in which sources of normative Islam have been interpreted to show that women are inferior to men.

i) *How was woman created?*

The ordinary Muslim believes, as seriously as the ordinary Jew or Christian, that Adam was God's primary creation and that Eve was made from Adam's rib. While this myth has obvious roots in the Yahwist's account of creation in Genesis 2:18-24, it has no basis whatever in the Qur'an, which, in the context of human creation, always speaks in completely egalitarian terms. In none of the thirty or so passages which describe the creation of humanity (designated by generic terms such as "an-nas", "al-insan" and "bashar") by God in a variety of ways is there any statement which could be interpreted as asserting or suggesting that man was created prior to woman or that woman was created from man. In fact there are some passages[21] which could — from a purely grammatical/linguistic point of view — be interpreted as stating that the first creation ("nafs in wahidatin") was feminine, not masculine![22] The Qur'an notwithstanding, Muslims believe that "Hawwa" (the Hebrew/Arabic counterpart of "Eve"), who — incidentally — is never mentioned in the Qur'an, was created from the "crooked" rib of "Adam" who is believed to be the first human being created by God. Here, it needs to be mentioned that the term "Adam" is not an Arabic term but a Hebrew term meaning "of the soil" (from "adamah": the soil). The Hebrew term "Adam" functions generally as a collective noun referring to "the human" (species) rather than to a male human being.[23] In the Qur'an, also, the term "Adam" refers, in twenty-one cases out of twenty-five, to humanity. Here it is of interest to note that though the term "Adam" mostly does not refer to a particular human being, it does refer to human beings in a particular way. As pointed out by Muhammad Iqbal:

> Indeed, in the verses which deal with the origin of man as a living being, the Qur'an uses the words "Bashar" or "Insan", not "Adam", which it reserves for man in his capacity of God's viceregent on earth. The purpose of the Qur'an is further secured by the omission of proper names mentioned in the Biblical narration — Adam and Eve. The term "Adam" is retained and used more as a concept than as a name of a concrete human individual. The word is not without authority in the Qur'an itself.[24]

An analysis of the Qur'anic descriptions of human creation shows how the Qur'an evenhandedly uses both feminine and masculine terms and imagery to describe the creation of humanity from a single source. That God's original creation was undifferentiated humanity and not either man or woman (who appeared simultaneously at a subsequent time) is implicit in a number of Qur'anic passages.[25] If the Qur'an makes no distinction between the creation of man and woman — as it clearly does not — why do Muslims believe that Hawwa' was created from the rib of Adam? Although the Genesis 2 account of woman's creation is accepted virtually by all Muslims, it is difficult to believe that it entered the Islamic tradition directly, for very few Muslims ever read the Bible. It is much more likely that it became a part of Islamic heritage through its assimilation in the Hadith literature. That the Genesis 2 idea of woman being created from Adam's rib did, in fact, become incorporated in the Hadith literature is evident from a number of ahadith. These are particularly important since they appear to have had a formative impact on how Muslims have perceived women's being and sexuality (as differentiated from men's). The *matn* (content[26]) of these ahadith — one from *Sahih Al-Bukhari* and one from *Sahih Muslim* — all ascribed to the Companion known as Abu Harairah,[27] is given below:

1. Treat women nicely, for a woman is created from a rib, and the most curved portion of the rib is its upper portion, so if you should try to straighten it, it will break, but if you leave it as it is, it will remain crooked. So treat women nicely.[28]

2. Woman is like a rib. When you attempt to straighten it, you would break it. And if you leave her alone you would benefit by her, and crookedness will remain in her.[29]

I have examined these and similar ahadith elsewhere[30] and have shown them to be flawed both with regard to their formal *(isnad)* and their material *(matn)* aspects. The theology of woman implicit in these ahadith is based upon generalizations about her ontology, biology and psychology which are contrary to the letter and spirit of the Qur'an. These ahadith ought, therefore, to have been rejected, since Muslim scholars agree on the principle that any hadith which is inconsistent with the Qur'an cannot be accepted. However, despite the fact that the ahadith in question contradict the teachings of the Qur'an, they have continued to be an important part of the ongoing Islamic tradition. Undoubtedly, one of the major reasons for this is that these ahadith come from the two most highly-venerated Hadith collections by Muhammad ibn Isma'il al-Bukhari (810-870 A.D.) and Muslim bin al-Hallaj (817 or 821-875 A.D.). These two collections known together as *Sahihan* (from "sahih" meaning sound or authentic) "form an almost unassailable authority, subject indeed to criticism in details, yet deriving an indestructible influence from the *ijma* or general consent of the community in custom and belief, which it is their function to authenticate."[31] While being included in the *Sahihan* gives the ahadith in question much weight among Muslims who know about the science of Hadith, their continuing popularity among Muslims in general indicates that they articulate something deeply embedded in Muslim culture — namely, that women are derivative[32] creatures who can never be considered equal to men.

Theologically, the history of women's subjection in the Islamic (as well as the Jewish and Christian) tradition began with the story of Hawwa's creation. In my view, unless Muslim women return to the point of origin and challenge the authenticity of the ahadith which make all representatives of their sex ontologically inferior and irremediably crooked, male-centred and male-controlled Muslim societies are not likely to acknowledge the egalitarianism evident in the Qur'anic statements about human creation.

ii) *Was Woman responsible for the Fall of Man?*

Many Muslims, like many Jews and Christians, would answer this question in the affirmative, though nothing in the Qur'anic descriptions of the so-called Fall episode would warrant such an answer. Here it may be noted that whereas in Genesis 3:6, the dialogue preceding the eating of the forbidden fruit by the human pair in the Garden of Eden is between the serpent and Eve (though Adam's presence is also indicated, as contended by feminist theologians) and this has provided the basis for the popular casting of Eve into the role of tempter, deceiver and seducer of Adam, in the Qur'an, the Shaitan (satan) has no exclusive dialogue with Adam's *jauj*. In two of the three passages which refer to this episode, namely Surah 2: *Al-Baqarah*: 35-39 and Surah 7: *Al-A'raf*: 19-25, the Shaitan is stated to have led both Adam and *jauj* astray though in the former (verse 36) no actual conversation is reported. In the remaining passage, namely, Surah 20: *Ta-Ha*: 115-124, it is Adam who is charged with forgetting his covenant with God (verse 115), who is tempted by the Shaitan (verse 120) and who disobeys God and allows himself to be seduced (verse 121). However, if one looks at all the three passages as well as the way in which the term "Adam" functions generally in the Qur'an, it becomes clear that the Qur'an regards the act of disobedience by the human pair in "al-jannah" (the Garden) as a collective rather than an individual act for which exclusive, or even primary, responsibility is not assigned to either man or woman. Even in the last passage in which "Adam" appears to be held responsible for forgetting the covenant and for allowing himself to be beguiled by the Shaitan, the act of disobedience, i.e., the eating from "the Tree", is committed jointly by Adam and zauj and not by Adam alone or in the first place.

Having said that, it is extremely important to stress the point that the Qur'an provides no basis whatever for asserting, suggesting or implying that Hawwa', having been tempted and deceived by the Shaitan, in turn tempted and deceived Adam and led to his expulsion from al-jannah. This fact notwithstanding, many Muslim commentators have ascribed the primary responsibility for man's Fall to woman, as may be seen from the following extract:

> In al-Tabiris *Tarikh* (1:108) the very words Satan used to tempt Eve are then used by her to tempt Adam: "Look at this tree, how sweet is its smell, how delicious is its fruit, how beautiful is its colour!" This passage is concluded by God's specifically accusing Eve of deceiving Adam. Later in the narrative (1:111-112) al-Tabari mentions a report that is also cited by other commentators, the gist of which is to say that Adam while in his full reasoning faculties, did not eat of the tree, but only succumbed to the temptation after Eve had given him wine to drink. Al-Tha'labi in citing the same report also stresses the loss of Adam's rationality through the imbibing of wine, and al-Razi (*Tafsir* 3:13) says that such a story, which he has seen in several "tafsirs", is not at all far-fetched. Implicit in this specific act, of course, is both Eve's culpability and Adam's inherent rationality. Lest any should miss the point that Eve is actively and not just innocently involved in Adam's temptation, Ibn Kathir asserts that as God surely knows best, it was Eve who ate of the tree before Adam and urged him to eat. He then quotes a saying

attributed to the Prophet, "But for Banu Isra'il meat would not have spoiled (because they used to keep it for the next day), and but for Hawwa' no female would be a traitor to her husband!" (*Bidaya* 1:84). [33]

There is hardly any doubt that Muslim women have been as victimized as Jewish and Christian women by the way in which the Jewish, Christian and Islamic traditions have generally interpreted the Fall episode. However, it needs to be pointed out that the Qur'anic account of the episode differs significantly from the biblical account, and that the Fall does not mean in the Islamic tradition what it means in the Jewish, and particularly in the Christian, tradition.

To begin with, whereas in Genesis 3 no explanation is given as to why the serpent tempts either Eve alone or both Adam and Eve, in the Qur'an the reason why the Shaitan (or "Iblis") sets out to beguile the human pair in "al-jannah" is stated clearly in a number of passages [34]. The refusal of the Shaitan to obey God's command to bow in submission to Adam follows from his belief that being a creature of fire he is elementally superior to Adam who is a creature of clay. When condemned for his arrogance by God and ordered to depart in a state of abject disgrace, the Shaitan throws a challenge to the Almighty: he will prove to God that Adam and Adam's progeny are unworthy of the honour and favour bestowed on them by God, being — in general — ungrateful, weak and easily lured away from "the straight path" by worldly temptations. Not attempting to hide his intentions to "come upon" human beings from all sides, the Shaitan asks for — and is granted — a reprieve until "the Day of the Appointed Time". Not only is the reprieve granted, but God also tells the Shaitan to use all his wiles and forces to "assault" human beings and see if they would follow him. A cosmic drama now begins, involving the eternal opposition between the principles of right and wrong or good and evil, which is lived out as human beings, exercising their moral autonomy, must now choose between "the straight path" and "the crooked path".

In terms of the Qur'anic narrative, what happens to the human pair in "al-jannah" is a sequel to the interchange between God and the Shaitan. In the sequel we learn that Adam and zauj have been commanded not to go near "the Tree" lest they become *zalimin*. Seduced by the Shaitan, they disobey God. However, in Surah 7: *Al-A'raf*: 23 they acknowledge before God that they have done *zulm* to themselves and earnestly seek God's forgiveness and mercy. They are told by God to "go forth" or "descend" from "al-jannah", but in addressing them the Qur'an uses the dual form of address (referring exclusively to Adam and "jauj") only once (in Surah 18

Ta-Ha: 123); for the rest the plural form is used which necessarily refers to more than two persons and is generally understood as referring to humanity as a whole.

In the framework of Qur'anic theology, the order to "go forth" from "al-jannah" given to Adam or the children of Adam cannot be considered a punishment because Adam was always meant to be God's vice-regent on earth, as stated clearly in Surah 2: *Al-Baqarah*: 30. The earth is not a place of banishment but is declared by the Qur'an to be humanity's dwelling place and a source of profit to it [35]. The "al-jannah" mentioned in the Fall story is not — as pointed out by Muhammad Iqbal — "the supersensual paradise from which man is supposed to have fallen on this earth". [36]

There is, strictly speaking, no Fall in the Qur'an. What the Qur'anic narration focuses upon is the moral choice which humanity is required to make when confronted by the alternatives presented to them by God and the Shaitan. This becomes clear if one reflects on the text of Surah 2: *Al-Baqarah*: 35 and Surah 7: *Al-A'raf*: 19, in which it is stated: "You (dual) go not near this Tree, lest you (dual) become of the 'zalimin'". In other words, the human pair is being told that *if* they go near the Tree, *then* they will be counted amongst those who perpetrate "zulim". Commenting on the root ZLM, Toshihio Izutsu says:

> The primary meaning of ZLM is, in the opinion of many of the authoritative lexicologists, that of "putting in a wrong place." In the moral sphere it seems to mean primarily "to act in such a way as to transgress the proper limit and encroach upon the right of some other person." Briefly and generally speaking "zulm" is to do injustice in the sense of going beyond one's bounds and doing what one has no right to. [37]

By transgressing the limits set by God the human pair become guilty of zulm towards themselves. This zulm consists in their taking on the responsibility for choosing between good and evil. Here it is important to note that the

> Qur'anic legend of the fall has nothing to do with the first appearance of man on this planet. Its purpose is rather to indicate man's rise from a primitive state of instinctive appetite to the conscious possession of a free self, capable of doubt and disobedience. The fall does not mean any moral depravity, it is man's transition from simple consciousness to the first flash of self-consciousness, a kind of waking from the dream of nature with a throb of personal causality in one's own being. Nor does the Qur'an regard the earth as a torture hall where an elementally wicked humanity is imprisoned for an original act of

sin. Man's first act of disobedience was also his first act of free choice; and that is why, according to the Qur'anic narration, Adam's first transgression was forgiven... A being whose movements are wholly determined like a machine cannot produce goodness. Freedom is thus a condition of goodness. But to permit the emergence of a finite ego who has the power to choose, after considering the relative values of several courses of action open to him, is really to take a great risk; for the freedom to choose good involves also the freedom to choose what is the opposite of good. That God has taken this risk shows his immense faith in man; it is now for man to justify this faith. [38]

There is no Fall in the Qur'an, hence there is no Original Sin. Human beings are not born sinful into this world, hence do not need to be "redeemed" or "saved". This is generally accepted in the Islamic tradition. However, the association of the Fall with sexuality, which has played such a massive role in perpetuating the myth of feminine evil in the Christian tradition, also exists in the minds of many Muslims and causes untold damage to Muslim women.

It is remarkable to see that though there is no reference to sexual activity on the part of man or woman even in their post-lapsarian state of partial or complete nakedness in either Genesis 3 or the Qur'an, many Muslim scholars have jumped to the conclusion that exposure of their *sau'at* (i.e., "the external portion of the organs of generation of a man and of a woman and the anus"[39]), generally translated as "shameful parts", necessarily led the human pair to sexual activity which was "shameful" not only by virtue of being linked with their "shameful parts" but also because it was instigated by the Shaitan. The following explanation by A.A. Maududi — one of contemporary Islam's most influential scholars — represents the thinking of many, if not most, Muslims on this point:

> The sex instinct is the greatest weakness of the human race. That is why Satan selected this weak spot for his attack on the adversary and devised the scheme to strike at their modesty. Therefore the first step he took in this direction was to expose their nakedness to them so as to open the door of indecency before them and beguile them into sexuality. Even to this day, Satan and his disciples are adopting the same scheme of depriving the woman of the feelings of modesty and shyness and they cannot think of any scheme of "progress" unless they expose and exhibit the woman to all and sundry. [40]

The initial statement leaves no doubt about Maududi's negative view of "the sex-instinct" which he describes as "the greatest weakness of the human race." Associating sexuality with the Shaitan's "attack on the adversary", Maududi assumes that on discovering their state of physical exposure, the human pair resorted irresistibly to an act of "indecency" i.e.

sexual intercourse. However, there is nothing in the text which warrants this assumption. In fact, according to the text, the human pair's first act on discovering their exposed state was one of "decency", namely, that of covering themselves with leaves.

That Maududi — like many other Muslims, Jews and Christians — sees women as the primary agents of sexuality which is regarded as the Shaitan's chief instrument for defeating God's plan for humanity, is clear from the way in which he shifts attention from the human pair to the woman, in the above passage. In turning his eyes away from the "nakedness" of the sons of Adam to focus on the "nakedness" of the daughters of Hawwa', he is typical of Muslim culture.

Though the branding of women as "the devil's gateway"[41] is not at all the intent of the Qur'anic narration of the Fall story — as the foregoing account has shown — Muslims, no less than Jews and Christians, have used the story to vent their misogynistic feelings. This is clear from the continuing popularity of ahadith such as the following:

> Narrated Usama bin Zäid: The Prophet said, "After me I have not left any affliction more harmful to men than women" (*Shahih Al-Bukhari*, Vol. VII, p.22).[42]
>
> Ibn Abbas reported that Allah's Messenger said: "I had a chance to look into Paradise and I found that the majority of the people were poor and I looked into the Fire and there I found the majority constituted by women" (*Sahih Muslim*, Vol. IV, p. 1431).[43]
>
> Abu Sa'id Khudri reported that Allah's Messenger said: "The world is sweet and green (alluring) and verily Allah is going to install you as vice-regent in it in order to see how you act. So avoid the allurement of women: verily, the first trial for the people of Isra'il was caused by women" (*Sahih Muslim* Volume IV, p. 1431).

iii) *Why was Woman created?*

The Qur'an, which does not discriminate against women in the context of the Fall episode, does not support the view — held by many Muslims, Christians and Jews — that woman was created not only *from* man but also *for* man. That God's creation as a whole is "for just ends" (Surah 15: *Al-Hijr*: 85) and not "for idle sport" (Surah 21: *Al-Anbiya'*: 16) is one of the major themes of the Qur'an. Humanity, fashioned "in the best of moulds" (Surah 95: *At-Tin*: 4) has been created in order to serve God (Surah 51: *Adh-Dhariyat*: 56). According to Qur'anic teaching, service to God cannot be separated from service to humankind, or — in Islamic terms — believers in God must honour both *Haquq Allah* (rights of God) and *Haquq al-'ibad* (rights of creatures). Fulfilment of one's duties to God and humankind constitutes the essence of righteousness. [44] That men and women are equally called upon by God to be righteous and will be equally rewarded for their righteousness is stated unambiguously in a number of Qur'anic passages such as the following:

> The Believers, men
> And women, are protectors,
> One of another: they enjoin
> What is just, and forbid
> What is evil: they observe
> Regular prayers, practise
> Regular charity, and obey
> God and His Apostle.
> On them will God pour
> His mercy: for God
> Is exalted in power, Wise.
> God hath promised to Believers,
> Men and women, Gardens
> Under which rivers flow,
> To dwell therein,
> And beautiful mansions
> In gardens of everlasting Bliss
> But the greatest bliss
> Is the Good Pleasure of God:
> That is the supreme felicity (Surah 9: *At-Taubah*: 71:72). [45]

Not only does the Qur'an make it clear that man and woman stand absolutely equal in the sight of God, but also that they are "members" and "protectors" of each other. In other words, the Qur'an does not create a hierarchy in which men are placed above women, nor does it pit men against women in an adversary relationship. They are created as equal creatures of a universal, just and merciful God whose pleasure it is that they live — in harmony and in righteousness — together.

In spite of the Qur'anic affirmation of man-woman equality, Muslim societies in general have never regarded men and women as equal, particularly in the context of marriage. Fatima Mernissi's observations on the position of a Muslim woman in relation to her family in modern Morocco apply, more or less, to Muslim culture generally:

> ...one of the distinctive characteristics of Muslim sexuality is its territoriality, which reflects a specific division of labour and a specific conception of society and of power. The territoriality of Muslim sexuality sets ranks, tasks,

and authority patterns. Spatially confined, the woman was taken care of materially by the man who possessed her, in return for her total obedience and her sexual and reproductive services. The whole system was organized so that the Muslim 'ummah' was actually a society of male citizens who possessed among other things the female half of the population. Muslim men have always had more rights and privileges than Muslim women, including even the right to kill their women... The man imposed on the women an artificially narrow existence, both physically and spiritually.[46]

Underlying the rejection in Muslim societies of the idea of man-woman equality is the deeply-rooted belief that women — who are inferior in creation (having been made from a crooked rib) and in righteousness (having helped the Shaitan in defeating God's plan for Adam) — have been created mainly to be of use to men who are superior to them.

The alleged superiority of men to women which permeates the Islamic (as also the Jewish and Christian) tradition is grounded not only in Hadith literature but also in popular interpretations of some Qur'anic passages. Two Qur'anic passages — Surah 4: *An-Nisa'*: 34 and Surah 2: *Al Baqarah*: 288 — in particular, are generally cited to support the contention that men have "a degree of advantage" over women. Of these, the first reads as follows in A.A. Maududi's translation of the Arabic text:

> Men are the managers of the affairs of women because Allah has made the one superior to the other and because men spend of their wealth on women. Virtuous women are, therefore, obedient; they guard their rights carefully in their absence under the care and watch of Allah. As for those women whose defiance you have cause to fear, admonish them and keep them apart from your beds and beat them. Then, if they submit to you, do not look for excuses to punish them: note it well that there is Allah above you, Who is Supreme and Great.[47]

It is difficult to overstate the impact of the general Muslim understanding of Surah 4: *An-Nisa'*: 34 which is embodied in Maududi's translation. As soon as the issue of woman's equality with man is raised by liberals, the immediate response by traditionalists is, "But don't you know that God says in the Qur'an that men are *qawwamun* in relation to women and have the right to rule over them and even to beat them?" In fact, the mere statement, *ar-rijal-o qawwamun-a 'ala an-nisa* (literally, the men are *qawwamun* in relation to the women) signifies the end of any attempt to discuss the issue of woman's equality with man in the Islamic ummah.

It is assumed by almost all who read Surah 4, verse 34, that it is addressed to husbands. The first point to be noted is that it is addressed to "ar-rijal" (the men) and to "an-nisa" (the women). In other words, it is addressed to all men and women of the Islamic community. This is further indicated by the fact that in relation to all the actions that are required to be taken, the plural and not the dual form (used when reference is made to two persons) is found. Such usage makes clear that the orders contained in this verse were not addressed to a husband or wife but to the Islamic "ummah" in general.

The key word in the first sentence of this verse is "qawwamun." This word has been translated variously as "protectors and maintainers (of women)," "in charge (of women)," "having pre-eminence (above women)," and "sovereigns or masters (over women)". Linguistically, the word "qawwamun" means "breadwinners" or "those who provide a means of support or livelihood." A point of logic that must be made here is that the first sentence is not a descriptive one stating that all men as a matter of fact are providing for women, since obviously there are at least some men who do not provide for women. What the sentence is stating, rather, is that men ought to have the capability to provide (since "ought" implies "can"). In other words, this statement, which almost all Muslim societies have taken to be an actual description of all men, is in fact a normative statement pertaining to the Islamic concept of division of labour in an ideal family or community structure. The fact that men are "qawwamun" does not mean that women cannot or should not provide for themselves, but simply that in view of the heavy burden that most women shoulder in child-bearing and rearing, they should not have the additional obligation of providing the means of living at the same time.

Continuing with the analysis of the passage, we come next to the idea that God has given the one more strength than the other. Most translations make it appear that the one who has more strength, excellence, or superiority is the man. However, the Qur'anic expression does not accord superiority to men. The expression literally means "some in relation to some," so that the statement could mean either that some men are superior to some others (men and/or women) and that some women are superior to some others (men and/or women). The interpretation which seems to me to be the most appropriate contextually is that some men are more blessed with the means to be better providers that are other men.

The next part of the passage begins with a "therefore", which indicates that this part is conditional upon the first: in other words, if men fulfill their assigned function of being providers, women must fulfill their corresponding duties. Most translations describe this duty in terms of the wife being "obedient" to the husband. The word *salihat*, which is translated as "righteously obedient", is related to the word *salahiat*, which means "capability" or "potentiality", and not obedience. Women's special capability is to bear children. The word *qanitat*, which succeeds the word "salihat" and is also translated as "obedient" is related to a bag for carrying water from one place to another without spilling. Women's special function, then, according to this passage, is that like the bag in which water is transported without loss to its destination, she carries and protects the foetus in her womb until it can be safely delivered.

What is outlined in the first part of this passage is a functional division of labour necessary for maintaining balance in any society. Men who do not have to fulfill the responsibility of childbearing are assigned the functions of being breadwinners. Women are exempted from the responsibility of being breadwinners in order that they may fulfill their function as childbearers. The two functions are separate but complementary and neither is higher or lower than the other.

The three injunctions in the second part of the verse were given to the Islamic ummah in order to meet a rather extraordinary possibility: a mass rebellion on the part of women against their role as childbearers, the function assigned to them by God. If all or most of the women in a Muslim society refused to bear children without just cause as a sign of organized defiance or revolt, this would mean the end of the Muslim ummah. This situation must, therefore, be dealt with decisively. The first step to be taken is to counsel the rebels. If this step is unsuccessful, the second step to be taken is isolation of the rebellious women from others. (It is to be noted here that the prescription is "to leave the women alone in their beds". By translating this line, "keep them apart from your beds," Maududi is suggesting, if not stating, that the judging party is the husband and not the Islamic community — an assumption not warranted by the text). If the second step is also not successful then the step of confining the women for a longer period of time may be taken by the Islamic community or its representatives. Here, it is important to point out that the Arabic word that is generally translated as "beating" has numerous meanings. When used in a legal context as it is here, it means "holding in confinement", according to the authoritative lexicon *Tal-al-'Arus*.[48] (In Surrah 4: *An-Nisa'*: 15, unchaste women are also prescribed the punishment of being confined to their homes.)

While Muslims, through the centuries, have interpreted Surah *An-Nisa'*: 34 as giving them unequivocal mastery over women, a linguistically and philosophically/theologically accurate interpretation of this passage would lead to radically different conclusions. In simple words what this passage is saying is that since only women can bear children (which is not to say either that all women should bear children or that women's sole function is to bear children) — a function whose importance in the survival of any community cannot be questioned — they should not have the additional obligation of being breadwinners whilst they perform this function. Thus, during the period of a woman's child-bearing, the function of breadwinning must be performed by men (not just husbands) in the Muslim ummah. Reflection on this Qur'anic passage shows that the division of functions mandated here is designed to ensure justice in the community as a whole. There are millions of women all over the world — and I am one of them — who are designated inaccurately as "single" parents (when, in fact, they are "double" parents) who bear and raise children singlehandedly, generally without much support from the community. This surely does not constitute a just situation. If children are the wealth and future of the ummah, the importance of protecting the function of child-bearing and child-raising becomes self-evident. Statistics from all over the world show that women and children left without the care and custodianship of men suffer from economic, social, psychological and other ills. What Surah *An-Nisa'*: 34 is ensuring is that this does not happen. It enjoins men in general to assume responsibility for women in general when they are performing the vitally important function of child-bearing (other passages in the Qur'an extend this also to child-rearing). Thus the intent of this passage, which has traditionally been used to subordinate women to men is in fact to guarantee women the material (as well as moral) security needed by them during the period of pregnancy when breadwinning can become difficult or even impossible for them.

The second passage which mentions the so-called "degree of advantage" that men have over women is Surah 2: *Al-Baqarah*: 228, which reads:

Divorced women
Shall wait concerning
For three monthly periods.
Nor is it lawful for them
To hid what God
Hath created in their wombs,
If they have faith
In God and the last Day.
And their husbands
Have the better right
To take them back
In that period, if

> They wish for reconciliation.
> And *women shall have rights*
> *Similar to the rights*
> *Against them, according*
> *To what is equitable;*
> *But men have a degree*
> *(of advantage) over them,*
> And God is Exalted in Power, Wise. [49]

As can be seen, the above-cited passage pertains to the subject of divorce. The "advantage" that men have over women in this context is that women must observe a three-month period called "iddat" before remarriage, but men are exempted from this requirement. The main reason why women are subjected to this restriction is because at the time of divorce a woman may be pregnant and this fact may not become known for some time. As men cannot become pregnant they are allowed to remarry without a waiting period.

In my judgment, the Qur'anic passages — in particular the two discussed above — on which the edifice of male superiority over women largely rests, have been misread or misinterpreted, intentionally or unintentionally, by most Muslim societies and men. A "correct" reading of these passages would not, however, make a radical or substantial difference to the existing pattern of male-female relationships in Muslim societies unless attention was also drawn to those *Ahadith* which have been used to make man not only superior to a woman, but virtually her god. The following hadith is particularly important:

> A man came in with his daughter and said, "This my daughter refuses to get married." The Prophet said, "Obey your father." She said, "By the name of Him Who sent you in truth, I will not marry until you inform me what is the right of the husband over his wife." He said,…"if it were permitted for one human being to bow down *(sajada)* to another I would have ordered the woman to bow down to her husband when he enters into her, because of God's grace on her." (The daughter) answered, "By the name of Him Who sent you, with truth, I would never marry!" [50]

A faith as rigidly monotheistic as Islam cannot conceivably permit any human being to worship anyone but God, therefore the hypothetical statement "If it were permitted…" in the above-cited hadith, is, *ipso facto*, an impossibility. But the way this hadith is related makes it appear that if not God's, at least it was the Prophet's will or wish to make the wife prostrate herself before her husband. Each word, act or exhortation attributed to the Prophet is held to be sacred by most of the Muslims in the world and so this hadith (which, in my judgement seeks to legitimate *shirk*: associating anyone with God — an unforgivable sin according to the Qur'an) becomes binding on the Muslim woman. Muslims frequently criticize a religion such as Hinduism where the wife is required to worship the husband *(patipuja)* but in practice what is expected from most Muslim wives is not very different from patipuja. In India and Pakistan, for example, a Muslim woman learns almost as an article of faith that her husband is her *majazi khuda* (God in earthly form). This description, undoubtedly, constitutes "shirk".

Most ahadith dealing with the subject of married women describe a virtuous woman as one who pleases and obeys her husband at all times. Pleasing the husband can, in fact, become more important than pleasing God. Putting it differently, one can say that most Muslims believe that a woman cannot please God except through pleasing her husband. Some ahadith are cited below to illustrate this point:

> The wife of Sufwan B. Mu'attal went to the Prophet when we were with him and said, "O Messenger of God, my husband... beats me when I perform my devotions, and makes me eat when I fast..." (The Prophet) asked Sufwan about what she had said and he replied, "O Messenger of God...she fasts and I am a young man and have not patience." Then the Messenger of God said, "From now on let a woman not fast except by permission of her husband" (Ibn Hanbal). [51]
>
> A woman whose husband is pleased with her at the time of her death goes straight to Paradise (Tirmidhi). [52]
>
> There are three (persons) whose prayer is not accepted nor their virtues taken above: the fugitive slave till he returns to his masters and places his hand in their hands; the woman on whom her husband remains displeased; and the drunkard, till he becomes sober (Baihaqi). [53]
>
> Hadrat Anas reported that the Holy Prophet had said: "For a woman her husband is Paradise as well as hell" (Ahmad and Nasa'i). [54]
>
> Hadrat Ibn Abi Aufi reported that the Holy Prophet has said: "By Allah in Whose Hand is my life, the woman who does not discharge her duties to her husband is disobedient to Allah, and the discharge of duties towards Allah depends on the discharge of duties towards the husband" (Ibn Majah). [55]

Man and woman, created equal by God and standing equal in the sight of God, have become very unequal in Muslim societies. The Qur'anic description of man and woman in marriage:

> They are your garments
> And you are their garments (Surah 2: *Al-Baqarah*:187)

implies closeness, mutuality and equality. However, Muslim culture has reduced many, if not most, women to the position of puppets on a string, to slave-like creatures whose only purpose in life is to cater to the needs and pleasures of men. Not only this, it has also had the audacity and the arrogance to deny women direct access to God. Islam rejects the idea of redemption, of any intermediary between a believer and the Creator. It is one of Islam's cardinal beliefs that each person — man and woman — is responsible and accountable for his or her individual actions. How, then, can the husband become the wife's gateway to heaven or hell? How, then, can he become the arbiter not only of what happens to her in this world but also of her ultimate destiny? Surely such questions must arise in the minds of thoughtful Muslim men, but Muslim women are afraid to ask questions whose answers are bound to threaten the existing balance of power in the domain of family relationships in most Muslim societies.

Qur'anic Islam versus Islam in history and issues of women's sexuality

The foregoing account provides much evidence to show that the Qur'an does not discriminate against women, whose sexuality is affirmed both generally and in the context of marriage. Furthermore, while making it clear that righteousness is identical in the case of man or woman, the Qur'an also provides particular safeguards for protecting women's special sexual/biological functions such as carrying, delivering, suckling and rearing offspring.

Underlying much of the Qur'an's legislation on women-related issues is the recognition that women have been disadvantaged persons in history to whom justice needs to be done by the Islamic ummah. Unfortunately, however, the cumulative (Jewish, Christian, Hellenistic, Bedouin and other) biases which existed in the Arab-Islamic culture of the early centuries of Islam infiltrated the Islamic tradition, largely through the Hadith literature, and undermined the intent of the Qur'an to liberate women from the status of chattels or inferior creatures and make them free and equal to men.

A review of Muslim history and culture brings to light many areas in which — Qur'anic teachings notwithstanding — women continued to be subjected to diverse forms of oppression and injustice, not infrequently in the name of Islam. However, there are also areas in which the message of the Qur'an has been heeded. For instance, in response to the Qur'an, condemnation of female[56] infanticide which was not uncommon amongst pre-Islamic Arabs. Muslim Arabs abolished the practice of burying their daughters alive. This means that when Muslims say with pride that Islam gave women the right to live, they are, indeed, right. However, it needs to be added here that though Muslims do not kill their baby daughters, they do not, in general, treat them equally with boys. Generally speaking, the birth of a daughter is met with resignation and even sadness. A woman who only produces daughters is likely to be the target of harsh and abusive behaviour and threatened with divorce. It will be interesting to see what change, if any, takes place in Muslim culture when the fact becomes widely known that it is not the mother but the father who determines the sex of the child!

Underlying the gruesome practice of female infanticide was the notion, prevalent amongst Bedouin Arabs, that the birth of a daughter meant not only additional drainage of extremely scarce means of survival, but also — and more importantly — a real hazard to their "honour". The concepts of "honour" and "shame", which have a profound significance in Bedouin culture (as also in Mediterranean societies) are linked with the idea of women's chastity or sexual behaviour. Pre-Islamic nomadic Arabs who lived in a state of constant warfare with the environment and with other tribes, had a separate word for the honour of women — *ird*, about which B. Fares observes:

> "Ird" from its etymology seems to be a partition which separates its possessor from the rest of mankind... This partition is certainly fragile since it was easily destroyed... (In the pre-Islamic jahiliyya period) 'ird' was intense and of momentous importance; besides it was the guiding motive in the acts and deeds of all the Arabs except those of the Yemen... on account of its sacred nature, it was entitled to take the place of religion; the Arabs put it in the highest place and defended it arms in hand.[57]

So fearful were pre-Islamic Arabs of the possibility of having their "ird" compromised by their daughters' voluntary or involuntary loss of chastity that they were willing to kill them. Obviously, to them their honour mattered more than the lives of their infant daughters. It is important to note that the "honour" killings still go on in many Muslim societies in which a woman is killed on the slightest suspicion of what is perceived as sexual misconduct. There are also many instances of women being killed for other reasons and the murder being camouflaged as an "honour" killing in order to make it appear less heinous a crime.

The term "ird" does not appear in the Qur'an. However, just as in the case of Bedouin Arabs, most Muslim men's concept of "honour" revolves around the orbit of women's sexuality, which is seen as a male possession. Commenting on how men's honour is intertwined with women's virginity (which symbolizes their chastity) in patriarchal Muslim culture, Fatima Mernissi observes:

> ...virginity is a matter between men, in which women merely play the role of silent intermediaries. Like honour, virginity is the manifestation of a purely male preoccupation in societies where inequality, scarcity, and the degrading subjection of some people to others deprive the community as a whole of the only true human strength: self-confidence. The concepts of honour and virginity locate the prestige of a man between the legs of a women. It is not by subjugating nature or by conquering mountains and rivers that a man secures his status, but by controlling the movements of women related to him by blood or by marriage, and by forbidding them any contact with male strangers.[58]

Since women's sexuality is so vitally related to men's honour and the self-image in Muslim culture, it becomes vitally important in Muslim societies to subject women's bodies to external social controls. One way in which some Muslim societies (e.g. in North Africa) have sought to do so is by means of female circumcision, which ranges from cutting off the tip of the clitoris to virtual removal of the clitoris and the sealing of the mouth of the vagina except for a small passage. The extent of physical, emotional or psychological damage done to women by the practice of female circumcision depends, among other things, upon the nature of the "operation" and how it was performed. Having heard personal testimonies from Muslim women who have experienced the horror of radical circumcision, I have no doubt at all that this practice constitutes an extreme form of cruelty towards women which must not be tolerated. Here it needs to be pointed out that though the Islamic tradition (following the Jewish tradition) requires male circumcision, it does not require female circumcision. Female circumcision practised in countries such as Egypt, the Sudan, and Somalia, is, thus, rooted in the culture of those regions and not in religion.

Another way in which Muslim societies seek to control women's bodies is by denying women access to means of birth control. Here it may be noted that though there are Qur'anic statements referring to the killing of one's living children[59], there are no Qur'anic statements on birth control. In the Hadith literature, examples may be found which support the practice of *azl*[60] *(coitus interruptus)* and which do not.[61] A similar ambiguity is found amongst Muslim jurists.[62] In view of the fact that there is no definitive statement on the subject of birth control in the major sources of the Islamic tradition, the issue — in a sense — remains open. Considering the overwhelming importance of the problem of expanding population in most Muslim countries, the subject of family planning or birth control should obviously be considered a high priority for discussion by the learned in the Muslim ummah. ("Ijma", or consensus of the community, constitutes a source of law in the Islamic tradition). However, family planning programmes have met with strong resistance in the Islamic world in general and most of this resistance appears to be rooted in religious grounds.

One Qur'anic passage commonly cited by opponents of birth control in Muslim societies is Surah 2: *Al-Baqarah*: 223, which states:

Your wives are
As a tilth unto you
So approach your tilth
When or how you will;
But do some good beforehand,
And fear God,
And know that you are
To meet Him (in the Hereafter),
And give (these) good tidings
To those who believe. [63]

The likening of a wife to life-containing soil has profound meaning but the average Muslim is not sensitive to the subtleties of the comparison or to the implications of the Qur-an's reminder to the husband that he should act righteously. Since wives are described as a "tilth" and permission has been given to the husbands to approach them "when or how you will", the average Muslim man believes not only that husbands have the right to have sexual intercourse with their wives whenever they choose, but also the right to impregnate them at will in order that they might yield a harvest.

Numerous ahadith attributed to the Prophet insist that a wife must never refuse to have sexual relations with her husband. For instance, Imam Muslim reports the following ahadith on the authority of Abu Huraira:

Allah's Apostle said: "When a woman spends the night from the bed of her husband the angels curse her until morning."

... Allah's Messenger said: "By Him in whose Hand is my Life, when a man calls his wife to his bed and she does not respond, the One who is in the heaven is displeased with her until he (her husband) is pleased with her." [64]

In view of this insistence that the husband's sexual needs be instantaneously satisfied (unless the wife is menstruating, fasting, or in some other exceptional circumstances) it is rather ironic to note that a large number of Muslim women suffer from "frigidity". Like the earth, all too often they are "cultivated" without love or proper care and never discover the wonder or joy of their own womanhood.

Undoubtedly the threat of unlimited pregnancies and childbirths with little or no health care available has made many Muslim women afraid of sex. But the manner in which Muslim societies have legislated that regardless of her own wishes a woman must always meet her husband's sexual demands as *duty* has also led to sexual intercourse becoming a mechanical performance which leaves both the man and the woman sexually unsatisfied.

A number of studies[65] conducted by social scientists indicate that Muslim societies put a high premium on female fertility. Among the reasons why this should be so is the belief, however unfounded, that birth-control and abortion are morally "wrong". A second reason is a hankering for a son and then more sons. A third and more traditional reason is the desire to keep women tied to the homestead and in a state of perpetual dependency upon men.

It has been assumed by conservative Muslim scholars (who form the majority of scholars in the Muslim world) that birth control is demonic in origin and its primary purpose is to facilitate immorality. A.A. Maududi's views cited below are typical of this viewpoint.

> Co-education, employment of women in offices, mixed social gatherings, immodest female dresses, beauty parades, are now a common feature of our social life. Legal hindrances have been placed in the way of marriage and on having more than one wife, but no bar against keeping mistresses and having illicit relationships prior to the age of marriage. In such a society perhaps the last obstacle that may keep a woman from surrendering to a man's advances is fear of an illegitimate conception. Remove this obstacle too and provide to women with weak character assurance that they can safely surrender to their male friends and you will see that the society will be plagued by the tide of moral licentiousness.[66]

In this day and age it hardly needs to be argued that a woman who has no control over her own body or who is compelled by social and religious pressures to play the part of a reproductive machine becomes less than a fully autonomous human being. Furthermore, there is a definite connection between the status of women and their ability to control or determine the number and spacing of children they will have, as a recent United Nations study has shown.[67]

While the issue of birth control is of great urgency and importance to many Muslim women, the issue of segregation and veiling seems to me to affect an even larger proportion of women in Muslim culture. In recent times, the heated, ongoing discussion in a number of Muslim societies (e.g. Egyptian, Iranian, Pakistani) as well as amongst Muslim minority groups (e.g. in Western Europe or North America) on whether Muslim women are required to veil themselves totally or partially, shows that the issue of veiling is at the heart of the greatest dilemma confronting contemporary Islam. It is necessary to understand that the most serious challenge to the world of traditional Islam is that of modernity. The care-takers of Muslim traditionalism are aware of the fact that viability in the modern world requires the adoption of the scientific or rational outlook which inevitably brings about major changes in modes of thinking and behaviour. While all Muslim societies want to have "modernization" (which is largely identified with science, technology and a better standard of living), hardly any Muslim society wants to have "Westernization" (which is largely identified with "mass" Western culture leading to moral and social laxity).

To the majority of Muslims in the world, perhaps the most undesir-able symbol of "Westernization" is a woman who does not honour the boundary between "private" space (i.e. the home which belongs to women) and "public" space (i.e. the world, which belongs to men) which they consider essential for preserving the integrity of the Islamic way of life in the face of endless onslaughts by erstwhile colonisers of the Muslim peoples. Muslims, in general, believe that it is best to keep men and women in their separate, designated spaces, and that the intrusion of women into men's territory leads to the disruption, if not the destruction, of the fundamental order of things. However, if it becomes necessary for women to intrude into men's space, they must make themselves faceless, or at least, as inconspicuous as possible. This is achieved through veiling, which is thus an extension of the idea of segregation of the sexes.

While it is beyond the scope of this paper to analyse all the Qur'anic statements which have a bearing upon the institution of *purdah* (i.e. segregation and veiling), a few observations need to be made. The Qur'an does not confine women to "private" space. In fact, in Surah 4: *An-Nisa'*: 15, confinement to the home is prescribed as a punishment for unchaste women! The Qur'anic law of modesty [68] — addressed to men as well as to women — does indeed discourage exhibitionism in dress or conduct. Its underlying message — addressed particularly to women who have, since time immemorial, been reduced to sex objects by androcentric cultures — is: do not dress or act like sex objects. The purpose of the Qur'anic legislation pertaining to women's attire or behaviour is not to confine them, spatially or psychologically, but to enable them to move round in "public" space without the fear of being molested.[69] Its larger aim is to transform women into *persons* who are secure and self-respecting and who do not feel that their survival depends on their ability to attract, entertain, or cajole those men who are not interested in their personality but only in their sexuality.

In evaluating the impact on Muslim women of veiling, it is necessary to clarify two points. The first is that "veiling" can be understood in a variety of ways, ranging from the wearing of a head-scarf to total covering of the body from head to foot. The second is that, in recent times, the veil has functioned not as a symbol of women's oppression but as an emblem of their political, economic and cultural emancipation and as a means of asserting their multi-faceted identities. The "veiled" revolutions which have taken place in Iran and Egypt in the 1980s illustrate this well.

While the wearing of a head-scarf by a Muslim woman, especially if she has worn the head-scarf as an act of free choice, does not restrict her autonomy as a person; total veiling of the body, especially if it is imposed externally, certainly constitutes a serious deterrent to the full and healthy development of Muslim women. While the Qur'an has given the Muslim woman the right to work, to earn[70], to go about her daily business without fear of sexual harassment, Muslim societies, in general, have imprisoned and entombed many Muslim women in oppressive veils and put them behind locked doors.

Nothing illustrates the obsession of Muslim men with women's sexuality and the desire to control it than the constant effort made by many of them to ensure that not a single hair on the head of any woman related to them is visible to a man who is not related to them! Not satisfied with "the outer garment"[71] prescribed for Muslim women in a specific cultural context, conservative Muslims seek the help of a weak hadith[72] to compel women to cover themselves from head to foot, leaving only the face and hands uncovered. Ultra-conservative Muslims have gone even further, requiring that a woman also cover her face[73]. Certainly there are no Qur'anic statements which justify the rigid restrictions regarding segregation and veiling which have been imposed on Muslim women in the name of Islam. If, for instance, the Qur'an had intended for women to be completely veiled, why would it have required Muslim men to lower their gaze when looking at them?[74]

Summary

Within the Islamic tradition both negative and positive attitudes are found towards women and women's issues. The Qur'an — which to me is the primary source on which Islam is founded — consistently affirms women's equality with men and their fundamental right to actualize the human potential which they possess equally with men. Seen through a non-patriarchal lens, the Qur'an shows no sign of discrimination against women. If anything, it exhibits particular solicitude for women, much as it does for other disadvantaged persons.

The attitude of the Hadith literature towards women is a mixed one. While there are a number of ahadith which recommend an attitude of kindness towards daughters and wives, there are also others — such as the following — which reflect a number of anti-women biases characteristic of Islamic culture.

> Narrated Abu Sa'id Al-Khudri: Once Allah's Apostle went out to the Musalla (to offer the prayers) of 'Id-al-Adha or Al-Fitr prayer. Then he passed by the women and said, "O women! give alms, as I have seen that the majority of the dwellers of Hell-fire were you (women)." They asked, "Why is it so, O Allah's Apostle?" He replied, "You curse frequently and are ungrateful to your husbands. I have not seen anyone more deficient in intelligence and religion than you. A cautious, sensible man could be led astray by some of you." The women replied, "O Allah's Apostle! What is deficient in our intelligence and religion?" He said, "Is not the evidence of two women equal to the witness of one man?" They replied in the affirmative. He said, "This is the deficiency in your intelligence. Isn't it true that a woman can neither pray nor fast during her menses?" The women replied in the affirmative. "This is the deficiency in your religion."[75]

In this paper many instances have been cited in which individual ahadith conflict with the Qur'an. However, there is one area in which the Qur'an and the Hadith literature seem to be in total accord. This pertains to attitudes towards one's mother. Surah 4: *An-Nisa'*: 1 commands human beings to revere God who created them, and next, to revere the wombs which bore them. There are also numerous ahadith on the subject of honouring one's mother. One of these — "Paradise lies at or under the feet of your mother" — cited by a number of Hadith collections, is probably the best-known of all ahadith in Muslim culture.

Muslims, in general, have been faithful to the Qur'anic commandment and in Muslim societies great love and respect is shown to one's mother. Here, it is of interest to note that the two most beloved names of God — Rahman and Rahim — come from the root-word "Rahm", which means "womb". Also, the word "ummah" comes from the root-word "umm", which means "mother". Hence, some of the most important symbols/images in the Islamic tradition are women-related.

But though respect for *one's own mother* is universal in the Islamic world, it must be noted that this respect is not necessarily extended al *all* mothers. In other words, though a Muslim may revere his own mother before all others, he does not consider motherhood as such to be worthy of the same respect that is given to his mother. The Qur'an, however, is concerned about all mothers and seeks to protect their rights. In Surah 2: *Al-Baqarah*: 233, for example, the Qur'an refers to the duties of a man towards his divorced wife who is the mother of his child or children:

> Mothers shall suckle their children for two whole years; (that is) for those who wish to complete the suckling. The duty of feeding and clothing nursing mothers in a surely manner is upon the father of the child. No one should be charged beyond his capacity. *A mother should not be made to suffer because of her child, nor should he to whom the child is born be made to suffer because of the child.* And on the (father's) heir is incumbent the like of that (which was incumbent on the father) if they desire to wean the child by mutual consent and (after) consultation, it is no sin for them; and if ye wish to give your children out to nurse, it is no sin for you, provided that ye pay what is due from you in kindness. Observe your duty to Allah, and know that Allah is Seer of what ye do. [76]

This verse shows, amongst other things, the way in which the Qur'an ensures that no one — mother, father, or child — is exploited or unjustly treated and how even in the event of a divorce the fundamental rights and duties connected with motherhood or fatherhood must be recognised. This verse also speaks of "mutual consultation" with regard to the weaning and nursing of the child — yet another acknowledgment of the right of the mother to be a party to every important decision affecting her child.

Although the Qur'an lays down that no mother should be made to suffer on account of her child, many millions of Muslim mothers — like non-Muslim mothers — suffer indescribable ordeals and hardships if they have the misfortune to be without means and without a husband or to have a husband who is not mindful of his duties.

A point of psychological interest needs to be made regarding the importance that is given to a Muslim mother when she has a grown son. This mother is the same woman who was discriminated against in her father's household and given an inferior position in the context of her own marriage. Her chance to "get even" with the world comes when she has a son who reaches manhood. The bitterness, resentment and frustration caused by a lifetime of repression, oppression and deprivation tend to find rather ugly expression when, at last, the son's mother becomes a mother-in-law and begins her (generally, not-too-benign) rule over her son's household. In Muslim societies the figure of the mother-in-law is feared as much as the figure of the mother is loved. However, as Fatima Mernissi has observed in the context of Moroccan society:

> It is the structure which sets up the roles for everyone and leaves specific outlets for the human individual's cravings and wishes. It is the structure which is vicious, not the mother-in-law.[77]

I want to end this paper with the hope and prayer that men and women — created equal by God — remembering that they are *zaujain* whose different sexualities complement each other, work together to construct that order in the home and in the world which reflects the justice and mercy, compassion and love of God towards God's creatures, and foreshadows that lasting Paradise from which the myth of feminine evil has finally been expelled.

NOTES

[1] Rahman, Fazlur, *Islam*, Doubleday and Company, Inc., Garden City, New York, 1968, p. 70.
[2] Ali, Cheragh ("The Proposed Political Reforms in the Ottoman Empire and other Muhammadan States", Bombay, 1883, pp. XIX and 147) quoted by Alfred Guillaume, *The Traditions of Islam*, Khayats, Beirut, 1966, p. 97.
[3] *Islam*, p. 73.
[4] *The Traditions of Islam*, p. 15.
[5] *Ibid*, pp. 12, 13.
[6] Hodgson, Marshall, G.S., *The Venture of Islam* (Conscience and History in a World Civilization), The University of Chicago Press, Chicago, 1974, Volume One (The Classical Age of Islam) p. 232.
[7] Gibb, Hamilton A.R., *Studies on the Civilization of Islam*, edited by Stanford J. Shaw and William R. Polk, Beacon Press, Boston, 1962, p. 194.
[8] *The Shorter Oxford English Dictionary* (Prepared by W. Little, H.W. Fowler, and J. Coulson; revised and edited by C.T. Onions), 3rd edition, Clarendon Press, Oxford, 1964, p. 1859
[9] Ali, A. Yusuf (Translator), *The Holy Qur'an*, McGregor and Werner, Inc., USA, 1946, p. 1056.
[10] Parwez, Ghulam A., *Tabwib ul Qur'an*, Idara Tulu' e Islam, Lahore, 1977, Vol. 2, p. 853.
[11] *The Holy Qur'an*, p. 1450.

[12] "Mari" is the rendering of "Al Insan" which is a generic term for humanity.

[13] *The Holy Qur'an*, p. 1653.

[14] Reference is made to "nafs in wahidatin" in a number of Qur'anic verses, e.g. Surah 4: An-Nisa': 1, Surah 6: Al-an'am: 98, Surah 7: Al-A'raf: 189, Surah 31: Luqman: 28, and Surah 39: Az-Zumar: 6.

[15] *The Holy Qur'an*, p. 905.

[16] The Qur'an is deeply concerned about issues raised by slavery and contains many recommendations aimed at the freeing of slaves and at their gradual absorption into the society of free believers. Marriage to a slave woman could serve several ends: it would free her from slavery and give her a socially respectable position, it would make it possible for a man with modest means to get married, it would rid society of the problems caused by illicit sex with slave women leading to illegitimate offspring who would also have the status of slaves, thus perpetuating the immoral institution of slavery. (See *Islam: A Challenge to Religion*, Idara Tulu' e Islam, Lahore, 1968, p. 346).

[17] *The Holy Qur'an*, pp. 187-188.

[18] Referring to the followers of Jesus, the Qur'an states in Surah 57: Al-Hadid 27, "...the Monasticism/Which they invented/For themselves, We did not /Prescribe for them." (*The Holy Qur'an*, p. 1507).

[19] Reference may be made in this context to the following hadith which is reported by both Bukhari and Muslim, the two most authoritative Hadith scholars of Sunni Islam: "'Abdullah b. Mas'ud reported God's Messenger as saying: 'Young men, those of you who can support a wife should marry, for it keeps you from looking at strange women and preserves you from immorality, but those who cannot, should devote themselves to fasting, for it is a means of suppressing sexual desire.'" (Robson, James, translation of *Mishkat Al-Masabih*, Shaikh Muhammad Ashraf, Lahore, 1975, Vol. I, p. 658).

[20] Reference here is to the following hadith: "Anas reported God's Messenger as saying, 'When a man marries he has fulfilled half of the religion; so let him fear God regarding the remaining half.'" (*Mishkat Al-Masabith*, Vol. I, p. 660).

[21] For instance, Surah 4: An-Nisa': 1, Surah 7: Al-A'raf: 189, and Surah 39: Az-Zumar: 6.

[22] In the aforementioned passages (as also in Surah 6: Al-An'am: 98 and Surah 31: Luqman: 28) reference is made to the creation from one source of being ("nafs in wahidatin") of all human being. Muslims, with hardly any exceptions, believe that the one original source or being referred to in these passages is a man named Adam. This belief has led many translators of the Qur'an to obviously incorrect translation of simple Qur'anic passages.

[23] "Adam" is used as a proper name in Surah 3: Al.'Imran: 35 and 59; Surah 5: Al-Ma'idah: 30; and Surah 19: Maryam: 58.

[24] Iqbal, Muhammad, *The Reconstruction of Religious Thought in Islam*, Shaikh Muhammad Ashraf, Lahore, 1962, p. 83.

[25] For instance, in Surah:75: Al.Qiyamah: 36-39. This passage reads: "Does 'al-insan' think that he will be left aimless/ Was he not a drop of semen emitted? Then he became something which clings. Then He (Allah) created and shaped and made of him two mates: the male and the female."

[26] Each hadith consists of two parts: "isnad" (or "sanad") and "matn". The "isnad" contains the names of persons who have handed on the substance of the hadith to one another. The "matn" is the text or actual substance of the hadith.

[27] Since the early centuries of Islam, it has been axiomatic for (Sunni) Muslim masses to regard the Companions of the Prophet as being totally above the suspicion of being untrustworthy in any way least of all as transmitters of the Prophet's ahadith. Given such

an attitude of absolute devotion, a critical examination of the credentials of the Companions as transmitters could hardly have been undertaken. However, in the earliest phase of the development of Islam, a more critical attitude prevailed towards the Hadith literature and its transmitters. Here it is of interest to note that according to the well-known Muslim scholar 'Abdul Wahab Ash-Shairani, Imam Abu Hanifah, considered to be the founder of the largest school of law in Sunni Islam, did not consider Abu Hurairah to be a reliable transmitter of ahadith (*Al-Mizan al-Kubra*, Cairo edition, Vol. I, p. 59).

[28] Khan, M.M., translation with notes of *Sahih Al-Bikhari*, Kazi Publications, Lahore, 1971, Vol. IV, p. 346.

[29] Siddiqui, A.H., translation with notes of *Sahih Muslim*, Shaikh Muhammad Ashraf, Lahore, 1972, Vol. II, p. 752.

[30] See note 21.

[31] *The Traditions of Islam*, p. 32.

[32] It is interesting to observe that while in the Genesis 2 story, woman is derived from Adam's rib, there is no mention of Adam in any of the ahadith under discussion. This is a further "dehumanization" of woman since she could — in the ahadith in question — have been created from a disembodied rib which may not even have been human.

[33] Simth, Jane I. and Haddad, Yvonne Y., "Eve: Islamic Image of Woman" in *Women and Islam*, edited by Azizah al-Hibri, Pergamon Press, New York, 1982, p. 139

[34] See Surah 15: Al-Hijr: 26-43, Surah 17: Bani Isra'il: 16-64, Surah 18: Al-Kahf: 50, and Surah 38: L U: 71-85.

[35] *The Reconstruction of Religious Thought in Islam*, p. 84.

[36] *Ibid.*

[37] *The Structure of the Ethical Terms in the Koran*, Keio Institute of Philosophical Studies, Mita, Siba, Minatoku, Tokyo, 1959, pp. 152-153

[38] *The Reconstruction of Religious Thought in Islam*, p. 85.

[39] Lane, E.W., *Arabic-English Lexicon*, Williams and Norgate, London, 1863, Book I - part 4, pl 1458.

[40] *The meaning of the Qur'an*, Islamic Publications Ltd., 1976, Vol. IV, p. 16, footnote 13(2).

[41] The famous expression comes from Tertullian (A.D. 160-225), a Church Father from North Africa who wrote: "And do you not know that you are (each) an Eve? The sentence of God on this sex of yours lives in this age: the guilt must of necessity live too. You are the devil's gateway; you are the unsealer of that (forbidden) tree: you are the first deserter of the divine law, you are she who persuaded him whom the devil was not valiant enough to attack. You destroyed so easily God's image, man. On account of your desert — that is, death — even the Son of God had to die." (*De cultu feminarum* 1.1, cited in *Biblical Affirmations of Woman*, p. 346).

[42] Also cited in *Sahih Muslim*, Vol. IV, p. 1431.

[43] Also cited in *Sahih Al. Bukhari*, Vol. IV, p. 305, Vol. VIII, pp. 362-363.

[44] The Qur'anic understanding of "righteousness" is described in Surah 2: Al-Baqarah: 177, which states: It is not righteousness/That ye turn your faces/Towards East or West;/But it is righteousness/To believe in God/And the Last Day/And the Angels/And the Book/And the Messengers;/To spend of your substance/Out of love of Him,/For your kin/For orphans/For the wayfarer/For those/who ask/And for the ransom of slaves;/To be steadfast in prayer/And practice regular charity/To fulfil the contracts/Which ye have made/And to be firm and patient/In pain (or suffering)/And adversity/And throughout/All periods of panic/Such are the people/Of truth, the God-fearing. (*The Holy Qur'an*, pp. 69-70).

128   *Women, Religion and Sexuality*

[45] *The Holy Qur'an*, pp. 174-175.
[46] *Beyond the Veil*, Schenkman Publishing Company, Inc., Cambridge, 1975, p. 103.
[47] *The Meaning of the Qur'an*, Vol. II (1971), p. 321.
[48] Shehab, Rafi ullah, *Rights of Women in Islamic Shariah*, Indus Publishing House, Lahore, 1986, p. 117.
[49] *The Holy Qur'an*, pp. 89-90. The emphasis is mine.
[50] Khan, Sadiq Hasan, *Husn al-Uswa*, p. 281.
[51] *Al-Hadith*, Vol. III, p. 80.
[52] Imran, Muhammad, *Ideal Woman in Islam*, Islamic Publications Limited, Lahore, 1979, p. 50.
[53] *Ibid*, p. 51.
[54] *Ibid*.
[55] *Ibid*.
[56] See Surah 81: At-Takwir: 8 and 9; Surah 16: An-Nahl: 57-59; and Surah 17: Bani Isra'il: 31.
[57] Article on "Ird", in *Supplement to the Encyclopaedia of Islam*, E.K. Brill, Leiden, 1938, pp. 96-97.
[58] "Virginity and Patriarchy", in *Women and Islam*, p. 183.
[59] See, for instance, Surah 6: Al-An'am, 137, 140, 152; Surah 60: Al-Mumpahanah: 12, Surah 71: Nuh:3.
[60] See *Mishkat Al-Masabih*, Vol. 2, pp. 677-678.
[61] *Ibid*.
[62] Rauf, M.A., *Marriage in Islam*, Exposition Press, New York, 974, pp. 65-66.
[63] *The Holy Qur'an*, p. 88.
[64] *Sahih Muslim*, Vol II, p. 723.
[65] For example, A. Aitken and J. Stoekel, "Muslim-Hindu Differentials in Family Planning Knowledge and Attitudes in Rural East Pakistan", in *Journal of Comparative Family Studies*, Spring, 1971.
[66] *Birth Control*, Islamic Publications Limited, 1974, p. 176.
[67] *Status of Women and Family Planning*, United Nations, New York, 1975, p. 4.
[68] See Surah 24: An-Nur: 30 and 31.
[69] See Surah 33: Al. Ahzab: 59.
[70] See Surah 4: An-Nisa': 32.
[71] Reference here is to Sirah 33: Al-Ahzab: 59.
[72] In this hadith, Ayesha reports that the Prophet Muhammad told Asma, her sister, when she appeared before him wearing thin clothes, "O Asma, when woman attains her puberty, it is not proper that any part of her body should be seen except this" and he pointed to his face and hands. (*Rights of Women in Islamic Shariah*, p. 4.)
[73] In this context, see A.A. Maududi, *Purdah and the Status of Woman in Islam*, Islamic Publications Limited, Lahore, 1975.
[74] Reference here is to Surah 24: An-Nur: 30.
[75] *Sahih Al. Bukhari*, Vol. I, p. 29.
[76] Pickthall, Muhammad M., *The Meaning of the Glorious Qur'an*, Muslim World League - Rabita, New York, 1977, p. 36.
[77] *Beyond the Veil*, p. 79.

Femaleness:
Akan Concepts and Practices

Elizabeth Amoah

Introduction

This study is an attempt to examine some of the traditional and contemporary views of the Akan — a large ethnic group in Ghana — on woman as a female being who goes through certain biological, physical and social processes such as menstruation, puberty, marriage, birth and widowhood rites. It is also an attempt to examine the effects these basic Akan conceptions of femaleness have on women as regards their roles and the rituals they go though in their lives.

The focus is on views derived from religion and custom. Both recorded and unrecorded materials are used as the sources of information. For example, oral traditions in the form of proverbs or wise sayings and songs were made use of. In addition to these oral sources, documented materials which have been listed in the bibliography are also used.

Ethnographers and geographers[1] define the Akan as comprising different ethnic groups such as the Ashanti, Akwapim, Aki, Fante, Wassaw and Nzema. These ethnic groups occupy the greater section of Southern Ghana with the exception of the area inhabited by the Gas-Adangbe and the Anlo-Ewe on the South-eastern coast. An essential feature of Akan social structure is matrilineal descent: for inheritance of property, tracing descent and succession to offices, the line used is that of the mother. However, among the Akwapim, some of the ethnic groups such as Mapong (in the Akwapim area) are patrilineal.

● Within the Ghanaian context, it was found difficult to give precise definition to the term "Female Sexuality and Bodily Functions".

It would have been useful to have a basically patrilineal group as another study model to bring out the basic differences on conceptions of women in these two types of society. Such differences do exist. For example, where descent is traced through the male line, male children are preferred. On the other hand, giving birth to female children who will extend the matrilineal clan is encouraged in a typical matrilineal group. But male children are also wanted in a matrilineal society, and it is not uncommon to hear a man quarrelling with his wife if she gives birth only to females. Apart from this basic difference, the plight of women in these two groups is the same. Women must ensure the continuity of the group by bearing and bringing up children. Thus, while this study concentrates mainly on a basically matrilineal group, the findings will largely be true for women in non-matrilineal groups.

The religion of the Akan

Platvoet[2] defines religion as a "process of communication by means of the exchange of messages between a human being or a group of human beings and one or more of the meta-empirical beings whom they believe to exist and to affect their lives... Religion as a process of communication takes place in a field or 'network' of culturally pre-set role-relationships modelled after the role-relationships which rule commerce among men. By these relationships the believers and their meta-empirical beings are constituted into a society and involved in an economy of reciprocal interests and expectations, rights and duties, responsibilities imposed, and liberties taken..."

That definition is very true of Akan religion. The Akan religion is a complex process of communication between human beings and numerous spirit beings which they believe exist and influence their lives. Some of these spirit beings and forces are:

1. *Onyame*, usually addressed as *Nana Nyankopon* who is believed to be the creator of the world and everything in it.

2. *Abosom* — gods and goddesses. They have their powers from *Onyame*. They are powerful, and they can use their powers either destructively or constructively depending on how human beings relate to them. There are priests and priestesses who act as spokespeople of these *abosom*.

3. The ancestors — they are known in Akan as *Nananom Nsamfo* — deceased grandparents, the spirits of recognised elders. In the Akan religion, it is believed that human beings after death continue to live a life similar to the present one. Depending on the type of life that people lead

on earth, some of the dead members of one's lineage group, the *abusua*, become ancestors or ancestresses. They are believed to acquire certain powers through death which they use to reward or punish the living members of the group, depending on how the latter relate to them.

4. Witchcraft — *Bayi* is another form of spirit power. It is believed that when the various types of witchcraft affect human beings they become very destructive. Witchcraft, therefore, is frowned upon by society. (The majority of people accused of being witches are women.)

5. Certain plants and animals are believed to possess spiritual power. Hence, plants such as the *Odum*, the *Tweneboa* and animals such as the leopard, are ritually pacified before they are used for religious purposes. Protective objects or "charms", i.e. *asuman*, and therapeutic medicines — *nnuru* — are made from these special plants and animals.

At the centre of these numerous spirit powers are human beings who are also believed to be endowed with certain spiritual elements. These are: (1) *Okra* which is believed to come from Onyame and so to be the source of life; (2) *Mogya*, which is believed to be transmitted to the child by the mother, determines the child's social status and links the child to the mother and her maternal *abusua* group. The *Ntoro* and *Sunsum* are believed to be spiritual elements which the father transmits to the child. They act as protective elements which at the same time determine the individual's personality traits and behavioural characteristics. It is generally believed that women have weaker and less effective sunsum than men. Hence it is that in most cases the man's sunsum are believed to give protection to the children. These spiritual elements possessed by human beings make them part of both the spiritual world and the human community. Hence it is said that through such religious rituals as divinations, women and men are able to transcend into the spiritual world and look into the past, present and future.

Conceptions of femaleness and maleness

Both women and men are believed to have the spiritual elements which have been discussed above. However, as has already been pointed out, men are generally considered to have stronger sunsum for protection and, in the indigenous Akan conception, there are clear distinctions between femaleness and maleness and there are clear terms for this distinction.

Femaleness is described by the term *bere* and maleness is described by the term *nyin*. They are basic terms used to describe the femaleness and the maleness of human beings, animals and even plants. Underlying the distinction is the concept of production. An animal or plant is described as *nyin* if that animal cannot produce its own kind or that plant cannot bear fruit. For example, among the Akan, the Fanti describe the pawpaw which only produces flowers but no fruits as *brosow nyin*. The clear attributes and characteristics which are associated with *bere-female and nyin-male* are listed in Table 1.

Bere-female	*Nyin-male*
1. Ability to reproduce (this is a basic attribute and requirement of every woman)	1. Virility
2. Caring and providing food; being kind and generous	2. Strength
3. Modesty	3. Authority — power
4. Dignity of bearing, perseverance	4. Leadership qualities
5. Obedience, submissiveness and conformity	5. Ability to offer protection and sustenance
6. Dependence, being in need of protection	6. Being the breadwinner
7. Beauty	7. Intelligence
8. Quarrelsomeness	8. Wisdom
9. Being a gossip	9. Ability to give counsel
10. Being dangerous	10. Ability to bear physical pain; ability to sustain emotions
11. Weakness	
12. Being emotional	
13. Envy	
14. Greed	
15. Desire for material things	

Such values and ideas on the characteristics which distinguish females from males are inculcated and absorbed from early childhood onwards. It is not unusual, for instance, to hear parents telling weeping male children: "Stop crying for men don't cry." Boys who frequent the kitchen, especially at times when meals are being cooked, are chased out for it is improper for men to be in the kitchen. Similarly, daughters are often told not to insult their brothers calling them fools or stupid. In fact, in most cases, any female who calls a male a fool or stupid receives a severe beating.

Those who seek to deviate from these social expectations are brought into line by a whole series of social devices including punishment, ridicule and gossip. A man who acts out of tune with the social expectations appropriate to his male role or is seen as effeminate is described as *banyin-basia*; literally a "male-female". No man likes to be called by this derogatory term. Conversely, a woman who is judged to be unduly forceful is described by the Wassa (an Akan group) as *babasia-kokonin*, literally "a female male", another derogatory term. A barren woman is known as *bonin*, and it is interesting to note the suffix *nin* or *nyin*-maleness at the end of that word.

Some of the traditional proverbs and sayings throw light on how femaleness is conceived. *Mmaa pe nea adee wo*, literally "Women like where things are": this means that women are generally attracted to places where they will easily acquire property or material things. The saying also implies that it is characteristic of women to prefer men with wealth. This desire for a comfortable life is considered as a bad feature in women. Another common saying is "Fear women so that you will live long"; or "If you want to live long, be careful of women." Yet another is "Women are ungrateful."

A critical examination of these traditional sayings conveys some of the negative concepts that the society holds about women.

Such conceptions about women form the basis of society's expectations of them. Certain jobs, for instance, are the peculiar preserve of women. In both traditional and contemporary societies, women plant the crops, maintain farms, collect water from rivers and wells, do the laundry, cook and provide food for the household, care for the children, make and sell pottery products, do the petty trading, and sometimes fish in the rivers but not in the sea. In short, women are expected to do the jobs which are centred on maintaining the home and bringing up children. These jobs, whether carrying big loads of fire-wood or farm products, or making several trips uphill for water while pregnant and/or carrying a baby on the back are judged light enough for women though society considers them as weak creatures.

Men are required to do all the jobs considered by the community as tougher. They are expected to build and maintain houses, clear the land, fell trees, weave cloth, do gold and iron smithery, make and beat the drums (one of the traditional means of communication). In other words, men provide the communicating tools. Men discuss or settle traditional court cases, they are responsible for politics, to hunt for meat and go to war and defend the town or village.

Some of the traditional sayings reinforce this sharp division of labour between the two sexes. "If the gun lets out bullets, it is the man that receives them on his chest." In other words, it is the men who face difficult problems bravely. "It is a woman who reproduces; a man is just like the corn stalk."[3] "If you buy a woman, pay a very high price for her for she has a whole town or community in her." In other words, the descendants of one woman can form a community. "Whether the woman's soup will be delicious depends on the man." That is, it is always the man who provides for the household meals; the woman's duty is only to cook what has been provided by the man. "The beauty of a woman (wife) depends on the man (husband)." "The hen also knows when it is dawn but it allows the cock to announce it." It is considered unnatural and a sign of misfortune for hens to crow. What this proverb indicates is that women have all the knowledge and capabilities possessed by men but, because of traditions and customs, they do not perform certain functions.

These are evident in specific social areas. In marriage, for instance, when both sexes are obviously needed for the purpose of procreation, one would expect to find mutuality of interests in at least the sexual relation of the wife and husband. This is not always the case. The woman's sexual role tends to be more or less marginal and passive. She does not take the initiative in sexual activities. Generally, women who take the initiative or express desire to have sexual intercourse are branded as *w'asee*, "bad", literally, "prostitutes". Of course there are exceptions. But the norm is that the husband or the man should take the initiative.

The fact that women generally do not take the initiative in sexual activities means that they have no opportunity for the full and free expression of natural human desires. The woman is normally not expected to give any indication that she is enjoying the sexual act. In fact, in most cases she is not even allowed to rest after the sexual act. It was reported that, in some cases, women are sent by husbands or male sexual partners to get them a glass of water or something to wipe themselves with soon after the sexual act.

Some gynaecologists and obstetricians are of the opinion that in cases where women do not conceive it could sometimes be because the male sperm may not have enough time to travel down to the womb for fertilization. Women are sometimes advised to lie down and rest for a while after the sexual act. This has worked for some women formerly considered barren or infertile.

An important traditional marriage counselling practice is to tell the bride never to refuse the husband sex on any condition (except while she is menstruating). This applies only to women. There seems to be no such restriction on men. The following sayings express this requirement: "It is the foolish woman[4] who has ten children in marriage." "It is the good (in

the sense of submissive) wife who sleeps on a good, comfortable mat."
"The beauty of the married woman is a credit to her husband."

These and many other sayings are part of the advice given to women,
especially adult women ready to marry. In fact, these sayings express
what society expects of and considers normal behaviour for women. For
example, "A married woman whose husband has not travelled must not
have her meal before the husband has his." This saying refers to the
wife's duty to make sure the husband has the best part of the meal and he
is properly fed before she and her children eat. "A woman should not take
a seat while her husband (man) is standing." There are no apparent
reasons for such restrictions other than that it is what custom or society
demands.

Among the Akan, rituals to mark the onset of puberty are associated
practically only with women. It is at this stage that the sharp distinction
between femaleness and maleness becomes obvious. Prior to this, parents
make an effort to instil the concepts of femaleness and maleness into the
minds of their children. But the separation of females and males is not
rigorously observed till the time of puberty. They may be seen, for
example, swimming in the village river or sleeping together in the same
room. This freedom ceases at puberty.

Then the child is considered to be ready to enter adulthood. Hence
puberty is considered as a very important stage in life. In spite of this, the
ritual recognition of puberty among the Akan is much less significant for
males than for females. Traditionally, however, on reaching puberty, the
male is given such tools as are necessary for the performance of men's
work. Among farming communities, the boy is often given a gun. This
symbolizes that he has achieved the status of a full grown male and is
ready to work on the farm, to marry, to have children and to be able to
care for his dependents. It is important to note here that impotency in men
is described as *w'agye ne tuo*, literally "his gun has been taken from
him". The gun is, therefore, a symbol of virility. Puberty rites and rituals
among the Akan have been extensively dealt with by such writers as
Rattray and Sarpong[5], and they agree that puberty rites are more significant in the case of the female and that their importance is reflected in the
fact that they generally extend over a number of days.

Puberty rites are held soon after a girl has had her first menstrual
period. In typical traditional communities, as soon as the girl tells her
mother that she has menstruated, the mother asks an older woman, in
some cases the queen-mother of the community, to examine her daughter.
This examination is done to make sure that the girl has genuinely

menstruated. It is also to make sure that she did not have any sexual relation before her first menstruation. After the examination, the girl is ritually washed and shown how to clean herself properly during menstruation. Then follow a few days of confinement during which her peer groups will be around, singing and playing.

Certain basic and common concepts underlie the puberty rites for girls. The symbols used in the rites reflect these concepts. For example, the sanctity of the girl's body is highlighted. It is believed that a girl's body should remain pure and undefiled until marriage, which generally follows soon after puberty. Thus there are severe ritual prohibitions on pre-puberty sexual activities and undue sexual precocity. This emphasis on sanctity and purity explains why the colour white is used a lot during the puberty rituals. For the Akan, white is believed to symbolize all that is pure and virtuous. Carrying the girl to the riverside for the ceremonial cleansing and then home again so that she does not touch the earth also reflects the belief in the sanctity of the girl's body.

Female fertility and procreation are stressed in the puberty rites. Many of the symbols used in the rituals emphasize the great importance attached to fertility and procreation. Among them are:

1) *Elephant's skin* — Interpretations of the elephant skin symbol vary from one Akan group to the other. Typically, when a girl's mouth is touched with the skin of the elephant, prayers such as the following accompany the act: "May the elephant give you her womb that you may bear ten children." "May you not come of age and be childless and (in consequence become as big as the elephant by reason of the children suppressed in her womb)". "May your womb not be as hard as the elephant skin."

2) *Roasted plantain* — This is used to signify that a girl's womb should not be as hard as the roasted plantain. Rather she should have a "soft womb", that is, a very fertile womb. That is why at a certain stage of the ceremony, an initiate is allowed to taste banana.

The songs and prayers also emphasize fertility and procreation. One such song is recorded by Sarpong: "O Lord Kwame"[6]

Earth Yaa[7]
Siore Kobi and you thousand and other gods,
Today is Monday,
And by your grace,
This grandchild of yours has come of age,
And we are now touching her mouth.
Stand well behind her

So that she may get a good man who has a name,
Life and prosperity to come, and marry her quickly.
Let her give birth to thirty children.
Girls and boys who will lead good lives and acquire property.
So that when in the future
Our grandfathers call us to their sides
We may get people to replace us
In the government of this land
Health to all of us who are assembled here.

Soon after going through the puberty rites a girl is expected to marry. In fact, one of the fears for girls who break the *kyiribra* is that they would eventually end up barren and infertile, a condition which is considered a curse.

Puberty is also a period when young girls are introduced to sexuality. Before this period, parents try as much as possible not to discuss anything about sex with their children. Direct mention of the reproductive organs is forbidden and euphemistic words are used in referring to them. For example, the male sexual organ is called a *dua* — stick, and the female sexual organ *Akosua kuma*.[8] But during puberty rites, reference to sexual organs and sexual activities is made without inhibitions. This is normally done through songs sung during the rites. An example of such songs is :

Kwaku Atta (name of a man)
I shall lie with my lover.
Kwaku Atta
I shall lie with my lover on my father's bed
You elderly women are having sexual intercourse with men;
Penises are enjoyable.[9]

The girl has now become an adult who is required to produce children, and she now has to be taught everything about sexual activities. It is said that, among certain Akan groups, the neophytes are taught the proper way of having sexual intercourse with a man by older and experienced women. It is believed that sexual intercourse is one of the contributing factors to a happy and successful marriage. This is why young brides are always advised never under any circumstances to refuse sex to their husbands.

Sustained advice and counselling during this period is centred on how to be a good wife, some of the criteria of which are the following:
— Cooking good and tasty meals for the husband and the household.
— Obedience to the husband, which implies not refusing him sex or food under any circumstances.

— Consulting the husband on any venture.
— Respecting and obeying her in-laws.

A wife who conforms to the above criteria is traditionally referred to as *Obaa kwasea*, literally, the "foolish woman" or *obaa pa*, a "good woman", that is, a woman who gives much or does everything to please her husband. Such wives are believed to be rewarded with many children. Having as many as ten children is the ideal of women in a typical, traditional union. It must, however, be emphasized here that, these days, because of economic and other factors, most Ghanaian women do not desire to have as many as ten children! In the past, ten was a sign of blessing and reward for good wives.

It is through puberty rites that girls for the first time receive sex education from experienced and successful wives. Young boys do not go through such elaborate puberty rites, nor are they offered any other kind of formal sex education. Sometimes the behaviour of adult men as husbands provides a model for the boys.

The prolonged ritual ceremonies associated with puberty rites for women may create much stress. The same can be said about the physical exposure of girls which is central to traditional puberty rites, among the Krobos for example. Although exposing the girl's nakedness is meant to emphasize the importance of fertility, it cannot be denied that the experience is somewhat demeaning, and that, in some respects, it comes close to advertising the girls for eligible husbands. No such advertising is done for men.

One can already observe some changes with regard to puberty rites. Within some Christian and literate groups, such rites have either been completely eliminated or even reformulated. When their daughters menstruate for the first time, some Christian and western-educated mothers just give them eggs and *oto*[10], mashed yam with or without palm oil, and no elaborate rite is practiced. Some Ghanaian Protestant churches arrange Christian confirmation rites to coincide with puberty among young people. In this way, traditional ritual procedures are replaced with the Christian ritual of confirmation. In both the Christian and the traditional rites, the idea of initiation into social and religious maturity is stressed. But certain features in the traditional systems need to be refined and injected into the Christian rites. For example, the important elements of sex education, with instruction in personal hygiene and emphasis on the responsibility of a mother and a wife, must receive emphasis. Christian confirmation should stress this not only for girls but for boys as well.

Menstruation

Puberty in females is closely associated with the onset of a girl's menstruation. Menstruation among the Akan is surrounded with many traditions. A menstruating woman is variously described as: "She has gone to the outskirts of the village"; "She has bent her hands behind her back"; "She has started her life"; "She has killed the elephant"; "She has turned aside."

Menstruation is considered unclean. Traditionally, women in such a condition were moved from their homes and settled in a house known as *bra-dan* — menstruation house — at the outskirts of the village. Because a menstruating woman is considered unclean, she should not: cook her husband's or any adult male's food; enter the stool house;[11] (Women who break this rule are severely dealt with. In some cases such women are killed);[12] cross or fetch water from certain rivers; greet or talk to the chief; (Wives of certain craftsmen such as weavers and blacksmiths should not address their husbands directly when they are menstruating. They must talk to their husbands through the medium of spokesmen who are usually young male children); touch some of the traditional musical instruments, such as the drums; touch or come into contact with protective or destructive medicine or objects known as the *asuman*.

A number of sayings and proverbs express such prohibitions. For example: "If a woman turns the soup pot upside down, she should not go to the chief's palace." In other words, if a woman menstruates, she should not go to a chief's palace. The image of overturning the soup pot indicates prohibition against cooking during menstruation, especially for husbands or adult males.

The basic belief underlying the numerous prohibitions associated with menstruation is that the menstrual blood is considered so dangerous and potent that any direct or indirect contact with it is believed to render all powers impotent and inactive. Therefore, besides the menstruating woman being unclean, she is also dangerous and must be isolated and avoided, especially by men and certain religious personalities. Even women who hold religious functions such as traditional priests are forbidden to enter religious shrines when they are menstruating. Ironically, menstrual blood is considered as a very important event in a girl's life. Menstruating is compared to the killing of an elephant — *w'akum-sono* — a deed considered dangerous, brave and important. There are fixed rules on *when* a girl should have her first menstruation. It is a misfortune for a girl to have her first menstruation at noon. Hence the saying: "It is the disobedient child (daughter) who menstruates in the afternoon". It was also a misfortune to have one's menstruation on certain days of the week. This is implied in the saying: "It is the child who disobeys her mother that menstruates on *Kurudapaawukuo*".[13]

Mothers tell their daughters about times and days, and they also try to hide daughters who do not conform to traditional expectations. If caught, the girls are punished because it is believed that menstruating at forbidden times will bring misfortune to the community.

Purification rites

It is also forbidden for a girl who has not yet had her first menstruation to have sexual intercourse. Such an act is considered a very serious offence which brings misfortune not only to those directly involved but to the whole community. A girl who has been caught committing this offence must undergo a purification rite known as *Kyribra*, literally "hate menstruation" rite.

Sarpong[14] reports on *Kyribra* rites:

When a queen-mother is satisfied that a girl is, or has been guilty of *Kyribra*, she summons the girl's parents to appear before her and she officially informs them of their daughter's misbehaviour. She impresses upon them the horrible nature of her 'moral depravity', and then orders them to have the ceremony of purification (of the girl, her lover and the community) performed, and this takes place outside the queen-mother's palace. In Offinso and some other chiefdoms, the girl is, in the first instance, taken to the paramount chief, and if the identity of the lover is known, he too is ordered to appear at the chief's house. The boy and girl are compelled to pay a certain amount of money[15] which their parents provide, if only because in the eyes of the people the parents bear the blame of the offence equally with their children, as it demonstrates the inadequacy of the parental education they received.

With the money, the spokesman of the chief purchases a sheep or two, a bottle of palm-oil, a small white chick (preferably just hatched), a pot of water and eggs. Then prayers are said to pacify the spiritual beings so outrageously offended. An old woman is selected to shave the recalcitrant girl, after which the leaf of a plant called *damram*, which is very red in colour is shown to the girl with the words: *Se akwadaa repeade kokoo ahwe a yede damram ahahan kyere no.* "If a child insists on seeing something red, it is shown the leaf of *damram*." Red is symbolic of danger[16] and so it is bad for a child to want to behold it. This common saying therefore is tantamount to a curse to the effect that a bad child (in this case the girl) who only does dangerous and forbidden things, should be prepared for the consequences of its action. The girl's palms are then joined together and the red leaf is inserted between them.

Then she is seated on the ground under the *akusia* tree which is usually found standing in front of the chief's house, and under which, in the past, criminals are said to have been executed. In full view of the crowd, she is stripped naked, except for a loin-cloth, and her legs are stretched and separated as widely as possible. A sheep is held over her head, and fiercely brandishing his sword and chanting some incantations (the words of which no informant knew, presumably because they are a professional secret), an executioner slaughters it, allowing its blood to gush on to the girl's head and trickle down her body. According to one informant, for the purification to be effective at all, blood should run down the girl's genitals. Otherwise the ceremony would be considered unsuccessful and another sheep would have to be killed. This information can hardly be disputed as it is the best explanation for the separation of legs which appears to be a general rule in the *kyribra* ceremony. The spokesman takes an egg and says: *Wo akwadaa yi woatena ho akyima, na woamma yeankyima wo, na woanyinsen; wo mmusuo mmo wo so.* "You have menstruated and have not waited to be initiated and have become pregnant. May your ill-luck be upon your own head". He then throws the egg at the girl's head, leaving yolk and shell thereon. Around Kumasi the egg is thrown on the ground in front of the girl with the words, *Bo gu ne tiri ne n'apampa so*, "Break upon her head and the crown of her head."

The spokesman pours the bottle of palm-oil over the girl's head and follows this with the pot of water. Next he puts the severed head of the sheep under her left armpit and its legs under her right armpit while saying: *Wo mmusuo mmo wo so*, "Let your ill-luck remain with you". Then the head or legs of the little white chick are put into her mouth with the rest of the chick hanging outside.

The girl is here helped to her feet and chased out of the village with the mob running after her, shouting, deriding and hooting, Huu. Huuu. Huuuu. They turn back at the outskirts of the village, and the girl's relatives who also have been silently and sorrowfully following her, take her to the nearest river and wash her. [17]

Where the foregoing ritual takes place in front of the queen-mother's house, another sheep is killed in the chief's stool-room to ask the ancestors for forgiveness of the offence. Then blessings and protection are sought for the girl so that she may have a safe labour and give birth to a live baby.

If the male culprit is known and he has not bolted, some of the blood of the sheep is poured on his feet before he too is driven away with the girl. His own matrilineage may hold a less severe and complex purification ceremony consisting merely in severing the head of a chick and allowing the blood to flow on his feet.

These ceremonies are principally meant to cleanse the "criminals" to pacify the spirits and to stay the execution of their punishments. It is now the turn of the whole community to be purified, and the spokesman takes mashed yam or plantain mixed with palm-oil and the lungs (cut into little pieces) of the slaughtered sheep, and goes round the village scattering them in all directions This is thought to rid the community of the evils brought about by the committing of the kyribra in it. [18]

The culprits are forced to live in a hut prepared for them in the forest, and to remain there until about 40 days after the birth of the kyribra child. While the boy and girl may not show their faces in the village, their mothers keep visiting them and supplying them with such things as they may need. In the event of the boy being at large, the girl's mother keeps company with her daughter.

The girl is made to go through a very shameful and demeaning ceremony. The man who made her pregnant is equally guilty of breaking a customary rule, but his punishment is much less severe. The rites are meant to purify the community, but the male partners get away lightly.

Infertility

What young girls go through during puberty rites emphasizes that fertility is the fulfilment of womanhood. Infertility is considered to be one of the greatest misfortunes for women. There is a derogatory term specially used for barren women — *obonin* or *bonyin*. As we have seen, the suffix *nyin* or *nini* refers to maleness. In other words infertility in women makes them no longer females but males! To be able to produce children is synonymous with being a woman. Some of the traditional folk songs portray how childless women are thought of in the community. The following is an example:

> What is the time of my death like today!
> Mother and Father have both died;
> When will I die?
> Woman without issue, the cursed one!
> When will I die?

In this song, a barren woman is portrayed as yearning to die for it is better to die than to live and be ridiculed for one's childlessness. In the majority of cases, instead of receiving sympathy from the community, childless women are ridiculed.

> Behold the barren woman,
> Alas! Alas!
> The childless woman
> Behold, behold,
> The childless woman!...

Infertility is seen purely as a woman's problem. In both government and private hospitals and clinics, traditional shrines and various centres which have specialized in curing infertility, almost all the patients one sees are women. Almost all the Spiritual Churches[19] specialize in curing barrenness and infertility. At a certain stage in their worship, some of these churches hold a special session for infertile members. The leader calls out for all infertile members of the congregation to come forward for special prayers to be said for them. It is always the female members who respond to this call, never the men. The impression one gets is that only women are infertile. It is now established that both females and males have infertility problems, but in Ghana and many other countries infertility is generally associated with women. Wives, and not husbands, are usually blamed for a couple's inability to have children. The reason of course is that men are generally able to hide their infertility.

Marriage

Most of the descriptive studies of Ghanaian societies establish very clearly that a high premium is placed on the institution of marriage. The elaborate rituals associated with puberty and growth are geared towards marriage and procreation. Among the Akan, as in many other societies, it is considered proper for every adult human person to marry and produce children who will continue the lines of the members of the community with whom she or he is related. Parents are worried when their children of marriageable age do not marry. The central purpose of marriage is procreation and all the forms of marriage — polygamy, infant betrothal, widow re-marriage (levirate) and concubine marriage — reflect the importance society places on procreation. Prayers said during traditional marriage ceremonies centre on couples having as many children as they can.

> Evil must go and good must come
> Evil must go and good must come
> Evil must go and good must come
> I bless you
> Have ten children
> So that you sleep on the mat of the tenth child
> I ask for life and health for you,
> I wish you prosperity, unity and the luck to have what you want
> I wish you the power to procreate.

Such great emphasis is put on children that, in certain situations, marriages which do not result in the birth of a child may be dissolved.

It is typical of some types of traditional marriage that the woman is allowed little or no freedom, though contemporary marriages tend to deviate from the old pattern. There is certainly need for change here; the right to choose one's marriage partner should be recognized as a basic human freedom. Many pre-arranged marriages prove to be unstable in the long run and result in much unnecessary unhappiness. Further, the increased inter-relations of people in the contemporary urban and indus-trialized settings encourage the exercise of personal freedom in this area.

In earlier times, much care was taken in relation to the choice of marriage partners and there was a series of ritual procedures relating to marriage. In some cases marriages were pre-arranged. Marriage very often brought together not only the two individuals but also the extensive kinship groups to which these individuals belonged. In this way a whole series of obligations, rights and responsibilities were incurred.

Yet, in the traditional relationship between the spouses, one cannot help noticing a certain discrimination. To start with, there is the tradi-tional division of labour at home. There is a sharp and strictly defined distinction between what a man should or should not do and what a woman should or should not do. Yet the contemporary situation often demands considerable adjustment to or even a complete departure from the traditional division of labour. It is not unknown in the contemporary Ghanaian urban situation for men to be called upon to babysit, wash and clean nappies, cook and do the laundry.

The traditional social division of labour issues from certain received conceptions about maleness and femaleness. As has been already indi-cated, maleness is associated with physical strength and the ability to offer security and comfort, whereas femaleness is usually associated with weakness in character and physical strength. Jobs are allocated to the sexes in the light of these beliefs. Underlying such allocation of work is the notion of the basic inferiority of women.

Another basic problem in Akan marriages relates to the inheritance of property, especially the husband's property. Traditionally, the matrilineal system supports the right of maternal relatives of the man to inherit his property on his death, thus excluding his own children and, even more so, his wife. Even if the wife contributed to the acquisition of the property, she has no claim on it. If they wish to do so, maternal relatives may look after the children. Otherwise, the wife and the children must look after themselves. This practice has resulted in untold bitterness and hardship to many widows and their children, as for example the termination of the formal education of the children. Attempts have been made through legal reforms to correct such injustices. One solution is to divide the total property among the three parties, namely the wife, the children and the deceased husband's maternal relatives. This will apply particularly to situations where the marriage is legally or traditionally recognized. However, there are difficulties in the implementation of such arrangements. For example, problems can arise in the case of a marriage without any issue or where the woman dies before her husband. No clear and generally accepted solutions seem to have been worked out for different situations.

The problem has engaged the attention of Christian and other progressive bodies in Ghanaian society. The Christian attitude has been that it is generally unfair for the husband's family to disinherit the surviving wife and children. The church has tended to recommend in all such cases that due recognition should be given to the wife and children as joint partners with the man in building their collective fortunes. Hence provision should be made for their survival in the case of the death of the husband or father. This is an issue of fairness and equity for which the Christian church has stood very firmly.

Widowhood

In many Ghanaian societies, and especially among the Akan, the death of one of the spouses sets in motion a whole series of ritual prohibitions and restrictions on the activities of the surviving spouse. Discriminatory practices against women are most in evidence in relation to widowhood. Some of the do's and don'ts which the widow has to observe in the traditional situation are:

1. The widow must be beside the dead body of the husband until the corpse is buried.

2. The widow must wear a girdle of fibre around which is hung a key or sometimes a locked padlock. This will prevent the ghost of the deceased husband from having sexual relations with her. It is also an indication that the widow is forbidden to have any sexual relations within at least a year of the husband's death. The symbolic meaning of the key is that the "vagina is closed" for one year. It is believed that if a widow breaks this, her husband's ghost will have sexual relations with her and this will result in her death or in her becoming barren.

3. The widow should not clean her body and, in some extreme cases, not even her teeth, for at least eight days.

4. She should not have any normal meal for eight days. Even if she is eating light food such as porridge, she should stop eating as soon as she hears anyone weeping or wailing. If she is so unfortunate as to be disliked by the husband's relatives, they will capitalize on this so that as soon as

she starts to eat, one of them will start wailing in order to stop her from eating.

No such strict restrictions are imposed on widowers. The period of ritual confinement prescribed for surviving widowers tends to be considerably shorter than for widows, or even nominal. The restrictions, which are mainly dietary in terms of movements and personal appearance, and of relationship with other people, all lead to situations of psychological stress and deprivation for the widow.

In many cases, these imposed deprivations derive from feelings of vengeance which the husband's people have been harbouring for a long time against the wife. In Kibi, for example, a woman was reported to have said: "When my brother dies, his recalcitrant, uncooperative and unfriendly wife will be taught some lessons in good human relationships." The relations may feel that the wife had prevented the deceased from performing his duties to his maternal relations while he lived; or that the wife prevented them from visiting the couple's home while the husband was alive; or even that the widow did not perform her obligations as sister or daughter-in-law to the husband's relations. Whatever the reasons, it is clear that the ritual obligations and taboos can be manipulated to the disadvantage of the widow. Society had formulated them and women are the agents for their enforcement, in the same way that they officiate and preside over the puberty rites. They are caught up in a system where they make sure that other women go through the discriminatory rites and customs which they as individuals would not wish to go through. They generally feel very strongly that indigenous customes and practices must be faithfully perpetuated, even when these bring misery and unhappiness to women. Sometimes too, when women have themselves gone through the bitter experience of widowhood rites, they want others to go through them too as some sort of revenge.

Inhuman treatment entailed in widowhood rites is viewed with great disfavour by the church in Ghana. In several cases, the church has taken punitive actions against erring members in this regard. The tendency has been for Christians to spurn such customary widowhood rituals openly, although in certain cases there still lurks the vague fear of untoward consequences. The period of widowhood has tended to be considerably shortened and the actual rites very much truncated and completely transformed. For example, a Christian widow may be asked simply to wash herself in the sea as soon as the deceased husband is buried. She is exempted from doing any work at least for a week; she is also expected to abstain from sexual activities for a year. The Christian church does not prevent its members from going through the widowhood rites, but they tend to do so in a relatively humane way.

The Government of Ghana has published an Act of widowhood rites. But it is doubtful whether many women have heard about it, especially in the rural areas where the majority of them are illiterate.

The Christian woman and traditions and customs

Christian women in the Ghanaian context face some peculiar problems with regard to these issues. This is because these traditions and customs apply particularly to the women in their positions as wives, mothers, sisters, widows — as people who occupy various positions within the social system.

We have already seen that in many Ghanaian societies rites associated with puberty were a requirement which established publicly the social and physical maturity of the female child who went through the ceremonies. The problem for the Christian woman is that while her new faith cuts her off from much of the traditional obligations in this respect, in practice, the strong forces arising from social and moral relationships would seem to incline her to adhere to them, so that very often she is faced with a dilemma. The church itself, as we pointed out, has recognized this. The solution of bringing together in one ceremony the traditional puberty rites and the Christian confirmation rites represents an attempt to resolve the apparent conflict. In this way the church acknowledges the important educative value of some of these puberty rites and makes an effort to pay equal attention to the socialization of boys within the context of the confirmation rites.

With regard to widowhood rites, the church has very little or no control over the decisions of the family of the deceased and thus its hold on women members with regard to such rites seems to be very weak. One must recognize the strong social pressures that are often exerted on the widows to go through the customary rites and some Christian women themselves tend to accept the necessity of performing these rites. There are some compelling reasons for this attitude. For example, it is a way of honouring the obligations and responsibilities that attach to them as wives. Further, by following the customary ritual requirements they escape criticism of their peers. Also it must be added that there seems to be a residue of fear of untoward consequences if one gives up such observances.

It may however to be noted that there are indications of bold rejection of these traditional requirements, mostly from women who attend some of the Spiritual Churches which are new Christian movements, most of them founded by both women and men. They put great emphasis on the power of the Holy Spirit.

The churches do not seem to have a strong enough hold on their women members in the matter of inheritance. In case of a man dying intestate, the church accepts the position of a tripartite division of property, that is among the relatives of the man, the surviving children and the wife. This seems to be a compromise on the part of the church. The women do not seem to have much to say against this arrangement.

In the case of menstruation and its accompanying prohibitions, there seems to be some ambivalence, both on the part of the church and of the women. For example, in some of the churches, such as the "Apostolic Revelation Society", women are specifically prohibited from participation in various activities of the church. Sometimes they are not even allowed to be present in the church building. On the other hand, practically none of the established churches have any known prohibition attaching to women during menstruation.

On the whole there are as yet no known rules or regulations based on traditions and customs regarding the full participation of women in the Church. Full participation of women in church activities, including positions of importance, tend to be influenced by prevailing anti-feminist prejudices and stereotypes rather than by any well-established traditional objections.

Discriminatory institutions in contemporary Ghanaian society

In spite of changes in society, many old ideas still underlie a number of the practices and institutions in contemporary Ghanaian society. Particularly significant among them are the following.

1. Issues relating to decision-making with regard to political and civil affairs: In the traditional courts of the rural areas where most of the Ghanaian women live, the majority of chiefs and those who surround them — the elders — are still men. In very rare cases, when no man competent enough to be a chief can be found, female chiefs are named, but they are surrounded by male elders who take important decisions in the community. It is very ironical that although the process of consultation out of which judgments emerge is still referred to as "consulting the old lady"[20], in practice some of these traditional processes continue to discriminate against women. In legal processes, women are always supposed to be represented by competent authorities, that is, the queen-mothers, and may not act on their own behalf. In contrast, once he is an adult, a man can initiate legal action on his own and go through all the legal processes by himself. He can also be asked to be a member of the court of elders to preside over cases. This means an unlimited exercise of legal freedom for a male adult. It would seem, therefore, that in the traditional practices, women tend to be classified with minors and, in this way, denied full expression of their basic freedom.

2. *Issues relating to religious roles:*. As far as certain religious rituals such as pouring libation are concerned, the practice in general has been for men to perform these rites, even when older women are present. If it should be necessary in specific cases for women to play crucial roles in such rituals, the practice has been to carefully select women who have reached their menopause, that is, who have ceased playing the traditional roles expected of them as wives, mothers and keepers of home — who have ceased to *be* women.

Certain criteria and standards have been set for women who hold ritual positions. These criteria vary from ritual to ritual. Generally, the following categories of women are selected to perform certain ritual functions: young virgins, women who have reached their menopause, widows, married women with lots of children, and mothers who have not lost any of their children.

Today women are breaking through tradition to play new roles outside the home. If such women are lucky enough to be able to combine these new with traditional roles such as procreation, caring for the home and children, society sees nothing wrong with the new roles. For example, many women share with their husbands the role of breadwinner, and serve as doctors, lawyers, church leaders, etc. At the same time they are expected to function as mothers, housekeepers, etc. It is when the old traditional roles are seen to be sacrificed for the new ones that conflicts arise. One of the numerous arguments people use against women being accepted into the church's ordained ministry is that it is unsightly to see a pregnant priest and that, therefore, these two roles are incompatible.

3. *Issues relating to adultery:* Society takes a harsher view and seems all too ready to blame and punish women more than men in cases of adultery. While the husband has conjugal rights over the wife, the reverse is not true. He has relative liberty to have sexual relations outside the marriage, whereas a woman has no such right. If a woman suspected of adultery denies it, the husband has the right to make her go though a traditional ordeal. Even if the ordeal has fatal consequences, the man will not be blamed for her death. A man who is caught in adultery is not required to pass a similar "test". All that he has to do is to pacify the

husband of the woman with whom he committed adultery. He owes no apology to his wife. A wife cannot seek divorce because her husband had committed adultery; a husband does have the right to divorce an adulterous wife. The effect of these rules is to encourage men to have sexual relations outside marriage while women are required to have sex only with their husbands.

The way forward

Discriminatory practices against women seem to constitute an important part of the beliefs, customs and practices in many Ghanaian societies. Although exceptions may be found in specific communities, particularly of the patrilineal type, it could still be maintained that the general trend works against women's progress and equality. Although there are changes taking place, there is little doubt that the individual's habits and behaviour are formed by those basic beliefs. Nor should we discount the importance of the traditional roles allotted to women. It is clear, nevertheless, that traditional attitudes with regard to the role and position of women in society need to be very actively reconstructed. It is essentially an educational task; it calls for the eradication of certain long-held ideas about the place and role of women in society vis-à-vis men. In this process, care should be taken to correct wrong ideas not only by instruction, but also by example. Thus, in addition to educational campaigns and activities, attempts should also be made to publicly reward and encourage women who stand up against oppressive customs and practices.

It should be possible for women who have been harmed through discriminatory customs to seek legal and other redress without hindrance. Specifically, women who have suffered bodily harm and injury in going through widowhood rites must be encouraged to seek legal claims against the persons involved in such practices. Religious and civic bodies as well as charitable organizations, foreign and local, must lend their weight for the achievement of such objectives. The end objective is the unlimited expression of the full potential of women as equal and free individuals in the community.

Attention should be drawn to useful examples from cultures which permit freer expression of the potential of women; useful lessons from such examples should be publicised. It should not be too difficult to organize visits by women *and* men so that they can see and appreciate alternate patterns of social relations with regard to women in society. Free exchange of ideas with regard to such issues should be encouraged internally, externally and cross-culturally.

The ideal of partnership poses a fundamental challenge to the traditional culture in terms of its beliefs, expectations, norms, attitudes and ideals relating to women. Already there are indications of change as a result of the spread of Christianity, urbanization, industrialization and education. Social legislation may help in certain directions, but a sustained process of education in the wider sense of the term is especially necessary among the women themselves. Such education should make especially the rural majority aware of their own potentiality as effective contributors to social development. Women must be encouraged to understand their physical and social environment. They must be helped to learn that the barriers that hold their own progress in check are, in the long run, artificial, socially created, and therefore surmountable. Educated and emancipated women should express concern for their less fortunate sisters and by example as well as instruction, seek to uplift them from conditions of social deprivation. Some existing organizations, for example, the Ghanaian Women Lawyers' Association (FIDA), have helped in drawing up proposals of new laws in favour of women. They should, however, maintain pressure on the government to enact these laws.

Existing organizations, including women's organizations, have a particularly urgent task in this regard. They should not only concern themselves with setting up rural and cottage industries to provide gainful employment for women, but should also hold frequent discussions on the very many instances where cultural practices work against the development and self-expression of women. The campaign should attack beliefs and practices which seem to have outlived their usefulness and are now stumbling blocks to progress. These discussions should be organized at local rural and urban community levels. Subjects such as the rights of women and children and the protection available under the laws should be discussed. Care should be taken to point out the particularly unfortunate cases where cruelty towards or discrimination of women is actively encouraged by other women. The paradoxical nature of the maltreatment of women by women should be stressed. Newspapers, particularly those of religious organizations, for example, *The Christian Messenger* and the *Catholic Standard* should publish interpretations of existing laws which affect interpersonal relationships and the rights of specific sectors of the community.

The ultimate object of all these reforms is the general improvement of the social conditions of women and to lift them to the status of equal partners in the process of social development.

152   Women, Religion and Sexuality

NOTES

[1] (a) Eva L.R. Meyerowitz, *The Akan of Ghana, Their Ancient Beliefs*, London, Faber 1958. (b) E.A: Boateng, *A Geography of Ghana*, Cambridge University Press, 1954.

[2] J.G: Platvoet, *Comparing Religions: A Limitative Approach. An Analysis of Akan, Para Creole and for Sanda Rites and Prayers*, The Hague, Bunnik, 1981.

[3] In this proverb a woman is likened to a plant (for example, the plantain socket) which can re-germinate. The man is likened to the corn stalk which cannot re-germinate.

[4] The woman is described as foolish in the sense that she is very submissive.

[5] R.S. Rattray, *Religion and Art in Ashanti*, London, 1959. P. Sarpong, *Girls' Nubility Rites in Ashanti*, Accra-Tema, 1977.

[6] God is addressed as *Kwame*, a name given to a Saturday-born boy. Saturday is believed to be the day of God.

[7] *Yaa*, the name given to the Earth deity, is the name given to a girl born on Thursday.

[8] Akosua is a female born on Sunday.

[9] Sarpong, *op. cit*, p.78.

[10] *Oto* is mashed yam or plantain mixed with palm oil. It is often used in most of the religious rituals.

[11] The stool house is where the sacred stools of dead rulers are kept.

[12] Rattray, p.12.

[13] Kurudapaawukuo — the Wednesday that precedes Adae, one of the great festivals in which the ancestors are remembered. This day is therefore considered sacred.

[14] Sarpong, *op. cit.*, pp.49-51.

[15] This may be anything from 7 pounds to 20 pounds (C14-C40).

[16] This will be elaborated on a little later.

[17] It is reported from Bechem that before the girl is chased away, a big ring is put on her head, as a pad on which a pot filled with water is placed.

[18] Anybody may ask for a piece of the meat of the sheep slaughtered for the ceremonies. But many people who consider it to be "meat of iniquity" of which one needs to be apprehensive, decline to have anything to do with it.

[19] These are new Christian movements, the majority of which have been founded by Ghanaians.

[20] Before verdicts are passed in traditional courts the elders or the councillors retire to deliberate over the case. They usually say *yeko bisa aberewa*, "We are going to ask the old lady's view on the case", although, in fact, they never consult any old lady.

BIBLIOGRAPHY

G.A. Acquaah, *Mfantse-Akan Mbebusem (Fante-Akan Proverbs)*, Wyman, London, 1943.

E. Amoah, *Moral and Social Significance of Proverbs among the Wassaw, an Akan People*.

B.A. Aning, *Nnwonkoro*. Tema 1975.

K. Antubam, *Ghana's Heritage of Culture*, Leipzig, 1963.

J.A. Annobil, *Mbebusem Nkyerekyero mu*, London, H. Watson & Viney Ltd., 1955.

Eva L.R. Meyerowitz, *The Akan of Ghana — Their Ancient Beliefs*, London, Faber, 1958.

J.H.K. Nketia, *Folk Songs of Ghana*, London, 1963, p.85.

J.G. Platvoet, *Comparing Religions: A Limitative Approach. An Analysis of Akan, para-Creole and for Sanda Rites and Prayers*, The Hague, Bunnik, 1981.

Rattray. *Religion and Art in Ashanti*, London, 1954.

J.M. Sarbah, *Fanti Customary Law*. A brief introduction to the principles of the Native Laws and Customs of the Fanti and Akan districts of the Gold Coast, with a report of some cases thereon decided in the Law Courts. London.

P. Sarpong, *Girls' Nubility Rites in Ashanti*, Tema, 1977.

Buddhist Attitudes:
A Woman's Perspective

Junko Minamato

Introduction

Buddhism, which coexists with Confucianism and Shintoism in Japan, does not deal specifically with the questions under discussion. Neither classical Buddhist sutras nor present Buddhist scholars touch on the subject. Both Confucianism, which came from China in the 6th century, and Shintoism, an ancient religion native to Japan, have more to say on matters which affect the daily lives of the people. Therefore, we will have to look at both of these religons before we attempt to explain Buddhist attitudes towards female sexuality.

According to the Shinto myth of creation, Izanagi (the male god) and Izanami (the female goddess) created the Japanese archipelago together. In this mythology the sun goddess Amaterasu played a primary role, while Tsukiyomi, god of the moon, was relegated to a secondary one. The oldest chronicles of Japan, Kojiki and Nihonshoki, also indicate that ancient Japanese society was a matrilineal one in which women exercised considerable authority. Before the advent of Buddhism and Confucianism in the 6th/7th century it was customary for the bridegroom to move to the house of the bride, and women had the right to initiate divorce proceedings and to remarry any number of times. Pre-8th century Japanese poetry reflects the liberal spirit on matters of sexuality: a separate but sacred house was maintained for women in childbirth, which was an occasion for celebration; no taboos surrounded the subject of menstruation.

Early Japanese history contains numerous examples of women rulers, but with the gradual change to a patriarchal society and the Tenno (emperor) system, women's influence waned and male domination became the norm.

Confucianism brought with it a partiarchal and male-centred system of ethics in which strict observance of the established hierarchy, loyalty to one's superiors and filial duty were of utmost importance. A son had filial obligations towards his mother, but at the same time a mother was expected to obey her son, especially the eldest son.

Absolute subordination was required of a wife, who could be divorced if she failed to bear a son. The menstruating woman and the woman in childbirth were considered impure. In short, woman's sexuality was largely seen as a negative quality. These attitudes gradually filtered down from the aristocratic class to become the norm for all of Japanese society.

Ritual practices concerning childbirth, purification after childbirth, wedding services and various fertility cults were characteristic of Shintoism. Buddhism, on the other hand, was primarily concerned whith the salvation of souls, although having come to Japan via China, it was already influenced by Confucian ethics. It became a state religion, but then underwent a reformation which gave rise to various sects such as Zen, Jodo and other Mahayana schools, which emphasized salvation for the masses. Mahayana Buddhism greatly influences life in Japan today. It is on this school that I will base my subsequent observations.

Early Buddhism

Buddhism began in India in 5 B.C. when Sakya attained enlightenment and Buddhahood. Sakya was a son of the ruler of the Sakya tribe, born into wealth and free from material worries. He married a cousin, Yasodhara, and they had a child named Rahula. He lived in three different palaces, one to protect them from each season — hot, cold and rainy. Although Sakya had no apparent problem in his life, he gave up his family and went into the priesthood.

No explanation is given for his entering the priesthood, but Sakya believed that the negation of sexuality was essential to the priestly vocation. It is said that he tried to make up for the loss of his mother who died during his childhood by finding sexual fulfillment and that he entered the priesthood because sexual life was unsatisfactory. Another possible explanation is that he chose this response because he could not find whatever it was he was seeking in life as a married man.

After attaining enlightenment, Sakya taught that by freeing oneself from self-centredness, both men and women could experience the enlightenment of Nirvana, as he himself had done. Buddha taught that all people can be equally enlightened through "Gyo" (disciplinary training), through which one can come to understand the pain felt in life.

Problems related to the institutionalization of Buddhism (Sangha)

The development of the principles of Buddha's teachings and the institutionalization of the religion facilitated the development of Buddhism, but it also contributed to the secularization of the religion. Buddha's step-mother, Mahaprajapatt, wished to become a priestess, and although she made tremendous efforts to do so, she was not accepted by Buddha. Finally, on the advice of Ananda, a disciple of Buddha, she was allowed to enter the priesthood. Some people see this as an indication of Buddha's discrimination against women; but I believe that Buddha allowed women to enter the priesthood because he rejected patriarchal principles.

However, for a woman to enter the priesthood, eight conditions had to be met. One of the primary ones was the principle of "Bhikusuni". This meant that women who entered the priesthood could not chastise or give advice to men who broke priestly rules. On the other hand, male priests were to discipline women who did not follow all priestly rules. Thus even a woman who had been a priest for many years still had to accept chastisement from a novitiate male priest. This clearly indicates the different attitudes towards men and women in the priesthood.

Furthermore, men were commanded to follow 250 different Buddhist precepts *(sila)*, while women were required to follow 350 silas. These differences seem to indicate discrimination against women, but there is another way to interpret the differences. Even though women, as priestesses, had more difficult Buddhist precepts to follow than men, they were able to follow the commands more easily than men and thus had fewer hindrances to attaining enlightenment. Buddha demanded from priests the complete negation of sexual desire, and he knew from his own experience that this was very difficult for men to achieve. The negation of sexuality became natural for Buddha, but for priests who later entered the priesthood for reasons other than those of Buddha, a way had to be found to strengthen the resolve to remain celibate: the idea that women were unclean thus came to be emphasized.

An example from the Sutta Nipāta (835), the sacred book of Buddha, indicates how this was done :

> Once when I went to hear about the higher perception of life, I saw the three witches of jealousy, hatred, and greediness. I had no desire to have sexual relations with them, for they were filled with unclean human wastes. I did not want to touch them even with the tip of my toe.

Using the most obscene words, women were also described as unworthy of men, as temptresses. Sutta Nipāta 703 says: that "Woman is

a temptress for the holy person. Let not woman be a temptress for man."
But no instances are found which describe man as a tempter. They are
considered blameless when they accept an invitation from the temptress.
This unfair attitude to women is based on the belief that it is difficult for
male priests to completely negate their sexuality.

The world of the Theri-gatha

Although Buddha imposed strict rules regarding women candidates for the
priesthood, an unexpectedly large number of women entered the priesthood
and attained enlightenment. They lived strictly in the way of Buddha. A
frank expression of their experiences was compiled in the "Theri-gatha".
"Theri" means monks who understood "dharma" and "gatha" means poems.
There were many women who became priestesses after leaving their beloved
children and husbands. The following story appears in the "Theri-gatha":

> I suffered and became confused because of my child's death. My thoughts
> were confused and disrupted. I wandered here and there without clothes and
> with uncombed hair. Then I went to a Buddhist service and began to regain my
> mind. I was taught "dharma" through the mercy of Buddha. Listening to his
> words, I left my family and entered the monastery. I came into the peace of
> Buddha by following his words. In this way my anxiety came to an end. I
> overcame the root of my anxiety (Theri-gatha 133-138).

The same benefits accrued to women who lost their husbands and
turned to Buddha. There are stories of prostitutes who, after much
suffering, became monks. They determinedly rejected all sexual relations
and followed Buddha's teachings wholeheartedly.

There are cases which indicate that male priests occasionally tempted
women. Stories in the Theri-gatha describe the experience of women
rejecting the advances of men. One woman, whose eyes were an object of
a man's desire, plucked out her eyes and gave them to the man. In this
way she followed Buddha's teachings.

Whatever the reason for entering the monastery, the women were
strong and continued to be followers of Buddha's footsteps. They may
have seemed a threat to patriarchal society, although we have no way of
knowing how these women who left their families, rejected their sex roles
and family roles, were accepted by society. We do know that sex
differences were not a factor in the attempt to reach enlightenment. When
one reached the stage of supreme understanding, no discrimination
remained. The experiences of women shared in the Theri-gatha prove that
women are capable of attaining enlightenment.

Mahayana Buddhism

Mahayana Buddhism is a systematized and theorized form of the original Buddhism. It was formed about 1 B.C. "Maha" means great and "Yana" means carriage. "Mahayana" was in other words a carriage by which to reach to the world of enlightenment from this world. The meaning of "Maha" was characterized by the teachings by "Bodissatta" (bosatu). Originally "Bodhisattva" meant a type of perception that comes with Buddha's enlightenment, or seeking enlightenment not only for oneself but also to save all living beings.

Another understanding was added later to the concept of "Bodhisattva": that attaining Buddhahood is associated with the salvation of all living beings. This "Tathagatagarbha" concept was based on the belief that all living things could become a Buddha.

The original Sanskrit for "Garbha" in "tathagatagarbha", essentially has two meanings: one meaning is womb, and the other is embryo. Thus it can be translated into "the womb which holds Buddha's embryo" or "Buddha's embryo which holds the womb". These interpretations seem to reveal the true meaning of Buddhism, especially as words describing women's bodily functions were used for the expression.

It could be argued that the attainment of Buddhahood is essentially to be feminine. The central concept of Mahayana Buddhism is "Sunya", or emptiness. Sunya does not mean nothingness, but rather the absence of substance. What is this substance? It may be defined as "words". Words create the idea of dualism, dividing selfhood from others. This dualism is the beginning of separation (*vikalpa*). Emptiness, "Sunya", negates the idea of separation, negates words and the division (dualism) they create. This process is called non-separation and leads to Nirvijnam, the wisdom of non-separation. Communicated by words, the teaching comes when the words are negated and transformed, transmitting life to living beings. It uses words which communicate to human beings; they may be understood by other animals in different forms.

By negating substance, the idea of carnal desire is equal to Buddha. There is a contradictory concept that human beings with carnal desire can be saved in Buddha. If carnal desire and Buddha each has its own substance, then both can never be equal. However, when both concepts negate substance and remain in emptiness, carnal desire and Buddhahood can become one. The same way of thinking can be applied to the birth and death concept, which is equal to Nirvana. The world of toil and enlightenment is empty essentially so that they can become one. When men and women can be empty themselves, can be without substance, there is no separation between them. This concept does not negate the difference in gender, but removes all discrimination against both genders.

The condition of women in Buddhism

Five reasons for barring women from the priesthood
Buddhism was affected and changed not only by changes made in the original principles but also by the social system.

India had a strong matriarchal tradition. Until the Aryan invasion of the country, women were involved in religious activities. In the period of the Vedas women were not despised, but with the development of patriarchy, women's status declined. The patriarchal system introduced five theories to bar women from achieving Buddhahood: Women were not able to be (1) Brahma, the creator, the highest god, (2) Sakra Deranam Indra, the main god protecting Buddhism, (3) Mara the devil who damages lives and people's goodwill, (4) the king of the four states — East, West, South and North — and king of gold, silver, copper and iron, and (5) Buddha.

Of these points, the most important is that women cannot be Buddha, in other words, cannot be saved. This theory was really not compatible with the basic teaching of Buddha. Buddha taught that all living beings were able to reach Buddhahood. According to it, animals could be saved, but not women. Buddhist thinking thus conformed to the mainstream social order which was organized under a patriarchal system.

In the *Manusmurti*, Law of Manu, the status of women declined even further. The teachings delineated three layers of submission: before marriage women were to be submissive to their fathers, after marriage wives were to submit to their husbands, then mothers were to submit to their sons. The role of women was that of being a mother. Unless a woman had a son she was divorced; women were only for bearing children. Woman as described in the *Manusmurti* was evil, unclean and to be used as a tool. As male power was strengthened, so too was the patriarchal system. The status of women was abject, and they were not treated as human beings.

The concept of rebirth as men
In the process of the development of Mahayana Buddhism, it was understood that any person could reach Buddhahood. The five theories which barred the salvation of women was an issue taken up and decided by male Buddhists. Mahayana Buddhists seemed to have difficulty in interpreting the five theories for women. However, no woman was

consulted in relation to the rule that women could not reach Buddhahood. Moreover, women could not find a way to solve the problem under the clever control of the patriarchal society. The theory that governed women's ability to reach Buddhahood was not a keen concern for men, who in any case did not believe that women were human beings. Male Buddhists who were concerned with Buddhahood for women held the theory that a woman had to be reborn as a man before reaching Buddhahood. This concept became famous as the Lotus Sutra *(Saddhar-mapundankasutra)*, explained in the following story from the sacred book:

> The King Sagara-raja had an intelligent daughter who had fine senses. With her wisdom she was a perfect person in many ways. She had wealth equal to the value of the universe and dedicated all her possessions to Buddha. When Buddha accepted the gift from her in front of all the elders, her female organ disappeared and a male organ grew on her. She was changed to a male before reaching the stage of enlightenment. Then she went to the South, the world of Uimala, and sat under the bodhi tree for "gyo" — disciplinary training, necessary to reach Buddhahood.

This specific and concrete example of a woman being changed into a man in order to obtain salvation represents a passive solution to the problem. As a Buddhist woman, this kind of solution makes me both angry and sad.

The idea of transmigration *(samsara)* existed in India during the development of Mahayana Buddhism. According to this concept, human existence does not end in death but is continued in a rebirth. With a worldview based on transmigration, birth is directly related to death, which is transformed to birth again, making it possible to be born again in a human body or in the body of an animal. There was no resistance to the idea of being born again as a male, but as far as I know there is not a single source indicating that a male might desire to be born again as a female. In a patriarchal society where males held superior status, no one had any desire to be reborn as a female.

The idea underlying the concept of Lotus Sutra was that women could be freed from physical suffering and social pressures in the long run by being reborn as men and thus achieving salvation. What, then, is the significance of the suffering of women? Generally speaking, the suffering is the pain of childbirth. This may involve real pain. However, from ancient times women have experienced great joy in the power of bringing new life into the world. The act of childbirth was seen as sacred, not simply a cause for suffering as it came to be defined by men who were physically incapable of bearing children. It is impossible to go back to the original form of Buddhism unless salvation for women solves the pain which causes the suffering.

Faith in Amida Buddha

In Mahayana Buddhism, the concept that unlimited numbers of Buddhas could exist emerged. This is similar to the "Bosatsu" concept.

The most beautiful region of Buddhahood was said to be a region in which people could live near the Buddha who would teach them, and thus lead them quickly to enlightenment. This was Amida Buddha. Amida Buddha has become the major current of Buddhist history, offering the attractive concept of altruistic vows and the "pureland" concept.

Amida Buddha was originated by Dharmakarabodhisatta (Hozo Bosatsu) who trained himself to reach Buddhahood and came up with the concept of the ideal state for the Buddhist country, "the Pureland". He established 48 vows for this purpose. Long ages have passed since Amida Buddha's time, but his vows are to lead all human beings to the true fulfilled land, the Pureland, located 100 million miles to the west. It symbolizes the ideal state. All who were born in the Pureland are equal, and experience no pain. Hozo Bosatsu pursued and accomplished all of his vows and became Amida Buddha.

The Amida faith is based on Amida Buddha's vows. By chanting the name, "Namu amida butsu", one can achieve birth in the Pureland. Anyone can embrace the belief, and easily chant the name. Through this teaching, people who are marginalized or frowned upon in society can also achieve salvation. This faith permeated to the lowest levels of Indian society. It also spread through another category of people — women — who could thus receive salvation. Faith in Amida Buddha had important implications for the salvation of women, who were suffering both physically and socially.

The 35th of Amida Buddha's 48 vows is directly concerned with women's realization of enlightenment. Buddha samyak sambodhi says:

> Sakymuni, when I reach the Bosatsu stage, all women who believed in the pure heart of Bosatsu who are in the mysterious and incomparable Pureland would dislike me as a woman. If all women left life in this world and received a woman's body again, I would not realize perfect enlightenment.

Once again, the message is that women who are determined to reach enlightenment and enter the Pureland of Amida Buddha must first change their sex. (In the Jodo sect of Buddhism, however, salvation was offered through the simple act of chanting the name — Myogo — and thus many women anticipated the realization of enlightenment.) But faith in Amida Buddha has been supported by women who dreamed of rebirth in the beautiful Pureland where there was no pain or suffering.

Japanese Buddhism

Zen (Suzuki Disetz and Beatrice Lane)

The main strand of Buddhism in Japan is represented by Zen Buddhism and the Jodo Kyo. The founders of Zen, Dogen and Eizai, are not discussed in detail here because they expounded a doctrine of salvation by Gyo, works, and were not laypersons but priests. The layperson with a spouse and children has difficulty relating directly to their teachings.

Dogen was a very fastidious person who could not accept the desires of the flesh, and was drawn to wealth and honour. Yet in his youth, before he moved to the Eiheiji Temple, he had a view of women quite different from the common understanding: "What kind of fault do women have? What kind of morals do men have? There are bad people even among men. There are good people even among women. The desire of people to hear the teachings of Buddha and to enter Buddhahood is not limited to men only but is also among women. When one does not cut off all doubts, men and women are in the same stage of perplexity. When one cuts off perplexity and realizes the truth (dharma), there is no difference between men and women" (from Raihai Tokuzu in "Shobo Genzo").

Thus Dogen's view was that women can achieve Buddhahood as well as men. When Dogen was young he believed in the equality of men and women and criticized the foolishness of the Mount Hiei and Mount Koya temples which barred women from entering. However, in later years, by the time Dogen built the Eiheiji Temple he no longer believed in the equality of men and women and prohibited their entry. This change of heart has repercussions on present-day society.

Zen is based on Dogen's teaching. It is based on meditation in the temple and detachment from the world and therefore has little significance for people today who must participate in society. A Zen Buddhist who can offer Zen's meaning to present social conditions is Suzuki Daisetz. He enriched Zen for the benefit of people in present-day society and also introduced Zen to other countries. His experience was not limited to the priesthood, as he lived truly and freely in the world of Zen. Because he experienced Zen in modern society, based on the original form of Buddhism, Daisetz may be as a Zen Buddhist superior to Dogen or Eizai, or at least equal to them.

Suzuki Daisetz was born in Kanazawa City in 1870. His father was a city doctor who studied Chinese and Dutch medicine, possessed many books, and interested himself in his son's education. However, his father died when Daisetz was 5 years old, leaving his family in financial difficulties. An elder brother died immediately after his father's death, his elder sister departed to marry, and two other brothers lived independently. Daisetz lived with his mother, a believer in Shin Buddhism. In the 1800's Jodo Buddhism was widespread in the Hokuriku area. It evangelized very simple but earnest believers, all of whom maintained a family altar at home. Every day they chanted the sutras before the altar, giving daily life a religious ambience. In later years, Daisetz said in his memoirs that his religious sensitivity was nurtured by his mother. His mother offered Daisetz's school record and other awards at the family altar and closely observed rituals for family ancestors.

When he was 21 years old, Daisetz entered Waseda University and visited Enkaku Temple in Kamkura for the first time to participate in Zen meditation. He questioned why his life did not flower like a tree which could grow and bear fruit unconsciously. This was the first step to entering the religious life. Meeting with Master Imakita Kosen in Enkakuji was the catalyst for Daisetz's decision to follow Zen Buddhism. After Master Kosen's death Daisetz learned from Master Soen Shaku. When Daisetz was 25 years old, he experienced internal unity of the subjective self with the object, Kensho. While meditating, he realized there is no difference between a large pine tree in the moonlight and the consciousness of self. He had reached the stage of true personhood.

In 1987 Daisetz went to the United States where he published various articles and translations. When he returned to Japan he taught English. Later, as a professor at Otani University in Kyoto, the main focus of his work was research and writing on Zen.

When he was 41 years old he married Beatrice Lane, an American. Born in 1878, in Boston, Beatrice graduated from Radcliffe College and continued studies in sociology at Columbia University. Not satisfied with traditional Christian faith, she became interested in oriental philosophy. When Daisetz was in the United States she learned much from him. Two years after Daisetz returned to Japan she followed him and they were married soon after.

Daisetz and Beatrice felt that it was their life's purpose to communicate oriental philosophy and religious ideas to the West and they placed importance on the exchange of opinions and ideas in writing. This was very rare in Japan. It was not common for a wife to be involved in the same work as her husband and this was possible not only because Beatrice was an American but because as a free-thinking Buddhist, Daisetz was not overly concerned about what others thought of him.

Most of Daisetz's writings relating to Zen are in English, and many people who come from abroad to Japan to study Zen become familiar with Daisetz's work. However, not many people know about Beatrice and their mutual influence.

Beatrice studied Buddhism throughout her life and was, of course, influenced by her longtime partnership with Daisetz. Most impressed with the thought on Bosatsu (Bodhisattva), she found great meaning for existence in the concept of "great mercy", or compassion, which made the existence of Bosatsu possible. Beatrice did not separate herself from other human beings. When she talked about ordinary living beings she included grass, trees, mountains and rivers as well as animals and human beings. In practice, she was an extraordinary protector for all animals, bringing home cats and sheltering dogs which came to her door. Beatrice thought the concept of Bosatsu particularly attractive for women, and she encouraged other women to practise the belief.

Beatrice said: "Our 'capacity for progress' depends not upon the masculine principle, but upon the feminine principle, if one wishes to call it so, of compassion and sympathy to all forms of life..."

"This 'Ewig Weibliche' — what can it mean but love, compassion, and sympathy, the eternal feminine spirit such as is manifested in the ideal of the Bodhisattva? It is the glory of Mahayana Buddhism that it has set itself unreservedly to this ideal and it holds it out to the world as the only antidote to all trouble, turmoil, and suffering induced by man and other beings" (*Impressions of Mahayana Buddhism*, p. 27, Kyoto, the Eastern Buddhist Society 1940).

The "Concept of Compassion" or mercy was the core of Beatrice's faith. She believed that one should not divide oneself from the other. The concept of compassion is not included in the male principles, because the male principles are the competitive ones. Compassion is a feminine trait. It is valuable to evaluate Buddhism from the feminist perspective which Beatrice found in Buddhism, although Buddhism was developed in a male-oriented social system.

The writings by Suzuki Daisetz, who was her master and husband, included this feminist perspective, for he truly lived as the liberated person who understood the core of Buddhism. He transcended the dualism of the world by avoiding any division of himself from the others. Daisetz and Beatrice practised the belief that men and women could not be divided throughout their lives. They attempted to help others to understand that they too could be free of dualistic thinking and thus experience the heart of Bosatsu.

Daisetz wrote after Beatrice's death that conversations with her never really came to an end. It is said that real communication can occur when the selfhood is liberated and when one recognizes the other's position. Daisetz wrote : "Beatrice's concern was not to be able to compile her 10-year study and to have to leave her partner alone. She often said we were united. But only half of the one remains now. Throughout my life my work was not completed without her help. But some day we may be united in Kairos. The mercy of Bosatsu is endless." Daisetz was able to transform the sadness of losing Beatrice into a joyful remembrance of the relationship that had existed between them.

Jodo Kyo (Shinran and Eshinni)

The major form of Buddhism in Japan is faith in Amida Buddha. The religion reached its climax in the person of Shinran, who lived in the 13th century and raised the Amida Buddha belief to the status of a popular religion. Applying Shinran's teachings to the present is the essence of the belief of the Amida Buddha. It may be asked why Shinran, who lived in the 13th century, should be important in the latter half of the 20th century. His faith experience was of a universal nature, but the concepts of the 13th century are not valid for solving problems that present themselves today.

Shinran was born in Kyoto in 1173. When he was nine years old he entered the Mount Hiei Temple for training in the doctrine of salvation. At that age the decision to enter the temple could not have been taken on his sole initiative. Scholars have different opinions as to why he entered the temple at such an early age, citing as reasons the many wars during that period, as well as chronic famine. Shinran's father's social status was such that Shinran had a very difficult and miserable life in his early years. In the Kamakura period (1192-1334) some influences of the matriarchal society still remained. When Shinran's mother died there was no one to care for him, and he was sent to the temple. In any case, to live in the environment of the temple, Shinran had to give up his ordinary secular life.

When he was 29 years old, Shinran left the Mount Hiei Temple and went to the Jodo Kyo, founded by the Priest Honen. The reason for this change is unclear, although he said in 1202 that he abandoned the difficult practices to take "the primal vow" in the Collection of Passages on Teaching, Practice, Faith and Realization of the Pure Land Way.

Letters written by the wife of Shinran, found in 1291, also explain why Shinran changed to the Jodo Kyo. They say that Shinran went down from Mount Hiei and stayed at Rokakudo, which was located in central Kyoto, 12-13 kilometres from Mount Hiei. He stayed there for 100 days and meditated on the direction of his life. On the morning of the 95th day he had a dream and went down the mountain in order to live with people practising the teachings of Jodo Kyo. The dream which Shinran received from the oracle Avalokitesvura Bodhisattva was the following: When the devotee finds himself bound by his past karma to come in contact with the female sex, I will incarnate myself as a beautiful woman and become the object of his love. Throughout his life I will be his helpmate for the sake of embellishing this world, and on his death I will become his guide to the Land of Bliss.

Why did Shinran not go into the sphere of enlightenment by overcoming life and death? One reason he was hindered from doing this was the problem of sexuality. This problem did not allow him to continue his self-training, which meant freeing himself from his ego. He had the internal desire to have a relationship with a woman, but was bound to follow the celibacy rule of the priesthood. Shinran thought seriously about the negation of sex for the priesthood. For him, having sexual relations with a woman violated the priesthood order and was therefore a sin. The dream oracle indicated that his sexual relation with a woman could be interpreted as finding Buddha contained in a female body. Therefore, his feelings against the celibate priesthood became strong. Out of a sinful situation and a growing sense of guilt, Shinran saw Buddha's salvation, which could lead him to Pure Land. With this confidence in the salvation of Buddha, Shinran decided to live in Jodo Kyo as a lay person with his wife and to establish a family. Shinran accepted what Buddha once rejected for his enlightenment and found his salvation in a different way from Buddha's.

The Buddhist life-style involves negating sexuality. Yet lay Buddhists and those who live in social relationships struggle with problems which are contrary to this precept and strengthen the ego — the opposite process of coming closer to Buddha's enlightenment. Shinran understood that the problem related to sexuality applied not only to him but was universal. The guilt involved in violating the vow of priesthood increased, while at the same time the joy of salvation was realized. It is similar to the belief which holds that the awareness of the fallen in hell is the realization of salvation. Shinran taught that "all sins of the past, present and the future are changed to good. To be changed does not mean the sin is erased."

According to Shinran, all beings are sinful, but receive "Other Power", which is more than the denial of self-power. *Tannisho*, a book written by Shinran's disciple Yuien fifty years after Shinran's death, says in this regard that "when a person overturns his heart of self-power and entrusts himself to the other power, he will realize birth in the true fulfilled land."

There are still few resources available to help us understand Eshinni, Shinran's wife. It is said that he might have had a few wives, but the number is not the issue here. What is important is that he married Eshinni as a Buddhist priest. Her life itself means a great deal for women today. She was born in 1182. There is no record of her birthplace or her personal history. The only information available to us today about their married life is contained in Eshinni's letters from Echigo (far away from Kyoto) to her daughter in Kyoto, written in Eshinni's later years. These suggest that she married Shinran in the expectation that theirs would be an ordinary marriage relationship. It was only later, in a dream whose meaning was confirmed by Shinran, that she learned that her marriage partner was not an ordinary person. She came to believe in him as Buddha. It is said that Eshinni actually saved Shinran and helped him to find Buddha through their physical relationship. At the same time, Eshinni was also redeemed and found her salvation. The awareness of Buddhahood grew between them, for the mutual relationship of man and woman can only be established when the man and woman have mutual faith.

Eshinni strengthened her faith by living with her family and relating to others. This is a faith model for people in present-day society. Eshinni's way of preaching the faith is specially understandable for women. She showed that man does not have a superior status when entering the faith and that woman is not inferior in any religious sense. Instead, Eshinni proved that women too can enter the faith and live within it.

Buddhism today

Although Buddhism started in India and came to Japan through China, Buddhism has been declining in those countries. In Japan Buddhism was adopted as the national religion in the 6th century and protected by the rulers of the time. It spread among upper-class elites. The number of adherents grew steadily. Policies for the protection of the religion emphasized the training of priests and involved the building of temples all over the country. The number of priests increased and the teachings of

Buddha spread among the people. The elite class protected Buddhism in order to secure their status in society. Ancestor worship was exploited to confirm their ruling power.

In the Kamakura period (1192-1334), evangelization depended greatly on the efforts of such masters as Dogen, Nichiran, Hogen and Shinran. Their teachings were easily understood by ordinary people who wanted to attain salvation. Through the offer of salvation to all, Buddhism attracted people caught in the difficult situations of war, famine and sickness.

Another reason for the success of Buddhism was the obligation for each family to belong to a temple (Edo era, 17-18 century). Faith was not a matter of individual devotion, and ancestor worship was enforced. Buddhist temples were supported by families through many generations and the control of the temple was passed down from one generation to the next in the priest's family. The religious organization stabilized in a pyramid formation. Each sect had a temple headquarters and a network of temples firmly organized under this family-based system, called the "Danka system". This remains the basis of Buddhist religious organization today, but the content of Buddhism has been distorted.

The primary purpose of Buddhism thus became ancestor worship, and the main emphasis was given to the observation of religious ceremonies. The numbers of followers of the major religions in Japan in 1982 were: Shintoism 50%, Buddhism 42%, Christianity 1%, others 7%. Buddhism is divided into 5 major sects: Tendai, Shingon, Joko, Zen and Nichiren. The relative size of each is given in the following table:

	Temples	*Members*
Tendai	4,000	3,305,643
Shingon	11,894	12,445,829
Jodo	29,851	20,283,420
Zen	20,513	8,610,094
Nichiren	6,548	32,626,405
Others	236	4,362,093
Total	73,042	81,623,484

Because 80 million of a total of 130 million Japanese call themselves Buddhists, Japan is called a Buddhist country. Generally speaking, Japanese go to Shinto shrines to pray for the safe delivery of babies. When the baby is one month old the parents take the baby to a shrine to ensure its healthy development. Young people go to a Shinto shrine for protection and to pray for success in entrance examinations for colleges and universities. Although some prefer Christian wedding services, the majority of marriages today are in the Shinto tradition. Major ceremonies in the year begin with New Year in a Shinto shrine. In March, during the week of the Spring Equinox, people go to Buddhist services and their ancestors' graves. In August and in the fall again they go to their ancestors' graves and some go to a Shinto shrine for celebrations. Even families that are not Buddhist perform Buddhist funeral rites for a deceased family member. There is a Buddhist service every day for 49 days after the funeral, with a final, main, service on the 49th day. This service is repeated, however, on the 100th day, then one year, 3 years, 7 years, 13 years, 25 years, and 50 years after the funeral. Every month on the day of the funeral the temple priest visits the family at home for services. In this way, people's lives are closely bound to Buddhism.

The local temple priest is supported by the family's adherence to the religion. The temple priest performs ceremonies for the dead. Most priests at present are married and have families. Before the Meiji Government lifted the law which prohibited the marriage of priests, the only exception was Jodo Shinshu, founded by Shinran. Until the Meiji period, Buddhist priests did not marry publicly. The negation of the sex desire stressed by Buddha is no longer practised.

In the Jodo sect, temples are operated by a master of the temple (jushoku) and his wife (bomori). The temple priest attends a ceremony called a "Tokudo" at the headquarters of his sect and receives special training to be qualified as a priest. There is no need for a woman to undergo training to become a bomori. She automatically becomes one upon marrying a temple priest.

The Jodo sect itself consists of ten sects. The biggest is called the Honganji sect, which consists of 10,460 temples, with 19,774 male and 5,285 female qualified priests. Women recognized by the Honganji sect for the priesthood are limited to those whose husbands have died or whose sons are still too young to be temple priests.

The Otani sect does not recognize women priests at all, and there are no examples of a wife assuming this position. Within the Otani sect a bomori is the same as an ordinary housewife, but she has to carry more responsibilities at home and at the temple. For example, she must welcome all members of the temple. She has to clean the building and the garden, and change the flowers on the altar. The bomori is expected to prepare for the numerous religious ceremonies which fall throughout the year and to take care of the monthly women's meeting held at the temple.

It is questionable whether busy priests and bomori who have to carry out so many ceremonies have time to study their faith. It is very rare to find temple priests and their wives who deepen their faith within the present context. In the management of the temple, they are too occupied with various ceremonies necessary for ancestor worship to be able to intelligently renew their faith. The present system of the temples shows various signs of crisis, for temples are not meeting the needs of people.

Why, then, do books on Buddhism sell so well? Why does the religion become the main subject at a cultural centre operated by secular groups? Why are women's meetings on Buddhism organized by the city so well attended? Keeping up various ceremonies for ancestor worship alone does not make one a Buddhist. The main problem for Buddhism in Japan is that the religion is supported by the family as its basic unit. The pyramidal organization formed and supported by the strong family system was established in modern times, largely based on the hereditary right of the priest's family. All temples follow this custom. The organization has the merit of transmitting Budhhist teachings, but at the same time, to sustain its organization, it has secularized the religion. As the secularization process continues, it will be more difficult to spread the true teachings of Buddhism.

Future tasks

Present-day Buddhism is not true to its original form. As feudalism forced women to be submissive, Buddhism oppressed women. Buddhism saw women as sinful beings, and the patriarchal system forced women to take on a role at the bottom of society. As a result, women were powerless. At present, a trend to renew Buddhism is developing among women. Since women have been severely disadvantaged by Buddhism in the past, one might ask why they would be interested in such a process of renewal. The principal reason is that the concept of equality between man and woman can be found in Buddhism. Also, religion is about life rather than about death, and human beings have a desire to seek the truth related to life. If the role of Buddhism is to seek the truth, then it should respond to the needs of all people.

In the renewal process it will be necessary both to evaluate the principles of Buddhism which discriminate against women and to achieve a new stage of religious understanding about men and women. Buddhism has the potential to develop a new form of feminism. The new understanding of Buddhism is that Buddha is neither male nor female, but has achieved the perfect state of both sexes. This allows all people to work towards the perfect state of being by achieving Buddhahood. The opportunity for such development is open to both sexes.

The Buddhist concept of "emptiness" means that the differences between the sexes are of little importance. The concept of emptiness, which is completely absent from Western thought, negates all horizontal relationships. It is a positive principle. This concept could open up a new way of thinking and help us to find a solution which responds to the needs of all people, and points the way for all to achieve perfect Buddhahood.

Orthodoxy and Women: A Romanian Perspective

Anca-Lucia Manolache

Introduction

It would be unjust to accuse the Christian church of not having transformed the status of woman. Christ himsèlf came to serve, to reconcile the world with itself and with God, and not to destroy existing structures; to prepare the world for the kingdom of God and not to establish a human reign; to modify the world's outlook so that it might understand its relation to God and the need to transform and be converted in its inner being.

It is for this that he came into a world which did not wish for his coming. He was born among a people who were not loved by their neighbours, and he chose a low social status that could confer on him no other authority than that which he already had, and which he would not exchange for earthly power. And the road he points to, by which human beings can reach this goal, is the cross. He does not propose a charter of human rights, but he recalls the freedom which is attained through truth, and the virtue of washing one's neighbour's feet. All people, without exception, are called to this duty, and blessed indeed are the meek, the gentle, the pure in heart. Through his Word — written or unwritten — through his attitude, through his attacks on hypocrisy and lies, by his gentleness towards those who suffer, he has set a new standard and a new criterion for the evaluation of the human life.

● This paper and the following response to it were prepared long before the overthrow of the Ceaucescu regime.

If his church, which is in the world but not of it — which obeys human laws though they are not its own — has not sought to confront the powers that oppress socially, yet it cannot be accused of making a pact with injustice. Always following its eschatological vision, it has responded to each call, keeping in mind the need to adapt newly created situations to the gospel message of salvation. And throughout the changes of each era, it interprets and applies the teachings of the Lord in accordance with the power of understanding and the ability to act which the Spirit of Christ inspires. The abolition of slavery only took place at the proper moment in history; racial segregation only disappears when society is ripe enough to realize the injustice of it. In the same way discrimination between the sexes will only be abolished when the human conscience recognizes it as nonsense, notwithstanding the fact that this has been a part of Christian doctrine for 2000 years. For the time will come, and "indeed it is now here", when the Spirit of God will give us the perfect understanding of the words and the acts of the Son of God in the world.

If the present society demands a favourable response from the church on the abolition of the age-old inequity which has condemned woman to a simple biological function, it is because Providence has decreed this moment so that the church can give new explanations, new interpretations and perhaps solutions for a better relationship between men and women. And this is proved by the great progress in our days made through medical sciences, biology, sociology, anthropology etc., all of which suggest that the church examine the need for a theological interpretation worthy of the new conquests of the human mind, both masculine and feminine.

The Romanian cultural tradition

Since this situation exists for women of all ages and in all corners of our planet the status of women in South-East Europe is no exception. In the land now occupied by the Romanian people, as among their neighbours, the social role of the woman has always been that of an auxiliary, and she has been deprived of the right to a place in history. Among our Romanian ancestors, the Dacians or Getae, according to historical works, "women were normally the servants of men".[1] Polygamy was the pride of Getae society[2] according to a great Romanian historian, and he adds: "The Getae and Dacian women were in the low state in which the weaker sex always found itself among uncivilized peoples; for respect for women is after all a sign of civilization."[3]

The conquest of Dacia by the Romans in 101-106 A.D., through introducing a certain civilization into the newly annexed province, could not change the situation. The continued attacks by invaders from the N.E. forced the Romans to abandon Dacia in 271-275 A.D. The successive waves of migrant peoples who flowed into the Daco-Romanian lands (Goths, Huns, Gépides, Avars, Slavs, etc.) forced the new people who had developed in the Carpathian-Danube area to live in a state of permanent struggle for 1000 years. In these conditions, in the centuries following the constitution of the Romanian people, both among the rulers and in other social classes, women's only role was to serve and obey. After the later migrations (Petchenègues, Cumans, Tatars, etc. in 1241) the creation of the first Romanian state represents an attempt to stabilize the Romanian people, without however bringing with it a modification of social conditions. Two centuries later the Turkish invasion began, and lasted for four centuries (1442-1826).[4] Romanian society suffered continually under Turkish oppression, and even in periods of relative calm there was a certain defensiveness vis-à-vis the Ottoman threat. Though the Romanian princes, the great founders of the church, encouraged Christian culture and kept in touch with their co-religionists in other countries (1451-1800), this did not bring about the slightest change in the status of women in Romanian society. The constant concern to maintain the fighting spirit needed to defend their people and their land left no room for religious and philosophical thought, especially since Ottoman domination was a permanent source of anti-feminism, even when it did not impose Islamic law by force.

It is not until the constitutional reform of 1913 that woman appears as a participant in social life. The constitutional changes of 1917 gave women the right to vote under certain conditions.[5] It was not until after 1944 that the constitution of the socialist state incorporated the right to vote for women, abolishing all discrimination based on race, sex or religion, and giving them equal rights "in all areas of economic, political, legal, social and cultural life" (Article 17), adding special measures for the protection of female and child labour (Article 18). Article 23 stipulates that in Romanian society "women have the same rights as men".

It has often been said that in the course of 2000 years of Christianity society has lost sight of a principle inherent in our religion: that each human being has a right to equal respect from others. On several occasions in the recent history of Europe, socialist ideas have constituted a warning to Christians,[6] drawing attention to age-old iniquities for which the rulers were responsible, as they continually oppressed the weak. And though social, national and religious segregation is a sign of a grave error of the human mind, it must be stressed that the injustice towards woman was even greater, since she suffered not only the consequences of the inferiority of the nation, the race and the religion, but was also condemned by her companion to an additional inferiority within that oppressed nation, religion and race.

We must recognize this strange discord between the Christian message and the practice of Christianity in the Church of Christ. Franco Molinari quotes a bitterly ironical remark of Georges Bernanos in the preface to his book *Chiesa feminista e enti* (Turin, 1977): "We, the believers, possess a wonderful message of liberation. What a pity that almost always it is put into practice by others."[7]

If this statement is true for all Christianity, it is even more true for the regions of Europe in which historical conditions did not favour the flowering of a superior civilization. Even today, when the Romanian woman occupies a position equal to man in social, legal and administrative life, and has equal pay and equal access to the highest level decision-making posts, it is not the same as regards her position in the Orthodox Church, nor indeed in the other churches on Romanian soil.

The faithful of our church, who come principally from a rural milieu, where traditions have remained unchanged for centuries, still consider it a sin for women to receive unction from the priest before men at religious services. And if she is standing near the priest by chance, the men around her try to prevent her preceding them for this last act of the service, even though some of the men have been standing outside and have just entered the church. And sometimes the priest himself invites the men to confession first, while women who came to the church long before the men are forced to wait their turn. This attitude is not confined to the men; many women in the church prevent other women from going before the men. This misogynous tradition can be found even among families with a more advanced culture and specially deep religious convictions. The attitude is so ingrained that boys and girls who in everyday life consider themselves equals, once they are in the church take a "non-conformist" position.

It is true that our clergy do not seem to be aware of this problem, but it is equally true that the Orthodox Christian women do not seem to raise the issue of the discrimination to which they are subjected in the church. An element which contributes to the situation is the absence of religious culture among young girls today, all of whom are familiar with the bitter joke describing institutes of religious teaching as "priest factories".

If woman figures in historical and artistic literature as a wife, a princess beside her husband, or as a simple courtesan, this only underlines her minor role. It is true that our women, like those in all societies in all ages, tried — and often succeeded — in escaping this constraint through the force of seduction, in order to redress the balance either for herself or more often for her sons, or else for the weaker members of her entourage. But this attitude is really a strategy of those who are weak or kept in an inferior position, in order to liberate themselves temporarily or partially from the situation of bondage.

Our religious practices show no tendency towards the liberation of woman. The question does not even arise, because the Orthodox woman is by far more orthodox than men, more submissive, more full of mercy towards the poor, and more faithful to the message transmitted by the clergy. Women are the large majority of those who go to church. It is they who hold services for the dead, who care for the sick and for abandoned children, who take care of cultural and historic buildings, and carry out lowly tasks which men rarely feel it their duty to do. In this spirit of humility — which is not necessarily Christian humility — women are often content with the gratitude that their sacrifice calls forth, without asking whether they cannot do more for the church of Christ. It does not even dawn upon them that they might fulfil an official function within the religious service; at the very most they fulfil certain functions in a convent, where the criteria for the role of women give them certain advantages.

The religious vocation of our women can only be realized by monastic life. There are many more women's religious communities in Romania than men's, although monasteries have always been the breeding ground for higher clergy. One cannot however speak of a cultural life in female religious institutions. Not having access to the priesthood, the nuns do not have access to religious teaching either. Since for the last 40 years religious teaching in the schools has been discontinued, the nuns today know even less about religious doctrine.

Given this state of affairs, a discussion of the problem of sexuality, and particularly feminine sexuality, stands very little chance of being taken seriously. The question has been taboo for centuries. For even if it were possible to overcome people's natural reticence, there is no background information and no tradition of personal opinions to get the discussion going. On the other hand, secular schools have started programmes of sex education, giving the young access to scientific thinking in our region. Nevertheless, a dialogue initiated with young non-believers was largely unproductive, because they do not take such questions seriously. A certain number of practising Orthodox whom we have approached have shown very little interest in the discussion, particularly since they feel that sexuality has nothing to do with religion. A dialogue initiated with medical personnel proved to be more fruitful. We were only able to have an open and useful discussion with a very small number of people: about 10 men and women doctors, all with sound professional background and general culture, and 5 or 6 ecclesiastics, all highly educated.

It is difficult to generalize on the opinion of other groups, since those who have a spiritual culture are old and have no interest in the problem of the social status of women, particularly the question of female sexuality. As for the younger generation, a new perception is now emerging of the relationship between men and women in our society. And although this perception is not deeply rooted spiritually to be able to lead to a just solution to the problem, in our day the number of women determined to protect their rights is increasing.

It may be asserted, however, that the problem of female sexuality cannot be raised officially in our church at the present time. And we are convinced that it would arouse the same opposition in all the Orthodox churches of the East. In our society there is a gap between the progress in the various anthropology-related sciences, and the alleged immutability of canonic law, which limits Orthodox theological thought, in spite of the dynamism and verve which has characterised it throughout history.

The glaring inequality between the status of lay women in our society, who can occupy the highest position, and that of women in the church, who are humiliated and put down by clumsy sermons quoting from the fathers passages critical of women, continues to amaze the average Christian. Non-Christians and non-practising Christians are right to ask us the question: "What has the church done to abolish iniquities in the world?"

The Orthodox liturgical tradition

In Orthodox worship books, we note that the passages on women tend to renounce the theology of Jesus and reflect the ancient Jewish tradition where women are considered responsible for all the evils from which humanity is suffering. The Orthodox Euchologion (Book of Sacramental Services) has close similarities with Chapter 12 and what follows in Leviticus. It is true that the priest prays for the woman and offers the blessings of the church, but the woman is considered impure and is not permitted to enter the church before a special purification ritual has taken place. For she has given birth "in sin", the Euchologion tells us as, according to the word of the Prophet David, we are conceived in sin and are all defiled. [8]

Have pity on your servant ... and pardon her sins ... purify her of her impurity, heal her of her suffering ... according to your mercy and cleanse her of her bodily defilement and the various internal pains... forgive your servant ... and those who have touched her.

After forty days other prayers are read for the same woman so that she may now enter "the temple of glory". God is called upon to "wash away all impurities from her body and from her soul at the end of these forty days and render her worthy of communion from your pure Body and Precious Blood".[9]

There is even a difference between the "sin" of having brought a boy into the world and the "sin" of the woman who gives birth to a girl. In the latter case her sin is double, as indicated in the Leviticus text.[10]

On the fortieth day after delivery, when the woman brings her child to the church for the prayers of purification (churching of the mother), there is discrimination in the way a female child is introduced. If it is a boy the priest takes him up to the altar, where he makes him bow at the four corners of the holy table. If the child is a girl it does not have this right. She is brought only to the entrance to the altar.[11]

Such practices, influenced by Mosaism,[12] are due to a misunderstanding of the biological realities of female nature in all the animal kingdom and of the nature of conception and reproduction. The fathers of the church and the faithful who contributed to the perpetuation of such discrimination have undermined the credibility of the Christian message in the modern world.

In reality some of the canon laws, established in antiquity and maintained today, have become outdated. They were formulated in the context of the culture and level of scientific knowledge of bygone times. For example, the seventh canon pertaining to Timothy of Alexandria prescribes that woman in her monthly purification state cannot have communion[13]. "Purification" here means menstruation; it refers to a woman's state of impurity, and means that woman becomes pure by eliminating this blood. As Evelyne Sullerot (23rd citation)[14] and others have pointed out, such ideas about woman's impurity during menstruation are due to ignorance. And those who consider woman impure during her menstruation also consider her impure when she gives birth, as we noted earlier.

That giving birth, especially giving birth to a male child, is the only justification for a woman's existence, is a view prevalent in the pagan and Jewish worlds and in the patristics. But in patristic ideology, which is followed by the majority of church-going Christians, this is not theologically significant, as we shall see later.

Maternity, and all forms of procreation in nature, are a miracle. But it is a "vocation" which the woman shares with animals, especially all mammals. With women, maternity no doubt means more. It involves, for example, certain obligations concerning the child and its social formation. Nevertheless, to limit the role and value of woman to maternity is to do her an injustice. The Jewish people have always considered maternity as a sign of blessing, but this is not commended in the teachings of Jesus. The understanding in Judaic messianism that every woman should become a mother, and this vocation justified marriage, reveals a desire to be saved "by one's sons"; every nascent family could be the place where the Messiah could be born. However, the Messiah was born in quite different conditions, and his mother was a virgin who conceived by the power of the Spirit.

New developments in the present context

The "International Women's Year" (1975) raised unexpected reactions in our church. This UN initiative was taken up by several religious organizations with conferences, consultations, round-table discussions, etc., and awakened interest in our church to find a solution to problems concerning the status of women in the church. During a whole decade (1975-1985) our ecclesiastics were obliged to give their opinions on the subject. The year 1975 marked the emergence of certain concerns in our country, which were dealt with in theological literature as much as in ecumenical meetings at different levels. In fact, a change of attitude has taken place — even if, at various meetings, our church spoke out against the ordination of women.

From the 17th to the 19th century, the Romanian princedoms were governed by a legislation based on doctrines inherited from Byzantine canonicity. Two important Codes: the *Book of Precepts* (1646) and the *Guide to the Law* (1652), governed Romanian religious and lay society. Although the civil and penal legislation was modified towards the middle of the 19th century and also at the beginning of the 20th, the ecclesiastical legislation underwent no change. On the contrary, it continued to influence legislative bodies until the separation of the church and the state which took place in the middle of the 20th century. None of the changes introduced over the last two centuries have improved the status of women, who are maintained in a clear state of inferiority vis-à-vis men, both in society and as a member of the family.

Chapters 211 and 364 of the *Guide to the Law* demonstrate this injustice, for there we read that "woman is more stupid (than man)" and that "because of inability" and "the weakness of woman" she must be ruled by man. It should be mentioned that the laws of the church (canons) which were applicable to the whole of Romanian society at all levels do not in the least appear to be inspired by Christian love, as far as women are concerned. Thus, a husband had the right to beat his wife and even to put her behind bars. On the contrary, if a wife "raised her hand" against her husband, she could be divorced. In fact divorce was easily obtained by a husband. In the case of a wife, divorce was granted only in cases of sexual perversion or if the husband became a heretic, or beat her with hate, leading to mutilation.

This legislation granted preferential treatment to men in all situations. Should a wife be ill for a long time, or should she disappear, the husband had only to wait for three years before a divorce was pronounced, whereas the wife, in a similar case, had to wait five years. And if a man pronounced guilty by the law chose to go into hiding his wife could not leave him, for "she is obliged to follow him" wherever he goes, whereas the husband is not obliged to follow his wife.

The *Guide to the Law* condemns severely negligence on the part of a woman leading to the death of her child: she is condemned to death. She is also condemned to death if she has sexual intercourse with a relative. In case of rape, the rapist is let off if he marries the victim; if not, he is fined 1/4 kg. gold. The rape of a nun is considered to be a more serious crime, which shows the esteem in which nuns were held. Even though the laws were changed, in Romanian society the status of women did not change, and continued to be influenced by the misogynous mentality of the East, which dominated all Orthodox Christianity until the 20th century (and does even up to the present day!). The church did little to make life easier for women. It may be mentioned that there is a monastery in our country (Frasinei — Olténie) where, like on Mount Athos, Greece, women are not allowed, and for this reason the monks who live there are considered to reach a higher degree of saintliness.

Over the past few centuries people's attitudes have undergone some change, due to contacts with the West. From 1848 liberal ideas originating in France were introduced by educated Romanians, leading to a certain overall liberalisation. Nevertheless, Romanian law being based on Napoleonic law, the status of women changed little, and especially in rural society. One could say that the rural mentality is largely influenced by monachism (in fact most monks and nuns come from villages) which shows a certain contempt for women.

Women in our country cannot hope to fulfill any function in the church; they may do some administrative work in the church and in so doing accomplish their Christian vocation. The problem of a female "diaconate" could provide a basis for discussion of the ordination of women at this level, but our church is not prepared to accept it. There has been no theological reflection on the role of women or on female sexuality.

As from 1975 onwards, our theological journals, in addition to articles where a woman is shown as a member of the family[15], began to include a few studies on the subject of women. As a result of participation in the Agapia consultation (1976), three Romanian Orthodox theologians were asked to give their opinions on the role of women in the church (with the accent on ordination). This consultation, organized by the WCC, presented diverging opinions on the female diaconate, but as far as the status of women in the church is concerned, nothing new emerged. In addition to foreign participants, (either present at the consultation or having sent in their studies) — Prof. Theodoru, Paul Evdokimov, Henri Rollet, and others — Romanian theology was represented by the work of the dogmatists: Fr. Prof. D. Staniloae[16] and Prof. N. Chitescu[17] and the Canonist Prof. I. Ivan[18]. But they provided no breakthrough. Women should be satisfied with maternity, the education of children and with providing the best conditions for man's development.

A few new ideas appear in articles written by female theologians, such as: *A Christian contribution to the problems of the International Women's Year*[19] or *The Mystery of the Virgin Birth.*[20] They deal with the equal vocation of women and men in sanctifying creation and bringing peace to the world, as well as with the anthropological importance of the fact that for the salvation of the world God bypassed man and chose human nature through the body of a woman, without any genetic masculine contribution.

Homosexuality in our country is considered to be an offence and is punishable by law. In the eyes of the church it is a sin, in the same way as all extra-marital sexual activity. The position is the same concerning birth control: the state does not permit abortion until after there have been four births in a family, or in cases of illness certified by a medical specialist. The other questions mentioned among "major problems of the project" of this study are not even considered by the church, and nothing can be found out about them, bodily female functions being left solely to medical science.

Conclusion
— For the Orthodox Christian sexuality still remains *taboo*.
— In our society women were not recognized as persons with legal rights until the middle of the 20th century, the legislation depending entirely on Byzantine canons.
— The misogyny in our society is that inherited from the patristic tradition of the church.
— Monachism, even though the masculine manifestation of it was a ferment for the cultural life of the Romanian society, maintained the concept of female inferiority.
— These concepts are due to physical conditions (masculine strength) and to a lack of scientific biblical exegesis.
— Another reason for misogyny in Romania is ignorance of female physiology (within religious thought) and an erroneous interpretation of "monthly bleeding", as well as an exaggerated view of maternity, inherited from the Old Testament.
— To this should be added the erroneous interpretation of the sacrament of marriage as having procreation as its sole aim.
Some remedies:
— Bringing a scientific viewpoint to bear on the problem in Christian religious spheres;
— More thorough Bible exegesis in Orthodox churches, study of biblical texts concerning women and general anthropology;
— Broader examination of Mariology in Orthodox theology;
— Theological consultations concerning women and religious studies undertaken by women.

NOTES

● In 1988 the inter-Orthodox theological consultation on the place of women in the Orthodox church and the question of the ordination of women called for a revival of the apostolic order of deaconesses. In addition to the diaconate for women, Rhodes recommended that women be given a specific blessing, as men are given, to enter other orders, such as reader and singer.

[1] A.D. Xehopol, *History of the Romanian people in Trajan Dacia*, (in Romanian) Iassiy, 1888, vol.1, p. 105.
[2] Idem, *ibid.*, p. 104.
[3] Idem, *ibid.*, p. 105.
[4] On this matter we consulted the book *History of the Romanian people from ancient times up to the present day*, (in Romanian) by C. Giurescu and D.C. Giurescu, Bucarest, 1971.
[5] Idem, *ibid.* pp. 609-611.

[6] Jean Marie Aubert considers that recognition of equal rights for men and women is due to the "industrial and scientific revolution" which "demystified the primacy of physical strength, muscular strength". *Antiféminisme et Christianisme*, Paris, 1973, p. 126.

[7] This book contains six contributions, of excellent quality, regarding the status of women.

[8] We quote the French translation of *Euchologion*, ch. A. "Prières de premier jour", p. 3.

[9] *Ibid.*, p. 7.

[10] These prescriptions are to be found in the Book of Leviticus (12:2-8) stipulating that the new-born be taken to the temple on the 8th day (date for circumcision of boys); if the child is a girl the mother remains "impure" for two weeks. The mother must stay away from the temple "in addition, seventy days to purify her blood". After that she will bring to the priest at the entrance of the Tent of Reunion a year-old lamb, a pigeon or dove to be sacrificed for the sin (12,6).

[11] *Euchologe* (in Roumanian), Bucarest, 1984, p.49.

[12] *Ibid.*, pp. 48, 49.

[13] *L'Homme et le Sacré*, (in French) Ed. Gallimard, Paris, 1950 & 1963, p. 19.

[14] Preface to the book *Le Fait féminin. Qu'est-ce qu'une femme?* (in French), under the direction of Evelyne Sullerot. Centre Royaumont pour une Science de l'Homme, collective work, with the collaboration of Odette Thibault, Paris, Fayard, 1978, p. 15.

[15] Pr.Mag. Dumitru Soare, *The Situation of Women in Islam and Christianity*, in Studii Teologice, no. 3-4, 1957; Prof. Const. Pavel, *Moral problems concerning marriage and the family*, in Biserica Ortodoxa Romana, no. 1-2/1967; Mag. Dan Miron, *Moral Principles concerning the Family in the Great Code*, Biserica Ortodoxa Romana. No. 11-12, 1969; Diac. Miron Mihut, *Romanian Legislation Concerning Marriage and the Family over the past two Decades*, in Biserica Ortodoxa Romana, No. 1-2/1967.

[16] *Women in Orthodox Theology.*

[17] *On Women's Ministry*

[18] *On the Acceptance of Women into the Ministry, in the light of Orthodox Canonical Doctrine*

[19] Anca Manolache, in Mitropolia Banatului, nr. 7-8/1975.

[20] Anca Manolache, in Mitropolia Banatului, nr. 5-6/1984.

Orthodoxy and Women in France

Elizabeth Behr-Sigel and Nicole Maillard

We have been asked to respond to the Romanian Orthodox contribution. As French women, we live in a country where the women's right to vote was not recognized until 1944. We were pleasantly surprised to learn that in Romania "the constitutional changes of 1917" had granted women "the right to vote in certain special circumstances".

Orthodox congregations in France are largely French-speaking. The members are mainly descendents of immigrants from Greece and Russia, but include a wide variety of people from other ethnic backgrounds. In our Orthodox women's groups immigrant women from Yugoslavia employed as manual workers or domestic help sit side by side with dissident intellectuals who have emigrated from the USSR, or mothers of families from Lebanon. Diversity of cultural background, language, social status and rite is thus a feature of our church life.

The other important factor which distinguishes our situation from that of women in Romania is the fact that we are a diaspora. The Orthodox represent a tiny minority of the population in France: from 40,000, a very approximate estimate of the believers with parish links, to 400,000 baptized Orthodox. No dependable statistics are available to allow a more exact estimate of the number of Orthodox in our country.

We have chosen to follow four main lines of reflection which strike us as particularly important in the study produced by our Romanian sister. These, in what we consider an ascending order of importance, are:
— the understanding of the history of relations between men and women;
— the attitude of Christian *men* to Christian *women*;
— the attitude of women to their own Christian commitment;

— and lastly, the possible underlying reasons for the existing discrepancy between the Christian message and Christian practice in relation to women.

A generalization about the status of women, which holds that they have been historically relegated to a subordinate position because of their biological functions, seems to us exaggerated. Ethnological findings and the history of civilizations have taught us to relativize all declarations in this very complex field.

We are likewise sceptical about the positive balance drawn by Anca Manolache in regard to the position of women in society in the recent years of her country's history. From reliable sources we know that many disparities still exist between the sexes in Romania today. For example, Romanian women are still paid considerably less than men for equal work. This is true in our country too. Another example is the prohibition of all abortions in Romania until a woman has given birth to four children, when we know that contraceptives are unobtainable in the country and that food and medecines are in short supply for everyone. The infant mortality rate (in the first six months) is extremely high and the suffering for the women forced to bring children into the world against their will is dreadful.

As regards the history of the church, we would slightly modify Anca Manolache's statement and would say "it is almost always women who have consciously obeyed Jesus' command to serve others". On the other hand, we cannot at all agree with our Romanian sister when she then immediately suggests that it would be unfair to accuse the church "of not in fact having transformed the status of women".

We believe there is no genuine inner conversion unless it is also translated into a new way of being and acting, that is, into new outward attitudes. The question of whether Jesus came to change hearts or to overturn unjust social relations strikes us as a non-issue. The church does not have to wait for "*the proper moment in history*" as though structures ripened of their own accord. The Holy Spirit is at work yesterday, tomorrow...and today! There is a prophetic dimension to the church which must not be forgotten in our view of history. And we must be bold enough to recognize that as far as the status given to women in the Orthodox church is concerned that dimension has been largely lacking. The *Domostroï* (a kind of set of rules for domestic life) of the Russian Orthodox Church did after all present it as a Christian duty for husbands to beat their wives!

On this same subject of men's attitude to women in the church, Anca Manolache nevertheless notes — rightly — "the strange discord between the Christian message and the practice of the Christian life". But we do not think she goes far enough. In our view there is more than a discord, there has actually been a regression: women enjoyed more scope and freedom in the early Christian communities of the first centuries than they have done subsequently in the imperial or national churches.

Sermons that are humiliating to women, denial of access to theological studies, precedence of the men always and everywhere in the church, even at communion — the list of unjust treatments meted out to Romanian Christian women by Romanian Christian men is extensive, Anca Manolache tells us.

Fortunately, in Orthodox parishes in France men's attitude towards the women is much more relaxed and open; reciprocity is the order of the day. Even though men are still in the majority on diocesan councils, the participation of women has long since been accepted. We believe, incidentally, that this was also still the case in Romania at the beginning of the sixties and that the ban on women studying in a theological academy is recent.

Anca Manolache considers that the inferior status imposed on women can probably be explained by "erroneous scientific concepts", but she does not really prove the point. Likewise unconvincing, to our way of thinking, is the reference to "Christian patristics", which is rejected en bloc as exemplifying "theological inconsistency". It is more complex than that. Though Tertullian, for instance, could write that "woman is the gate of hell" both women and men were nevertheless baptized in the church from the very beginning: one of the innovations of Christianity — and by no means the least important — was to regard woman no longer just in terms of her (sexual, reproductive) function, but as a person — and hence to recognize a woman's right not to marry. Fathers of the Church like Gregory of Nyssa, Basil of Caesarea and Maximus the Confessor affirmed the conviction that men and women are made in God's image and that men, women (and children) are recreated in the Spirit. It was in relation to trinitarian theology that they had the intuition to develop the idea of the Person which has gained such importance in the 20th century as the foundation of the inalienable nature of every man, woman and child. Today's Orthodox would benefit from knowing more of their own theological roots: they would be "purified" by it.

How do women see their own situation? It seems that in Romania, according to Anca Manolache, they have internalized their position of inferiority in the church. One explanation suggested by our Romanian sister is "the absence of religious culture" among women. Our situation is very different. In France one does not "naturally" become Orthodox. One does so as the result of a personal quest — often a very long one. And so one educates oneself: by participating in liturgical life, by reading books on theology and spirituality, attending congresses, etc. In France the people who still hold religious convictions today — and they are few in number — strive constantly for a deeper understanding of their faith through prayer and study.

At least as many women as men take the courses at the St Sergius Institute in Paris, either in person or by correspondence (*hundreds* of students for such a minority confession!); some women go on to complete doctorates and some are already teaching theology at St Sergius itself. There are women catechists and choir directors; women engaged in the media, women giving lectures, etc...

Greater theological competence enables women to be vigilant and not to take at face value certain theoretical or practical "distortions" in force in our respective churches. Thus Mariology, for example, can, when distorted, become a straitjacket of the worst kind for women, as when "Mary, humble servant of the Lord" is all too quickly interpreted to mean "women, be the servants of your husbands or of men in general!"

Let it be remembered in this respect that the *Theotokos* is the prototype of the *actively* (not passively) welcoming attitude to the Spirit for all Christian women *and men*, and not of an attitude supposedly reserved exclusively for persons of the so-called weaker sex.

Ministry — on this particular point Anca Manolache's remarks largely correspond to our own: as with Romanian women, so with Orthodox women in France the idea that they might come to have an official function, a ministry in the context of a religious service, simply does not cross their minds. The explanation of this is to be sought not so much in theological ignorance as in the psychological domain. For one thing, the present liturgical customs have been in use for many centuries and it is tempting — and reassuring — to think of them as eternal! For another, these women feel at ease in the warm liturgical atmosphere of the parish; they are in a comfortable cocoon and ask no questions, as though their social life outside had no connection with the rituals of the liturgy. We agree with Anca Manolache's analysis of the situation: "It is out of laziness rather than Christian humility on their part that women do not bother to ask themselves whether their Christian responsibility does not require them too to play a more active part in the spiritual guidance of the community."

In France there are other women — "elegant intellectuals" — who are all the happier in the cocoon of the church in that they do in fact exercise power of a more or less hidden sort, using charm and seduction. These women would feel they were denying their "femininity" if instead they could play an officially recognized role — which would then, of course, be open to scrutiny by everyone.

Different again are the women — not only intellectuals — among whom there is an increasingly clear tendency to demand ministerial recognition, and not just some fine phrases at the end of the liturgy thanking them for their "devoted service" and "spirit of sacrifice". At present very few of these women would aspire to the priesthood for themselves, but more of them are increasingly openly asking the fundamental question: why not, one day, Orthodox women priests? Lastly, a growing number would like to see *as of now* the restoration of the women's diaconate. Their aim is not power but recognized authority. There are still questions to be discussed: blessing or ordination? Diaconate with or without participation in liturgical services? Sometimes, too, women say, "What's the point of a title? I'm doing the work anyway, without the title!"

This rather colourful panorama of the situation of Orthodox women in France contrasts starkly with the grey picture of the situation of Romanian women. This is largely due to the fact that the taboos still persisting in our church circles are fewer and less rigid than in Romania. At Orthodox congresses, or even in the Sunday homilies, sexuality, love inside and outside marriage, maternity, and even abortion are often dealt with. In the liturgy and in the litanies it is quite common to hear a prayer for "those who are expecting a baby".

This freedom dates from as long ago as the thirties when ACER (Russian Student Christian Movement) was already organizing mixed camps for young people and children — a revolutionary educational method for those days. The French-speaking theologian Paul Evdokimov, following in the line set by his forerunner Bukharev (Russia, 19th century) also made a major contribution through his writings to the acceptance of sexuality as a naturally spiritual subject.

Moreover, the Orthodox church in France does not see itself cast in the role of moral censor. It is always very cautious where others' morals are concerned, considering these to be a matter of individual personal situations ("economy") to be examined in the light of pastoral conversations *and* participation in the whole liturgical life of the community. One major taboo remains deeply rooted, however, and that is homosexuality, which is generally considered implicitly or explicitly as a grave sin which does not call for any further research. To raise the subject of homosexuality openly and without a negative approach at a parish meeting, for example, is still felt to be shocking.

Another area where Orthodox women in France react differently from Romanian women is that of rites: women are prohibited from communicating during menstruation; at baptism the priest will not carry (or take) a female baby (or adult) behind the iconostasis round the altar, as he does for every male person baptized; after giving birth the woman is not entitled to come to the church and communicate for a period of forty days, after which she must undergo the rite of purification.

Because of its immense diversity, the Orthodox community in France represents — albeit not deliberately — a kind of experimental laboratory. Practical pluralism is the rule. The rites mentioned above are increasingly falling into disuse. Adolescent girls have never heard of the prohibition on communicating during menstruation; so they do not observe it, any more than do their mothers who do still know about it, but take no notice of it. Compromises are made. While some priests persist in not taking a newly baptized girl behind the iconostasis, others — with a fine disregard for paradox! — dare to do so provided she is a baby, but not when she is adult. Some parishes still practise the rite of purification but others have not been observing it for decades unless a woman asks for it.

How is one to explain the existence in the church of all these discriminations, taboos and rites? Is it not true that in Christ there is neither male nor female? That everything without exception is renewed in Christ and illuminated by Christ? Why, then, do so many grey areas remain among us, as though we somehow wanted to withhold them from God's infinite love?

We are touching here on the difficult sphere of the unconscious and irrational. It is as though for two thousand years our collective unconscious had still not been evangelized by the gospel; in other words, in the Orthodox churches, without wanting to admit it to themselves, people continue to believe that eros, menstrual blood, childbirth — in short, all that is most characteristic of woman — belong to the "powers", that is, unclean or dangerous things that are beyond our control.

In fact, it is as though the Orthodox continued to believe that there are two orders of the Holy, even after Jesus Christ: the cosmic, natural holy order which is supposed to include eros, and the holy order of God's kingdom, the eschaton, life in Christ through the Holy Spirit. Woman is unconsciously assimilated in the cosmic, natural order of the Holy. At most she may participate in the holy order of Christ's kingdom if she is consecrated and a virgin, or humble and submissive in the extreme.

That being so, we believe we are right in our understanding of one essential aspect of the Orthodox rites concerning women, mentioned above: they are not to be thought of as moralizing or apportioning blame to women (even though many Orthodox do make this mistake). The "sin" from which the woman is to be purified after childbirth is not some moral fault she is supposed to have committed, but her involvement in another order of the sacred, namely, the cosmic. Rather, according to our interpretation, the prayer of purification indicates that she is returning once more to the holy order of the kingdom of God.

It is not, therefore, an indication of any moral contempt for the woman, but rather an unconsciously dualistic approach to reality and life. Orthodox Christianity, like all popular religions, is syncretistic in character. It is a mixture of the gospel and ancient beliefs, transmitted in particular through the Book of Leviticus — or having found some semblance of justification in that Old Testament book — but which in fact go back far beyond that, to the neolithic age!

This is true in particular of the idea of the "uncleanness" of a woman's menstrual blood and in general the "taboo" surrounding everything to do with sexuality, the physical union of man and woman, and the transmission of life: where the Holy is ambivalent and exerts both attraction and repugnance. Anca Manolache brings out this ambivalence very well.

Thus, for instance, the rite of purification after childbirth is derived from very complex influences. Its intention is not, however, to make the woman feel guilty. In the cultural context of ancient times it was more a matter of healing and reassuring the woman who felt "unclean" after being in contact with a "taboo". It is therefore not a question of accusing the church because it practised this rite, but of asking it whether it can appropriately continue to do so when in broad sections of society this taboo has been exorcised through the combined influence of scientific knowledge of the processes of procreation and of the unconscious and, long before that, of a spiritualization of the notion of sin begun by the prophets of the Old Testament and accomplished by Christ.

It is a question of exhorting church leaders (priests and bishops), to fulfil vis-a-vis popular religion the prophetic educative role required of them by their office. There is a tension between the need for inculturation of the gospel and the prophetic call to conversion, that is, the transition from a syncretistic "religion" to the purity of the gospel. That gospel has to be constantly rediscovered in the living Tradition, in other words, under the influence of the Spirit.

In this field we have to proceed carefully and with tact, but also with *courage*, as did St Paul, and the Fathers like St John Chrysostom. This does not mean mechanically repeating what they said, but rather showing the same boldness and faithfulness to the gospel as they did in our approach to the new situation. We would cite as an example an extract from the homily on marriage by St John Chrysostom, which was revolutionary for those days:

> Through fear you may bind a servant, though he will not be long in escaping: but it is not by fear or threats that you can bind the companion of your life, the mother of your children, the well-spring of your happiness, but only by love and affection. What is a household where the wife trembles before her husband? What joy is there for a husband when he lives with his wife as with a slave and not with a free woman?[1]

NOTE

[1] Quoted by Jean Meyendorff in *Le mariage dans la perspective orthodoxe*, YMCA Press/ O.E.I.L., Paris, 1986, p.120.

Roman Catholic Teachings on Female Sexuality

Maria-Teresa Porcile-Santiso

The original purpose of this essay was to make a compilation of the present documents relating to Roman Catholic theological teachings and practices concerning feminine sexuality and bodily functions. As a Roman Catholic I was asked to explain the internal logic of this teaching. I can say that I have found the logic, specifically in three aspects: the primacy of life, a personalized philosophy, and a social ethic which leads to a sexual ethic.

Roman Catholic literature on the subject is vast, and one must select. I limit myself to an explanation of the basic information contained in the existing documents, which are usally known to the wider public only through references made to them in newspapers. What is presented here is mainly from my Latin American perspective. Yet another limitation relates to the fact that most of this work was done in 1984, following the Sixth Assembly of the WCC in Vancouver, and prior to the 1985 world conference of the UN Decade for Women in Nairobi (Forum '85).

The body — corporality

We live today in the "age of the body" and it is impossible to discuss sexuality without touching on the subject of the body,[1] and by implication, of anthropology. The traditional Roman Catholic interpretation of the body was influenced by an idea characteristic of Greek anthropology: body and soul, more or less dualistic in nature, according to the prevailing current of thought.[2] Influenced by the Semitic understanding of the human being rediscovered by biblical studies, corporality has been recovered as a topic for theological reflection. In this biblical conception the human being is a unity of "animated body" or "embodied, incarnate soul", on which life depends. That life, moreover, is a breath which comes from God and establishes human beings in a continual relation with their Creator and with the environment in which they are placed and which they must change through culture-cultivation.

In the RCC the Second Vatican Council echoes this new synthesis, and speaks very clearly on the dignity and worth of the body:

> Though made of body and soul, man is one. Through his bodily composition he gathers to himself the elements of the material world. Thus they reach their crown through him, and through him raise their voice in free praise of the Creator. For this reason man is not allowed to despise his bodily life. Rather, he is obliged to regard his body as good and honourable since God created it and will raise it up on the last day. Nevertheless, wounded by sin, man experiences rebellious stirrings in his body. But the very dignity of man postulates that man glorify God in his body and forbid it to serve the evil inclinations of his heart (*Gaudium et Spes*, 14).

Pope John Paul II has worked out a whole theology of the body, in which it is actually regarded as *sacramental*. Thus, the theological teaching about the body has undergone a surprising development; we have passed from a certain mistrust of the body to an appreciation of the human dimension of corporality in terms of expression, communion and relationship, as constitutive of being a person. What is needed is a philosophy of the body and at the same time a theology of resurrection of the flesh, and not just of the immortality of the soul.

Today, perhaps as never before in history, we are in the most favourable condition for the integration — at least from the point of view of consciousness — of spirit, soul and body, so that "the God of peace may sanctify us wholly and keep us sound and blameless at the coming of our Lord Jesus Christ" (1 Thess. 5:22).

Sexuality

Sexuality, like all human phenomena, is experienced within a particular culture.[3] However, as a specialized branch of biology and medicine sexuality is a new field of study. This has influenced the way human sexuality is experienced, especially by women, who have traditionally played a more "passive" and less involved role. In the cultural and ethnological domain also reliable sexual discoveries began to be made only in recent years. To all this was added the discoveries of depth psychology, especially by Sigmund Freud, who uncovered the presence of sexuality in the subconscious and in the early stages of the human being's growth.

All this made it possible to distinguish sexuality from genitality, and to realize that the sexual as such can be a kind of axis of identity comprising physical, physiological, psychological and social components.

What is necessary today is the full integration of sex as a *value* within the concept of the human person.[4] Consequently, in speaking of *human* sexuality the ethical and sociological aspect is inescapable; it is a matter of choice, responsibility and values freely adopted. Consequently we should consider two general topics related to human sexual life, namely the sense of shame and the subject of pleasure.

Modesty[5]

The sense of modesty is the human sentiment of shyness and reserve, habitually but not exclusively connected with the sexual domain; it represents a fundamental element of the personality. In itself it is a rather complex concept, involving a sense of privacy. Some of the early Christians, in contact with the Greek civilization, tended to a rigorist interpretation of modesty. As the role of sexuality is being rediscovered and affirmed, there is a tendency today to deny the value of modesty in favour of a sort of complete liberation of the body and of sex, dissassociating it from its deep human perspective and from its connection with ethics.

In contemporary thought, above all among phenomenological, spiritualist and personalist currents, a new basis of and justification for modesty is emerging. Modesty is coming to be seen as a mode of relation with others and of individual persons with themselves. It thus becomes an essential constitutive element of the human person. Emmanuel Mounier said: "Man could be defined as a being capable of modesty".[6] In other words, modesty is a distinctive feature of humanity as compared with the non-human animals, which are not capable of modesty.

When the sense of modesty has been lost, the person is inevitably subjected to a process of depersonalization. But it is only personal life that makes love possible, revealing it only to the degree that modest reserve can hide the depths of self. This love, says Kierkegaard, springs from intimacy, and consequently from the sense of shame and modest reserve, for "love loves mystery, love loves silence".[7]

Pleasure[8]

The reality of pleasure is profoundly human and licit. It comprises innumerable modes, from material to spiritual, to moral pleasure, aesthetic pleasure, etc.

From the point of view of moral theology, the concept of pleasure has given rise to various schools of thought. There has been a negative attitude to pleasure, probably as a result of the dualistic influence already mentioned. A word concerning abstention from sexual practice. It is important to distinguish two types of abstention: the abstention practised by certain persons who are the object of special grace, and those whose abstention from sexual practice is influenced by dualist philosophies. It is essential today to be quite clear that pleasure and virtue are not contradictory notions. Another false opposition, for instance, is that of pleaure and duty, which could be termed an exaggeration of the Kantianism of the 18th century.

Sexuality and the church — historical aspects

Here too to there is a dualist position similar to the one we have noted towards the body and corporality. An Argentine philosopher, E. Dussell, has written: "The Christian understanding of man took shape within the horizon of Hebrew thought and developed homogeneously in primitive Christianity; yet when Christendom (which is a culture, and must not be confused with Christianity) came into existence, through hellenization of the primitive experience, it changed its language and logical instruments of interpertation and thus fell into a mitigated dualism."[9]

In general, however, the most important contribution the New Testament makes to sexual morality is to be found on the plane of basic principles and motivations: fundamental equality between man and woman, the indissolubility of marriage, the intimate relation of marriage to the union of Christ and the church, the eminent worth of celibacy, the holiness of the body as temple of the Holy Spirit destined to rise again and united so closely to the Lord as to form only one spirit with him.[10]

Strictly speaking it is not possible to find in the gospel any valid foundation for dualism, yet in varying shades we come across it at various times in the history of Christian thought. There is however a threatening dualism which in the first centuries was manifested in numerous sects, such as Gnostics, Encratites, Montanists, Manichees, Priscillians. In the Middle Ages there were the Cathars, the Alumbrados, the enthusiast mystics of the Renaissance and more recently the exaggerations of Jansenism.[11]

It is important to mention St Augustine, whose influence on sexual morality was enormous, and continues to be considerable both among Catholics and Protestants.[12] Augustine asks himself what reasons God could have had for creating the human race male and female: "If we ask ourselves why God created Eve as Adam's helpmate, we find no likely reason except the need to beget children, just as the soil is a help for the seed, since the new plant is born from both..." Against the Pelagians, however, he says that sin has brought concupiscence with it. "If it were not for original sin, shameful concupiscence, would not exist... Matrimony would indeed exist even if no one had sinned, and the immortal body would have begotten children without morbid sexual desire... ".[13]

Nevertheless, Augustine acknowledges that the "goodness of marriage does not consist solely in the procreation of children,... but also in the natural society formed by the two sexes". But he also says that "the most sublime state of marriage is to love one another without making use of marriage".

In defence of marriage, Augustine is chiefly concerned to emphasize three matrimonial values: the good of offspring (procreation and upbringing of children), the good of mutual fidelity (conjugal charity freed to the utmost from concupiscence and making adultery impossible), and finally the good of the sacrament (inasmuch as conjugal union is a sign of the union of Christ and the church and consequently incompatible with divorce).

During the Middle Ages there were still many groups with a dualist tendency. The preoccupation, however, was not with sexuality as such but marriage, and in the 18th century two different concepts of matrimony existed (at least after Peter Lombard). The first, classic concept is related to concupiscence, which inevitably leads to mistrust of sexuality. The other conception presupposes a profound change of perspective in the approach to marriage, related more to St Thomas, who bases his arguments on Aristotle and on the biological nature of the human being. The latter conception is more optimistic than the former, since it recognizes the inherent goodness of nature.

Sexuality is always seen as ordered towards procreation. The procreative aspect is so fundamental that its negation is a graver sin than would result from not respecting sexual structures, so that, for example, contraception and masturbation are judged to be graver sins than fornication and adultery because of their *contra naturam* character. This is the approach which gives rise to the matrimonial ethics of St Thomas, influenced by the idea of natural law. In this view there is in humankind a natural law which we have in common with the animals. For example, this natural law requires that sexual intercourse should be between partners of different sex; that the sexual act is directed to the procreation of offspring; and that parents should bring up their offspring. In addition to this "generic" natural law common to animals and humankind, there is another "specific" one, proper to humankind alone, and not found in the animals, for example in regard to the openness of marriage to God and the need to establish some social relations with the marriage partner. Some authors see in this distinction between generic and specific natural law a loophole for dualism, since the *primary purpose* of procreation would belong to the generic law while the *secondary purpose* of mutual aid would belong to the specific law.

Among medieval authors, only Albert the Great regards the marriage act not only as a biological act adapted to procreation but also a personal human act. In practical terms, however, he holds the typically dualist Augustinian view of the morality of the sexual act, though in a moderate form. Martin Le Miastre, a professor at the University of Paris in the late 15th century, maintained that sexual intercourse could be had for motives other than procreation, and thus broke the chain that linked sexuality to biological generation. [14]

Then, in the 16th century, Cayetano, following in the footsteps of St Thomas, held that the sexual act is good if done with a view to procreate. With the Council of Trent, the totality of marriage, including its physical aspect, is evaluated in a sacramental perspective. "Grace perfects that natural love" (Denz 1799). For a time Augustinian pessimism is overcome, but later this was strongly emphasized by Protestants (Luther was, of course, an Augustinian monk) and especially by Calvinist puritanism which installed itself along the Rhine from Geneva to Rotterdam. In the Low Countries another dualist movement emerged, Jansenism, which exerted a strong influence on Catholic ethics. Jansen believed that his sexual ethics would not be censured because he was following Augustine. For Jansen, the rule of sexual life is that "Procreation alone justifies the use of marriage". [15]

Even today the West and the Catholic Church suffer the consequences of this dualism. In the Catholic Church, the Second Vatican Council opened up new vistas of inquiry, as we shall see.

Sexual morality

The etymology of the word "moral" relates it to the customs (mores) and standards governing human behaviour in various societies, but that does not imply (as a merely socially derived morality would) that a social phenomenon has become the moral standard. Nor is situation ethics acceptable, despite the need to take into account the degree of contingency supplied by the historical context in which moral values are held. Yet a total denial of this historical dimension would be, in the final definition, a denial of human culture.

The boundary between what is permissible and what is not, which has always existed for the Roman Catholic Church and still does, is delimited by the idea of sin. Traditional morality has clearly defined sexual sin. Any activity which is individual and solitary (masturbation), or with persons of the same sex (homosexuality), or without love (prostitution), or extra-institutional (pre-marital relationships), or which is an evasion of procreation (contraconception), or a denial of marital fidelity (adultery), is always considered sinful. This morality is in the official terms of Catholic doctrine the *same* for men and women.

From an anthropological standpoint, the integration of the person at the bodily, mental and spiritual levels is here presented to us in an unusually harmonious way. The questions arise on the level of morality. Various answers are proposed. For some, this integration at the anthropological level, which is the product of a personal philosophical vision, a psychology of the conscious and sub-conscious, and a theology with a strong biblical emphasis, is an idealistic response. Others say that it is a philosophy which is biological in tone, dualistic and compartimentalized, and one which does not take into account human reality. Still others say that it is a beautiful theory but impracticable in the conditions of today's world. It is difficult to reconcile these positions, but we should remember some fundamental points:

a) The Bible regards sexuality favourably. And as sexuality includes relationships with others, it is part of the context of the full person: heart, love, intellect and responsibility for one's neighbour.

b) In order to reach an exact understanding of Christian sexual morality it is important to remember that love is the standard.

c) There are four basic principles which are essential for this relationship to be fully human. *The principle of equality.* Men and women have the same nature with a divine origin and relationship and double morality is rejected (Gen. 1:27). *The principle of sexual differentiation.* The two sexes are not different in value but in function, and maleness and femaleness are not superior or inferior to the other, but simply different from each other. *The principle of the drive to union*, or the principle of integration. Just as the sexes are equal and different, they tend to union. *The principle of sublimation* (occasional, or permanent in the case of celibacy). The final Christian principle concerning sexuality is the possibility of surmounting it through sublimation.

In order to examine in greater detail the teaching of the Roman Catholic Church on sexual behaviour, let us consider three main divisions :
1 Heterosexual behaviour
2 Homosexual behaviour
3 Auto-erotic behaviour (masturbation)

HETEROSEXUAL BEHAVIOUR

This is, in fact, the only sexual relationship which the RCC considers valid, but its validity depends on certain conditions for it to be legitimate: sexual relations are only possible within marriage. This principle derives from the understanding of marriage as a *sacrament*. Based on these presuppositions about the sacramental nature of marriage, the church has derived norms concerning conjugal relations which themselves derive from natural law and from revealed law, and which deal with the purpose of sexual activity.

Throughout this discussion we find the principal stress being placed on the transmission of life and the birth of new life as the fruit of conjugal union. In the present century, in which science has discovered the internal rhythm of female cycles, a whole new area of enquiry has opened up, giving rise to polemical debate on the choice between natural regulation of births, and artificial birth control (or contraception) which the RCC does not accept. (Within contraception, abortion is a special case and is dealt with in a later part of this paper.) I thus limit myself here to the basic issues in heterosexual relations: sexual relations within marriage and premarital sexual relations.

The two distinctive features of the RCC in the area of sexual morality are a) the voice of the magisterium, and b) the thinking of moral theology.

a) *The voice of the magisterium:* The RCC is the only Christian church which has an official magisterium, which the church considers as a development of the revelation and of tradition. The magisterium does not only deal with matters of faith and dogma, but also of morals and "natural law" and it has various organs: Councils, Supreme Pontiff, Synods, Bishops' Conferences, etc. Within the RCC structure, the magisterium is a progressive response to the new concerns arising in the course of history in various ways: through issuing warnings, establishing norms, exercising discipline, etc. But, apart from the official magisterium, there are other theologians in the church who are not always in agreement with the church's official voice. In various ways these theologians relate to the magisterium. There are times when they are in disagreement with the official teaching. The seriousness of the disagreement depends on the organ of the magisterium in which there is disagreement. It is one thing to disagree with a Council and another to disagree with a letter or a statement of a dicastery of the Roman Curia. What is important to understand is that it is the magisterium which determines the direction the church takes at the level of doctrine.

b) *The Roman Catholic Church and the reflection on moral theology:* The other distinctive feature is that the church has a real corpus of doctrine on morality, with teachings, definitions, documents, statements, of a size no other church possesses. This has led it to develop a whole elaborate discipline within the specific field of theology — moral theology. The reason for this immense development of moral theology is perhaps the discipline of the sacrament of confession.

Official doctrine of the Roman Catholic Church on sexuality

The teaching of the church on sexuality takes into account a call to saintliness in married life. This includes the "army of virtues", among which chastity is considered the unifying force of an ordered and free love in the perspective of the Spirit. Chastity carries with it the discipline of periodic abstinence, a question of discipline. From this derives moral behaviour in the family and in the marriage for the couple. Outside of marriage sexual practice is disorder and sin.

We concentrate on developments in the 20th century, because they have largely shaped the present situation and practice. Because of the new scientific developments during this period the magisterium has had to make repeated pronouncements in this field.

St Thomas considered marriage to have two aims, procreation and love. As scientific discoveries are made they are taken into account by the teaching of the church. For example, the discoveries regarding the infertile period in the female menstrual cycle marked a fundamental advance, since it led to the natural rhythm method of birth control, "natural" in the sense of being based on the nature of human beings or, rather, women, since the menstrual cycle was theirs. In 1930, Pope Pius XI issued the encyclical *Casti Connubii*, in which he reiterated the primary aim of procreation and the subordination of all else to it. Any action to prevent procreation in any way is illegitimate.[16] For, in effect, "the primary end of marriage is the procreation and the education of children". As teaching, this proved to be somewhat conclusive, but despite that moral theologians continued their research and published some studies. Professors of moral theology, such as Doms, Kempel and von Hildebrand, emphasize a personalist concept of sexuality. The fundamental basis of this teaching is an analysis of human sexuality which, in its intrinsic nature, is different from the sexuality of animals. In animals, sexuality is related to procreation, whereas in the human couple it affects the deepest and most spiritual levels of the human person and is the most comprehensive form of communion between persons. For this reason, they claim, it is dehumanizing to use the same criteria for fertility for human beings as for lower animals. The logical deduction from their premises was that the morality of sexual relations cannot be measured against the yardstick of biology but against human purposiveness as expressed in sexual union. The Holy See acted against these theories and on 1 April 1944 the Holy Office banned these publications. [17]

The Pontificate of Pius XII. On 29 October 1951, Pius XII intervened in a famous speech to the midwives of Rome: "Every attempt on the part of the married couple during the conjugal act or during the development of its natural consequences to deprive it of its inherent power and to hinder the procreation of a new life is immoral... This prescription holds good today just as much as it did yesterday. It will hold tomorrow and always, for it is not a mere precept of human right but the expression of a natural and Divine law." [18]

However, he did admit the legitimacy of the Ogino-Kraus rhythm method, provided that the order of aims was maintained, i.e. that the biological nature of the sexual act be observed, and, therefore, remain open to the possibility of a new life, even when it was intentionally excluded precisely by choosing only the infertile period for intercourse.

In 1956 the famous "pill" was discovered as a cure for infertility. The pill opened up the possibility of separating fertility and love. Its use began to become widespread, mainly due to some notable moral teachers, who accepted a personalist concept, according to which human beings have dominion over their own nature, and the biological integrity of the sexual act is safeguarded. [19] On 12 September 1958, in a speech to the "Haematology Congress", Pope Pius XII declared it lawful to use the pill to prevent ovulation, provided that it was for therapeutic purposes. On the subject of the therapeutic use of the pill, more progressive moral theologians considered its use to regularize the menstrual cycle (if that was really possible) as perfectly legitimate. Some even considered that the natural rhythm method could thus be reinforced and safeguarded. [20] On that basis the use of the pill during lactation was also envisaged. What is undeniable is that great stress was laid on the act of procreation.

Up to this point the issue was being approached from an individual standpoint, but during the 1960s the problem of the world's rapid population growth began to assume prominence and from then on there was another aspect to the problem — the social aspect. Pope John XXIII took this aspect very seriously.

The Pontificate of John XXIII. In 1961 John XXIII, in the encyclical *Mater et Magistra*, recorded that "the transmission of human life is entrusted by nature to a personal and conscious act" which should be linked, and consciously linked, with other factors, including social and psychological factors.

> We realise that in certain areas and in the political communities of developing economies really serious problems and difficulties can and do present themselves, due to a deficient economic and social organisation which does not offer, therefore, living conditions proportionate to the rate of population increase; as also to the fact that the solidarity among the peoples is not operative to a sufficient degree...
>
> The true solution is found only in the economic development and in the social progress which respects and promotes true human values, individual and social; an economic development and social progress, that is, brought about in a moral atmosphere, conformable to the dignity of man and to the immense value the life of a single human being has; and in the cooperation, on a world scale, that permits and favours an ordered and fruitful interchange of useful knowledge, of capital and of manpower.
>
> We must solemnly proclaim that human life is transmitted by means of the family, the family founded on marriage, one and indissoluble, raised for Christians to the dignity of a sacrament. The transmission of human life is entrusted by nature to a personal and conscious act and, as such, subject to the all-wise laws of God; laws inviolable and immutable that are to be recognised and observed. Therefore, it is not permissible to use means and follow methods that can be licit for the transmission of plant or animal life. Human life is sacred. From its very inception, the creative action of God is directly operative. By violating His laws, the Divine Majesty is offended, the individuals themselves and humanity degraded, and likewise the community itself of which they are members is enfeebled. (*Mater et Magistra* n.50-51)

Carrying this forward, and from the explicit consideration of the "personal and conscious act", it would be impossible to think of an "individual" sexual morality devoid of social morality; this is a total compromise: of the person and of the society, or of the person as social subject.

The Second Vatican Council

The Second Vatican Council commenced in 1962. In it the personalist conception of sexuality predominated. No clear-cut distinctions were established between primary and secondary aims. The Council speaks of "intimate partnership of married life and love" (*Gaudium et Spes* n.48); conjugal love was extolled in that "it can enrich the expressions of body and mind with a unique dignity" (n.49), and it was declared that "children are ... the supreme gift of marriage" (n.50). It finally indicates the golden rule to harmonize love with responsible parenthood: "objective standards... based on the *nature of the human person* and his acts" (n.51). There is no longer any mention of the biological nature of the sexual act. The Council expressed itself in these terms:

> Therefore when there is question of harmonising conjugal love with the responsible transmission of life, the moral aspect of any procedure does not depend solely on sincere intentions or on an evaluation of motives. It must be determined by objective standards. These, based on the nature of the human person and his acts,... (*Gaudium et Spes* 51)[21]

Relying on these principles, sons of the Church may not undertake methods of regulating procreation which are found blameworthy by the teaching authority of the Church in its unfolding of the Divine Law.[22]

The Pontificate of Paul VI. Paul VI acknowledged the complexity of the problem.[23] The fundamental problem concerned the practical consequences for the moral life of believers, especially of the teaching pertaining to the use of contraceptives. Would their use be permitted, or would the church always condemn them?

It is important to take into account the social dimension of the problem noted by Pope John XXIII in *Mater et Magistra*. Paul VI echoes these concerns in his famous speech at the United Nations on 4 October 1965.

> You proclaim here the fundamental rights and duties of man, his dignity, his freedom — and above all his religious freedom. We feel that you thus interpret the highest sphere of human wisdom and, we might add, its sacred character, for you deal here above all with human life, and the life of man is sacred. No one may dare offend it. Respect for life, even with regard to the great problem of birth, must find here in your assembly its highest affirmation and its most reasoned defence. You must strive to multiply bread so that it suffices for the tables of mankind, and not rather favour an artificial control of birth, which would be irrational, in order to diminish the number of guests at the banquet of life.

This, too, is part of the background against which the same Pope's encyclical, *Humanae Vitae* (1986), appeared. In it the Pope reaffirms the teaching which derives not only from divine law as shown by Revelation, but also from natural law. In his encyclical the Pope was seeking "a new and deeper reflection upon the principles of the moral teaching on marriage", indicating that it is "intrinsically dishonest" to prevent conception artificially, "because of the intrinsic ordination (of human generative faculties) towards raising up life". The central affirmation of the encyclical is: "Every conjugal act must be open to the transmission of life."

Many see the kernel of the encyclical's teaching in the practical and moral part: "Similarly excluded is every action which, either in anticipation of the conjugal act, or in in its accomplishment, or in the development of its natural consequences, proposes, whether as an end or as a means, to render procreation impossible" (H.V. n. 14). The reason for such condemnation is the respect due to the natural biological order. Concretely, this means the natural rhythms in women with their alternating periods of fertility and infertility. These periods are invested with an authentic normative value, and there is no possibility of intervening in the process by deliberately and artificially creating periods in which conception can take place. Section 17 states:

> It is also to be feared that the man, growing used to the employment of anticonceptive practices, may finally lose respect for the woman and, no longer caring for her physical and psychological equilibrium, may come to the point of considering her as a mere instrument of selfish enjoyment, and no longer as his respected and beloved companion. (H.V.n.17)

These arguments have been considered by theologians, and by women — who were beginning to discover that they were not only objects of pleasure but that they also had the right to the conscious control of their natural functions. They enrich the reflection on the subject, especially when it is realised that at its very outset *Humanae Vitae* takes into account the change in understanding of women's personality: "A change is also seen both in the manner of considering the person of woman and her place in society, and in the value to be attributed to conjugal love in marriage, and also in the appreciation to be made of the meaning of conjugal acts in relation to that love."

It seems that the natural rhythm method presupposes a deep human relationship in which both husband and wife share. The problem often arises at the practical level, and that is where many Catholic theologians and pastors offer solutions which do not correspond to the explicit teaching of the encyclical. Others, on the other hand, see *Humanae Vitae* as having the virtue of seeing that developing countries need to be defended from a covert neo-colonialism, which would attempt to promote indiscriminate birth control among them for more or less disreputable reasons. In this regard, it refers to the encyclical *Populorum Progressio* which the same Pope, Paul VI, issued in 1967: "No solution to these difficulties is acceptable 'which does violence to man's essential dignity' and is based only 'on utterly materialistic conception of man himself and of his life'. *The only possible solution to this question is one which envisages the social and economic progress* both of individuals and of the whole of human society, and which respects and promotes true human values."

It is important to interpret *Humanae Vitae* in the light of *Populorum Progressio* so as not to fall into the argument based on social and individual morality. This explains why *Humanae Vitae* has generally been better received in certain third world quarters than in the developed countries although its application has created serious problems of conscience for many Christians.[24]

In the Roman Catholic Church this whole subject area is intrinsically connected with family planning and responsible fatherhood and motherhood. "Children are the supreme gift of marriage", declared the Second Vatican Council. *Gaudium et Spes*, from Vatican II, gives criteria (n.50 and 51) on which a right judgment can be made, which take into account the welfare of the parents and the children already born, the conditions of the times and the parents' state in life (material and spiritual); and the welfare of the community (the family, the society, and the church).

Family planning involves and is implemented by birth control. It is here that we find ourselves fully in the area of methods. Concerning these, the Council states:

a) All methods which are certainly or may be considered abortion are ruled out: "... from the moment of its conception life must be guarded with the greatest care".

b) Methods must be selected according to "objective standards (which are) based on the nature of the human person and his acts": the word "person" is used, and not simply "human nature", so as not to lapse into exclusively biological criteria. The word "nature" (of the human person is used) so as not to lapse into personalist relativism. His or her "acts" are mentioned, so that they are not seen in isolation but as an expression of the person as a whole.

c) The constitution adds that the "sons of the Church may not undertake methods of regulating procreation which are found blameworthy by the teaching authority of the Church in its unfolding of the divine law".

Because of the many repercussions which *Humanae Vitae* had, it had to be followed up (according to the understanding of the Pontificate of John Paul II) with a more wide-ranging document on sexual matters — "The Declaration on Certain Questions Concerning Sexual Ethics", issued on 29 December 1975 by the Sacred Congregation for the Doctrine of the Faith. The Declaration makes clear that in the church it is the task of the hierarchy to illumine the upright conscience, and the mention of "confessors" shows that possible situations of conscience, emotions, and sin are envisaged. The church "ceaselessly preserves and transmits without error the truths of the moral order, and she authentically interprets not only the revealed positive law but 'also... those principles of the moral order which have their origin in human nature itself'". [25]

It thereby confirms the foundation of the doctrine of natural law and divine law, based on St Thomas. The Declaration has a double aim: on the one hand it takes a positive view of sexuality, which it sees as integral to the human person and having integrative force: "According to contemporary scientific research, the human person is so profoundly affected by sexuality that it must be considered as one of the factors which give to each individual's life the principal traits that distinguish it. In fact it is from sex that the human person receives the characteristics which, on the biological, psychological and spiritual levels, make that person a man or a woman, and thereby largely condition his or her progress towards maturity and insertion into society."

For this reason the Declaration goes on to deal with particular aspects of sexual morality. [26] The end of paragraph 11 is of some importance for this study: "The more the faithful appreciate the value of chastity and its necessary role in their lives as *men and women*, the better they will understand, by a kind of spiritual instinct, its moral requirements and counsels. In the same way they will know better how to accept and carry out, in a spirit of docility to the church's teaching, what an upright conscience dictates in concrete cases."

The church lays down the same moral values for men and women. The Declaration describes chastity "as a virtue which does honour to the human person and which makes him capable of love which is true, disinterested, generous and respectful of others". It places love in the context of liberation from the painful conflict between "the law of the mind and the law of the sin which dwells in his members", quoting St Paul. The Declaration concludes by referring to the importance of educating and encouraging children and adolescents to weigh moral values with an upright conscience, echoing the doctrine of the Second Vatican Council (cf Declaration on Christian Education I).[27]

The Pontificate of John Paul II. The Pontificate of John Paul II began in 1978. He was already known for his interest in issues of family life, conjugal love, the sacrament of marriage, and problems concerning conception.[28] Various aspects of these questions can be discerned during his pontificate which can be ordered both chronologically and thematically. From 1979 to 1983, practically continually at his Wednesday catecheses to the people of God, the Pope outlined and commented on the biblical passages on the creation of man and woman, and marriage. He was thus preparing the ground for the Synod of 1980 on "The role of the Christian Family in the Modern World".

As for the catechesis on the language of the body (1979-82), some words are repeatedly cited which indicate the Pope's position: words such as "mutuality", "reciprocity", "responsible parenthood", "language of the body", "sacrament of the body", "nuptial significance of the body".

What is striking about "The Apostolic Exhortation Regarding the Role of the Christian Family in the Modern World" (November 1981)[29] is the way in which the situation is explicitly and frequently mentioned: "God's plan for man and woman", "interpersonal relations in marriage,... promoting the dignity of women", "the new culture calls for acknowledgement of the true values, for defending the rights of men and women...".

Sections 22 to 26 emphasize the rights and duties of women, and refer to offences against women's dignity: "Above all, it is important to underline the equal dignity and responsibility of women with men." "There is no doubt that the equal dignity and responsibility of men and women fully justifies women's access to public functions."

> Unfortunately the Christian message about the dignity of women is contradicted by that persistent mentality which considers the human being not as a person but as a thing, as an object of trade, at the service of selfish interest and mere pleasure: the first victims of this mentality are women.
>
> This mentality produces very bitter fruits, such as contempt for men and for women, slavery, oppression of the weak, pornography, prostitution — especially in the organized form — and all those various forms of discrimination that exist in the fields of education, employment, wages, etc.
>
> Besides, many forms of degrading discrimination still persist today in a great part of our society that affect and seriously harm particular categories of women, as for example childless wives, widows, separated or divorced women, and unmarried mothers.

The Document of the Sacred Congregation for Christian Education on "Educational Guidance in Human Love", published 10 November 1983, was considered a contribution to the harmonious development of persons in relation to their ultimate goal through positive and prudent sexual education (cf. *Doc Gravissimum Educationis* n.1, of the Second Vatican Council). It refers to the cultural and social differences between various countries and acknowledges the significance of sexuality as characteristic of human beings, men and women, on the physical, psychological and spiritual planes in a world which "in large part banalizes human sexuality". It proposes putting sex education into practice.[30]

In 1986, the Sacred Congregation for the Doctrine of the Faith published a document entitled "Encyclical to the Bishops of the Catholic Church on the Pastoral Care of Homosexuals".

In 1987 the document "Educational Guidance on the Respect for Emerging Human Life and the Dignity of Procreation" (22.II.87) was published. It lays down moral principles which today could be applied to the field of gene technology. It is a key document concerning the present position of the Catholic Church, which requires careful study. It takes into account fundamental principles related to the Christian understanding of man and his sexuality from the perspective of the integration of the whole person.

The Pontificate of John Paul will certainly continue to produce material to stimulate thought on this matter. Of course within the RCC itself there is often disagreement in this area. There seems in fact to be a real disparity between the official teaching of the church and the actual practice of the faithful. In many cases, individual situations are resolved according to differing pastoral criteria depending on the views of the local churches.

Pre-marital relations

In general, conditions pertaining in society today do not favour pre-marital sexual abstention.[31] The contemporary situation in pre-marital relations dates from the Second World War, whereas at the beginning of the century interest centred on free love or trial marriage.[32] The RCC condemns pre-marital sex for both men and women. There are three aspects to the problem: the moral-theological, the socio-legal, and the psycho-anthropological.

The argument of moral theology uses a biblical approach, although the Bible contains no specific references to pre-marital relations. In general the passages quoted are 1 Cor. 9:10; Gal. 5:19-21; Eph. 5:3-5; and Lev. 19:20; Deut. 22:21; 22:14 and 23:18.

There is also the approach of *natural law*. Catholic moral theology sees itself as related to natural law. It would seem that in accordance with natural law, it is inadvisable to enter into pre-marital relations because of the demands placed upon us by society. As early as St Thomas we find guidelines: "It is clear that to bring up children, not only is the role of the mother in feeding them essential, but much more the collaboration of the father who instructs and defends them, and moreover encourages both their spiritual and physical development. It is thus against nature to engage in conjugal union independently of all bonds. Such union should take place between particular individuals bound to each other in a stable relationship... Fornication, thus, as conjugal union outside the law, is intrinsically sinful." [33]

The encyclical of Pius XI, *Casti Connubii*, rejects temporary and trial marriages.

The socio-legal argument against pre-marital relations is based on the view that sexuality and love have a considerable dimension of social responsibility. *The psycho-anthropological argument* is based on the view that love involves the whole person. It is believed that love between unmarried couples leaves open the possibility for the relationship to be broken off. This possibility is not acceptable since no formal commitment has been made. [34]

Another argument concerns the potential child born of this union. In that case, the position taken by the couple will depend on the culture and society of which they are part, but from the point of view of the church, what is envisaged is a stable family setting. [35] The most recent documents of the church confirm this position. [36] It was reiterated in the Document on Sexual Morality (1975) which we have already mentioned.

HOMOSEXUAL BEHAVIOUR

We will limit our discussion to the magisterium of the church, which distinguishes between homosexual behaviour and homosexual tendencies: homosexual practice is not acceptable, but pastoral care is called for.

The church holds that there is a biblical basis for its position. Various texts are cited: the first series considers homosexuality as a part of the history of sin and growing alienation of humankind (Gen. 19:1-29 and Judges 19:22-30). Another textual tradition condemns the pagan practice of male cultic prostitution in shrines (Deut. 23:18-19; 1 Kings 14:24; Job 36:14). Leviticus condemns cultic prostitution (Lev. 18:22, cf. Lev.

20:13). In the New Testament various passages refer to the punishment of the sin of Sodom (Mt. 10:15, Mt. 11:23-24; Luke 10:12, Luke 27:29; Peter 2:6-8; Jude 6-7). In 1 Corinthians 6:9-10, sodomy is enumerated as one of the sins which exclude people from the kingdom of God. And in 1 Tim. 1:8-11, it is also reproved as one of the vices which are opposed to "sound doctrine". The classic text is Romans 1:18-32. These texts, taken as a whole, witness to the struggle of Israel, and later, of the apostolic church against the trend in paganism to attempt to justify homosexual behaviour. At the present time there is also a trend, even among Catholic authors, who would wish to reinterpret or evade these biblical texts. [37]

The official response of the Roman Catholic Church to homosexuality is to call for individual conversion, renewal of the whole of society and social therapy and prophylaxis. For many Catholic authors, in most cases homosexuality has to do with a neurosis, and it is often almost impossible to effect a "cure", which is due, in the majority of cases, to the fact that homosexuals do not wish to change their tendencies or cannot break free from their circle. [38]

In the ancient world, certain groups of misogynist or endocentric philosophers exalted homofilia as a form of friendship superior to that of marriage. Historically, however, most European nations have treated homosexuality as a crime and punished it severely, which shows that it has been rejected not only religiously, but also culturally and ideologically. Homosexuality between women does not seem to have been so severely punished. [39] Considerable thought is being given today to somatic causes of homosexuality. It seeems that there are also other causes, or extra-somatic situations such as social permissiveness, dehumanizing leisure, environmental influence, possessiveness by one or both parents, or experience of a tense or uneasy heterosexual relationship in others, and inadequate sexual education.

For most Catholic educators, homosexuality, or homosexual fixation, is to be considered as an abnormal situation which should be cured to the extent possible. The official teaching of the church continues today in this vein, as reflected in the Document on Sexual Morality, the "Educational Guidelines on Human Love" of the same year, and the "Encyclical to All the Bishops of the World on Pastoral Care for Homosexuals" (1986).

AUTO-EROTIC BEHAVIOUR

In Catholic theology, masturbation, which is usually defined as erotic self-stimulation until orgasm is achieved, has been for a very long time the object of harsh moral condemnation.

Some authors deduce this condemnation from Genesis 38:9 and the sin of Onan, which is the practice of *coitus interruptus*; onanism is not masturbation, although they have long been confused. In fact, it seems that there is only one Old Testament text which makes reference to masturbation, and it does so in a context which is, if anything, poetic (Eccl. 23:16). In the New Testament there are various texts which have been interpreted in this sense, particularly in St Paul (1 Cor. 6:9-10; Eph. 5:3; Gal. 5:9-21). None of these texts specifically mentions masturbation. In 1 Cor: 6:9-10 the Greek term *malakoi* (a weak or effeminate person) was interpreted as an allusion to masturbation, as the Vulgate translation of *malakoi* is *molles*, and since the Renaissance the custom has grown up of calling masturbation by the Latin term *mollitis*. It is possible that we have here an error of translation, but despite the differences and nuances in translation, the teaching of the church is clear. [40]

The practice of masturbation has been known from very early times. The Egyptians knew of it, and condemned it, as did the Greeks, although they rarely mentioned it. In writings dating from the Middle Ages, masturbation is most frequently mentioned in the penitential books. [41] St Thomas laid down a standard of judgment when he said, "the sins of lust are sins against one's neighbour" (*De Malo* 15.2.4). Their seriousness derives from the fact that they are opposed to love. Sexual disorder contains a selfish attitude which destroys the balance of the individual. [42] Pius XII, fearing that subjective guilt, which is at its height during adolescence, was being too easily eliminated, said, "We thus reject as erroneous the view of those who consider relapses in the years of puberty as inevitable...." [43] Exceptions for therapeutic purposes are also not admitted, because they underline the basic foundation of sexual morality: that genital pleasure must be exclusively directed towards its procreative purpose. [44]

In 1975, the Document on Sexual Morality of the Sacred Congregation of the Faith repeated the same teaching, as did the Educational Guidelines on Human Love, issued in 1983 by the Sacred Congregation for Catholic Education.

Abortion

In this study we have examined only the active use of sexuality. Let us now take a brief look at how the Catholic Church treats the subject of abortion, which on its own merits a whole ecumenical, intercultural and inter-religious investigation. [45]

It is impossible to look at all the ways in which abortion is defined. In general terms (and these vary according to legislation in various countries) abortion refers to the interruption of pregnancy before the foetus is viable. A distinction is made between spontaneous and induced abortion, and the latter may be legal depending on the cases recognized by the law in different countries, or criminal, when motives are considered illegal (i.e. when done clandestinely). The magisterium of the Catholic Church prohibits abortion. For the church life exists from the moment of conception.[46]

Catholic moral terminology distinguishes between foeticide (killing of the foetus in the mother's womb), abortion (expulsion of the foetus when living but not viable), and birth (expulsion of the foetus when living and viable). The Catholic Church's view is based on certain biblical texts such as Job 10:10-15, and Lk. 1:41-44. Textual criticism shows that there is no explicit teaching on abortion in these texts but they use language which speaks of life in the mother's womb and permit us to draw moral consequences on the implications of that life.

In scholasticism there were two different positions according to the view held on life and the soul. On the one hand there was creationism, which St Thomas took from Aristotle, according to which every form requires the pre-existence of matter suitable to receive it; hence the body existed first and the soul then came into it. The other position held that the body and soul were generated together, a position upheld by certain fathers such as St Gregory of Nyssa, St Basil and Tertullian.

The magisterium of the church speaks of the creation of *each* soul, but without going into details about the moment at which it is created.[47] At the same time the magisterium has consistently condemned abortion.[48] The teaching is echoed in recent texts of the magisterium issued since the Second Vatican Council: "Life once conceived must be safeguarded with extreme care from the moment of conception. Abortion and infanticide are horrible crimes."

And the Declaration on induced abortion states: "From the moment in which the egg is fertilized, a new life begins which is not the life of the father nor of the mother, but that of a new human being which evolves on its own. It will never become a human being if it has not already been one from the beginning. The science of modern genetics confirms this age-old evidence. It shows that from the first moment the programme for that which is to become a living individual is fixed: a human being, an individual being with its own well-defined characteristics. Fertilization is the beginning of the adventure of a human life. Time is needed for it to develop its abilities and its power to act."[49] The Encyclical on the Rights of the Family, published by the Holy See, underlined that "human life must be respected and protected absolutely from the moment of its conception".[50] More recently, in response to what the magisterium sees as the risks of genetic engineering, this teaching has been reaffirmed: "The human being must be respected — as a person — from the first moment of his existence".[51] The teaching of the church continues along the same lines: human life is present from the moment of fertilization.[52]

It was Christianity that first called to the attention of society the question of abortion and the defence of human life. In 1803 in Protestant England the first civil legislation barring abortion was passed. In the last 50 years, partly due to the emergence of the feminist movement, the call for women's right to abortion has grown.

Teaching and practice

We have looked at the official teaching of the church on sexuality, and will now examine the relationship between this teaching and the practice of RC believers.

The RCC's teaching on sexual morality has been the object of substantial criticism, and still is, both from inside and outside the church. Some critics accuse it of being an individualistic morality, thus bearing the marks of bourgeois morality. For others, it is a morality presupposing too high a level of education for it to be followed. According to such a viewpoint, it is directed to an elite social class. Still others consider it misogynous and patriarchal, a mark of the only church in which the clergy and the hierarchy are celibate males.

The individualistic and bourgeois aspect: Morality presupposes responsibility for one's acts, and thus the ability to do right or wrong, which implies the existence of sin. In fact, when the Catholic Church speaks of morality, it also speaks of sin, i.e. given the fact of norms of conduct which conform to the "nature of the person", the possibility exists of obeying or disobeying them. The consequences of such acts of disobedience cannot be indifferent from the moral point of view: they are considered sin. In today's world, talking about sin may seen inappropriate, obscurantist or obsolete. Today, everything is being studied, observed, tried. Tacitly, our secular society has trouble to admit the existence of order/disorder or grace/sin; nevertheless, from the perspective of the faith, and the theology of faith and redemption, these are irrefutable realities. In the face of disorder and sin it is essential to reaffirm the possibility of conversion, improvement, pardon, humility and compassion.

Such expressions could be considered "ecclesiastic" in contemporary society, which is more or less secularized and materialistic; but in fact this is the language of the Bible. The existence of sin and of forgiveness of sin is not only a human reality, but is both human and divine. For the RCC, sin is objective and personal, with one exception: situations of sin which are created by the sum-total of individual sins. Such "social sin" is the fruit, sum or consequence of individual sins. Individual behaviour always has social repercussions and vice-versa.

Today the teaching of the church on sexual morality is being challenged by society. In a world in which the great majority of people are faced with grim socio-economic situations that must be solved urgently, is it possible to leave the regulation and/or control of births to the decision of individuals, or couples? Should not national measures be taken? Is it even possible to consider natural regulation of births, with all that it presupposes by way of education and all that education presupposes in the form of the investment of time, specialist staff, etc.?

Those are the questions posed by the socio-economic argument, and they constitute a severe and very serious accusation. At this stage of the discussion it is important to recall the main developments in the recent official teaching of the church. Pope Paul VI addressed the United Nations in 1964, pleading for peace, against the arms race, and for the transmission of life. It is a matter of justice and the just distribution of material resources, a position which was repeated in the Document *Populorum Progressio* in 1967. In 1968 Paul VI published his controversial encyclical, *Humanae Vitae*, which attributes a detailed role to rulers and public authorities in addressing the terrifying demographic problem.

When the statements of 1964 and 1968 are placed side by side, we can see a clear consistency between the regulation of birth by natural means and the social implications. In fact, since the publication of *Mater et Magister* during the Pontificate of Pope John XXIII, the official documents of the church have always taken into account both the individual and the society.

The educational challenge: Decisions concerning "mastery of self" and personal relations obviously presuppose the capacity to act as free persons, and thus a certain level of development and maturity. Does this imply that it concerns only a socio-economic "elite" class, or does it mean simply making possible the full human development of the ordinary rural inhabitant or manual worker?

Is it possible to believe that "simple people" are not capable of handling such complexities of human development as the integration of "natural law" and "culture"? It seems that the real problem is much more complex. It is striking that, while today there is a widespread acceptance of everything that is "natural", there is, at the same time, a rather indiscriminate acceptance of artificial or even unnatural methods, abortion being a case in point. There is today a great challenge for education and for communication. Perhaps the real point for friction between the official documents of the church on moral theology and the practice of Christians and Catholics is also one of *content*, language, teaching and pastoral implementation.

It is interesting to note that sexual moral teaching, above all on the natural regulation of births, has in fact been more readily accepted in the third world than in the industrialized countries. One is tempted to ask whether the industrialized world is not finding it inconvenient that the poor increase in number and so exports all sorts of pills to them! In Latin America many documents, films and studies are devoted to this question. In Central America, the World Health Organization authorizes centres for the natural regulation of births, in view of the negative experience of the pill, which has even proved damaging to the health of many women. The pharmaceutical industry does not generally distribute the male pill, which exists but is practically unknown, because, they say, "there is no market for it." This is only the tip of the iceberg of cultural machismo. The psychological resistance of men is much greater than women's when they know that something will make them sterile or infertile, because cultural fear causes them to confuse sterility with impotence. Thus, women, who are victims of machist ideology, naively accept such male immaturity and prefer to be the ones to take the pill, even though their bodies and future motherhood can be much more seriously affected than would be in the case of men.

This is a basic issue, because, if in speaking of contraception we can speak of parallel methods affecting men and women indifferently, why is it that artificial birth control methods are mostly practised on women? The answer lies in the fact that natural methods understandably depend on the woman, since it is her body which has alternating cycles and natural rhythms. Yet the fact that artificial methods are mostly practised on woman is not based on nature but on culture. And in Latin America it is a culture characterized by male predominance.

This brings up another question: Would it be unrealistic to think of a development of the couple in which both male and female freely accept the reciprocal language of their bodies? There are people who speak of the transformation from human beings "governed by their instincts" to human beings who can exercise control of their bodies as they enter into mutual dialogue with their partner's body naturally and humanly.

A misogynous morality? Arguably, the strongest criticism against the sexual morality of the church is that which comes from the feminist movement and from feminist theology. A whole symphony of connotations of female sexuality affects women's participation in the church, to which responses are only slowly being formulated. This is understandable, because of the cultural diversity which exists in the church. In fact there is a serious problem of communication at the level of preparing documents and other written materials which affect the community and the church. An official document of the church, *Christifidelis Laici* (1989) mentions this problem. It is perhaps not realistic to believe that the problem can be solved or that dialogue and agreement among the very diverse theological positions can be found. Nevertheless, I believe it is necessary to build bridges between these river banks which at the moment seem unbridgeable: the documents of the magisterium and the practice of many Christian and Catholic lay persons. Many are unaware of or indifferent to this teaching. They therefore substitute or follow positions taken by other Catholic clergy in various local churches which do not agree with the magisterium. It is impossible to ignore these facts today, since the communications media make a point of publicising them widely. What can be done about this problem? There is no easy answer, especially because it entails doing something which we find very difficult in today's world: to listen to the world, the society and to the human being, male and female, at the same time as we remain attentive to the word of God.

Conclusion

Let us review the two types of criticism directed against the Roman Catholic Church in this matter:

a) Criticisms of form which question the need for such a minute and detailed regulation of so personal a matter which is a matter for the individual conscience. It is a serious criticism and often comes from an ecumenical context. No other church has anything comparable to the magisterium. Other churches, including the Orthodox Church, entrust to the couple the observance of the sacramental aspect of marriage. From the ecumenical point of view it is hard to see any response which could be satisfactory. The only possible reply is that there is a magisterium and a standard of obedience to it. That does not mean that theological research and study are disdained, because it is through them that the magisterium itself can advance (cf. Vatican II, Constitution on the Church, n. 25, and Constitution on Divine Revelation n.10).

b) The second criticism is directed at the content itself. This criticism, while not ignoring the question of form, is directed at a sexual morality which seems to resolve itself into methods, birth control, marital fidelity and the transmission of life. This criticism comes both from inside and outside the Catholic Church and might even be termed a caricature.

For the magisterium of the Church, the essential reason is the option for life and the understanding of the gospel message, in communion with tradition. The church feels that it cannot fail to proclaim what it perceives as the perfection of love. As a society at once human and divine, it must maintain the delicate balance between pedagogy, dialogue and understanding on the one hand and the call to holiness and godliness on the other.

NOTES

[1] W. Work, Sentido Biblico del Hombre, Marova, Madrid 1970; G. von Rad, Old Testament Theology I, Sígueme, Salamanca 1972; W. Eichrodt, Old Testament Theology, Göttingen (1965,88); R. Bultmann, New Testament Theology, 1961, 204-211; J. Schabert, Fleisch, Geist und Seele im Pentateuch, Estocarda 1966. 80-82; J.A.T. Robinson, The Body, A Study in Pauline Theology, Barcelona 1968. The question of anthropology of women has a special history which is still being researched. I have developed this theme in another paper.

[2] Original research on this question was done by Margaret Miles, professor of historical theology, Harvard University. Cf. Miles, M., Fullness of Life, Philadelphia 1981.

[3] Cf. H. Schelsky, Sociología de la Sexualidad, Buenos Aires 1963: P. Cuny, Aspects socio-culturels de la sexualité: Lumière et Vie, No. 97 (1979), 25-32; J. Thiel, La Antropología cultural y la Institución matrimonial: Concilium No. 55 (1970), 169-182; M. Vidal, El Objecto del consentimiento matrimonial: Concilium No. 787 (1973), 92-102; Antonio Hortelano, Problemas Actuales de Moral, Ed. Sígueme, Salamanca 1980, Vol. 2. p.288.

[4] E. Lopez Azpitarte, S.J., Sexualidad y Matrimonio Hoy, Ed. Sal Terrae, p.35. Cf. B. Malinowski, La vida sexual de los salvajes, Madrid, 1932; J.J. Lopez Ibor, Mystique et continence, Bruges, 1952; A. Bharati, Analisis antropológicos con enfoque cultural de la sexualidad humana: Folia Humanística 10 (1972), 505-515 and 649-662. J. Cl. Sagne, La mutation des modèles de l'échange dans une société en changement: Supplément 27 (1974), 480-489.

[5] G. Campini, article Pudor, in: Diccionario Enciclopédico de Teología Moral, Ed. Paulinas, Madrid 1978, pp.913-920.
R. Le Senne, Tratade de Moral General, Ed. Gredos, Madrid 1973.

[6] E. Mounier, Introducción a los existencialismos, Ed. Guadarrana, Madrid 1967, pp.130 ff.

[7] Cf. S. Kierkegaard, Diario do un Seductor, Ed. 29, Barcelona, 1971.

[8] M. Villegas, Article Placer, in: Diccionario Enciclopédico de Teología Moral, Ed. Paulinas, Madrid 1978, pp.1447-1454.

[9] E. Dussel, El Dualismo en la Antropología de la Cristianidad, Buenos Aires 1974, p.17.

[10] Cf. A. Humbert, Les Péchées de sexualité dans le Nouveau Testament: Studia Moralia 9 (1970), 182-183.

[11] A synthesis of the various systems may be found in: V.J. Bourke, Historia de la morale, Paris 1970, which contains a vast bibliography.

[12] K. Borresen, Subordination et Equivalence, Ed. Monesi, Paris 1967.

[13] P. Grelot, El Problema del Pecado Original, Barcelona 1969. This work is a valuable aid for study of the doctrine of original sin and for appraisal of the influence of St Augustine.

[14] J.T. Noonan, Contraception et Marriage, Paris 1960, p.391.

[15] C. Jansenius, Augustinus II/2, Louvain 1640, 335.

[16] Casti Connubii. AAS (22 Acta Apostolicae Sedis) (1930), 548, 549, 560.

[17] Decree of the Holy Office, AAS 36 (1944), 103.

[18] Pius XII, Address to the midwives of Rome, 29 October 1951, 843; cf. Pius XII, Catholic Documentation (1951), p.1554.

[19] Cf. P. Palazzini, D. Huerth, F. Lambruschini, Stud. Catt. (1961) p.62-72. 10.

[20] Cf. L. Janssens, L'inhibition de l'ovulation est-elle moralement licite? ETL 34 (1958) 358 ff.; and P.W. Gibbons, Physiological control for fertility: The American Eccl. Rev. (1958), 246-277.

[21] Second Vatican Council, The Pastoral Constitution on the Church in the Modern World (Gaudium et Spes), n.51.

[22] Ibid.

[23] Paul VI, Address to the Sacred College of Cardinals, 23 June 1964, AAS 56, 588.

[24] C. Curran, Contraception, authority and dissent, London 1969. On the publication of Humanae Vitae, Cardinal O'Boyle, Archbishop of Washington, was confronted with a revolt by some 20 priests in his diocese who refused to apply the encyclical literally. They expressed their thoughts in a statement of conscience of the church. The Cardinal suspended them a divinis. As the problem showed signs of being insoluble because of the hardening of attitudes on both sides, the Sacred Congregation for the Clergy in Rome intervened in a communiqué published in L'Osservatore Romano on 20 May 1971. "The particular circumstances which supervene in an objectively evil human act, even though they cannot render it objectively virtuous, can render it *blameless, less blameworthy*, or *subjectively defensible*".

[25] The same section 4 in note 7 lists the preceding Pontifical documentation on this subject: Dignitatis humanae, 14: AAS 58 (1966), p.940. Cf. Pius XI, Encycl. Casti Connubii, 31 Dec. 1930: AAS 22 (1930), pp. 579-580; Pius XIII. Address 2 Nov. 1954: AAS 46 (1954), pp.671-672: John XXIII, Encycl. Mater et Magistra, 15 May 1961: AAS 53 (1961), p.547; Paul VI, Encycl. Humanae Vitae, 25 July 1968, n. 4: AAS 60 (1968) p.483.

[26] The Declaration echoes the constant teaching and pastoral practice of the Roman Catholic Church on this subject in its Magisterium and tradition (Decl. n.9, note 19): Leo IX, Epos. Ad splendidum nitentis, a. 1054, DS 687-688: Decree of the Holy Office, 2 March, 1679, DS 2149; Pius XII, Address, 8 Oct., 1953, in: AAS 45 (1953), pp. 677-679; 19 May 1956, in ASS 48, (1956), pp.472-473.

[27] Regarding the extent to which this Document is accepted in *practice* in the Roman Catholic Church, it should be acknowledged that if anything, it has produced a negative reaction — the reason being not so much what it says but the dualist basis which many commentators continue to see in it: Cf. L.M. Weber, Gewissensfreiheit als Problem nachkonziliaren Ehepastoral: Wahrheit und Verkündigung, 1967, 1.631-1.655; R. Trevett, La Iglesia y el sexo, Barcelona 1967; J. Dominian, The Church and the sexual revolution, London 1971; J. O'Riordan, Evoluzione della teologia del matrimonio, Assisi 1974; various authors, la "Dechirazione sull'etica sessuale". Interpretazioni teoligichi e prospettive pastorali, Brescia 1976; J. Elizari, Un ano después de la declaración sobre algunas cuestiones de ética sexual: Pentecostés XV (1977) 77-78; Catholic Theological Society of America, Human sexuality, New York 1977. Quoted by Hortelano, op. cit. p.521.

[28] Woijtila, Karel, Love and Responsibility, BAC. (1965).

[29] The role of Christian family in the modern world, Synod of Bishops, 1980, OR n. 618 (1980) p.11.

[30] The Document makes this acknowledgement in its very full note 5. In his encyclical Divini illius Magistri, of 31 December 1929, Pius XI declared as erroneous the sex education of his day, which was mere biological data imparted indiscriminately at an early age, AAS 22 (1930), pp.49-86. In this light the Decree of the Holy Office of 31 March 1931, AAS 23 (1931), pp.118-119, should be read. However, Pius XI did consider the possibility of positive individual sex education by those who have received from God the mission of education and the grace to fulfil it, AAS 22 (1930), p.71. The positive value of sex education, mentioned by Pius XI, has been gradually developed by successive Pontiffs. Pius XII, in his speech to the 5th International Congress of Psychotherapy and Clinical Psychology on 13 April 1963, AAS 45 (1953), pp. 2768-286, and in his Address to the Women of Italian Catholic Action on 26 October 1941, AAS 33 (1941), pp.450-458, which gives concrete details of how sex education should be carried out within the family. Cf. also Pius XII to the Carmelites, AAS 43 (1953), pp.734-738; to French fathers of families, AAS 43 (1951), pp.730-734. The Magisterium under Pius XII paved the way for the conciliar declaration Gravissimum educationis.

[31] M. Vidal, Moral del Amor y la Sexualidad, Ed. Sígueme, Salamanca 1971, p. 376.

[32] Pius XI, Encycl. Casti Connubii, see note 16.

[33] Suma Teológica, II, II, q. 154, a 2. Cf also Suma Contra los Gentiles, I, III, Chapter 122; De Malo, 2.15, a 1 and 2.

[34] For this separate treatment on the arguments I am indebted to Rossi, L. in his article on Pre-marital relations in the Diccionario Enciclopédico de Teología Moral. Ed. Paulinas. Madrid 1978, pp.923-925.

[35] Cf. Gaudium et Spes, no. 47-52, which in fact incorporates the whole tradition of teaching on the family, but that would be to go beyond the scope of this paper!

[36] The German espicopate, Sexual guidelines for the spiritual care of young people, 1964, n. 14. Letter to the clergy by the Austrian bishops, 1967. The Italian espicopate, Matrimonio y Familia hoy, n. 18. The French episcopate, cf. Doc. Cathol. 67 (1979) 923. The Swiss episcopate in its documents on the Pfürtner case in 1972, which also encouraged other episcopates to state their position. The German episcopate, again, in Doc. Cathol. 70 (1973), 576.

[37] Cf. A.M.J.M.H. van de Spijker, Homotropie, Ueberlegungen zur gleichgeschlechtlichen Zunciguug, Munich 1972, p.24. Cited by Häring B., article Homosexuality, Diccionario de Teología Moral, op. cit. pp.457-458. An extensive bibliography can be found in North America.

220   *Women, Religion and Sexuality*

[38] Häring, op. cit. p.458.

[39] Cf. the different legislation on homosexuality in various countries in W.J.Senger, Se reconnaître homosexuel? Vers une situation nouvelle, Paris, 1970, pp.177-185. In the field of sexuality, R. Pellegrini, Sexologia, Madrid, 1955, pp.753-799, with an appendix on Spanish law, and F.V. Harper, El sexo y la ley, en Reproducción humana y conducta sexual. Barcelona, 1966, pp. 477-510. And in a wider context, G. Marafini. La societá permissiva e la morale, Rome, 1974.

[40] Greek has a wide terminology to describe the phenomenon of masturbation: *depho*, meaning "to work with the hand"; *Kanmoai*, "to scratch oneself"; *tribei*, "to rub". St Paul does not use this terminology when he condemns the "impurity" of pagans. To describe nocturnal emission of semen the Greek uses the workd *exoneiromos*.

[41] Cf. Ple, A. La Masturbación, Ed. Paulinas, Bilbao 1979. p.25.

[42] Ple, op. cit. p. 28.

[43] Pius XII, AAS 44 (1952), 275. See also the address to the pyschotherapists in AAS 45 (1953), 279-280.

[44] Cf. Decree of Holy Office on masturbation to obtain sperm for analysis, AAS, 21 (1929), 490. The same teaching is found in the Address of Pius XII to the Congress on Urology, AAS.45 (1953), 378, and to the participants to the Second World Congress on Fertility and Sterility, AAS 48 (1956), 472. Cf. Rossi, L. op. cit. p.634.

[45] Cf. Davanzo, G, article Abortion, Diccionario enciclopédico de Teología Moral, Ed. Paulinas, Madrid 1978, pp. 13.17.

[46] The feminist movement and feminist theologians call for "the right of women to control their own bodies". This position of Catholic women is in radical disagreement with the official Magisterium of the Church. Catholics for Free Choice, a movement which began in the USA, has set up an office for Latin America in Montevideo, Uruguay. It publishes a quarterly, "Conciencia Latinoamericana". A group of Latin American feminist Catholic women has published a book on the subject, Mujeres e Iglesia, Sexualidad y Aborto en América Latina, Mexico 1989.

[47] Cf. Statement of Faith of Leo IX, (Denz 685); Pius XIII, *Humani Generis* (Denz 3896); and the Profession of Faith of Paul VI, June 1968.

[48] Cf. Holy Office 1889 and 1895 (Denz 3719 and 3721); Pius XII, Address to the Association of Midwives of 29 October 1951; *Gaudium et Spes* no. 27 and 51; *Humanae Vitae*.

[49] Declaration on induced abortion, 12-13, of the Sacred Congregation of the Doctrine of the Faith, 1974.

[50] Encyclical on the Rights of the Family, art. 4. (O. Romano, 25-XI, 1983).

[51] Guidelines on Respect of Emerging Human Life and the Dignity of Procreation, of the Congregation for the Doctrine of the Faith, 1987.

[52] Paul VI, Letter to Cardinal Villot, 3 September 1970.

Catholicism, Women, Body and Sexuality

A Response

Rosemary Radford Ruether

Maria-Teresa Porcile-Santiso's paper on "Roman Catholic Teachings on Female Sexuality" is a clear and well-documented account of the official Roman Catholic position on sexual questions, as this has developed in the twentieth century. But it is somewhat apologetic towards these teachings and ignores a great deal of contrary tradition, as well as alternative views widely held among respected Catholic moral theologians.

Another tradition

Porcile says that the RCC has always taught the full equality of women with men in the image of God. The only question has been one of differences of social function between men and women, not of differences of value or status of women from men in creation or nature. However this declaration suppresses a great deal of contrary tradition. In fact, classical Christian and Roman Catholic tradition has been much more ambivalent about women's equivalent dignity or status in nature or creation.

St Augustine, in his treatise on the Trinity, which is based on the image of God in the human soul, denies that women possess the image of God in themselves. Women are included in the image of God only under the headship of their husbands.

> When she (woman) is referred to separately in her quality as a helpmeet, which regards the woman alone, then she is not the image of God, but as regards the male alone, he is the image of God as fully and completely as when the woman is joined with him in one. [1]

This theological anthropology reflects the legal situation of men and women in patriarchy. In the patriarchal system the male head of family or *pater familias* represents both himself as an individual and also the whole family as its collective head. Women, children and slaves fall under this collective headship of the patriarch. But sons can grow up and become heads of family and male slaves can be emancipated and become heads of family. Only women remain "by nature" permanent dependents, lacking the possibility of autonomous or civil personhood in society.

In Augustine (and implicit in biblical and Christian thought before his time) this patriarchal concept of headship is used to interpret the biblical doctrine of the image of God. The term "image of God" is understood to mean sharing in God's dominion over the lower creation. Only the male head of family is understood to possess such dominion not only over non-human creation, but also over the subordinate persons in the family. Therefore only the (free propertied) male possesses the image of God. Since woman can never be in this position of dominion, she is excluded from the image of God in herself.

This denial of women's equal human status with men is extended in the teachings of Thomas Aquinas, who remains the normative theologian for the Roman Catholic tradition. Thomas took over a (false) biological theory from Aristotle that taught that the male alone contributed formative potency in reproduction. The female is only the passive incubator of the male seed which is identified with the embryo. Aristotle believed that every male seed would normally produce a male. Females are born only through a defect in gestation in which the male seed fails to fully form the female matter. The result is a defective human being or woman. Women are physically weaker, less capable of moral will power or intellectual acumen than males. Their defective nature, morally, mentally and physically, makes them non-normative humans, unable to represent the fullness of human nature. They cannot exercise dominion in society, but must be governed by the male as their head.[2]

This Aristotelian anthropology was taken over by Aquinas. It shaped fundamentally his view of women both in the order of creation and in the church. Woman is defined as a necessary evil in creation. She is necessary to the male only as a helpmeet in procreation. But for any helping relation of a more spiritual or cultural kind, a man is better helped by another male than by a woman. This view reflects the classical understanding of friendship as a relationship only possible between peers. One cannot have a real friendship with inferiors, such as slaves. Since women are inferior to men by nature, they can only have a servile helping relationship to them, not the helping relation of an equal.[3]

Aquinas' Christology and ecclesiology were also shaped by this use of Aristotelian biology. For him, the maleness of Jesus Christ is not just a contingent historical fact. Christ's maleness is an ontological necessity. Only the male represents "perfect" or normative human nature. Only the male can represent the human. Therefore Christ had to be male in order to be the collective representative or "head" of humanity. It also follows that women cannot represent Christ. Therefore women cannot be ordained. Since ordination also is a position of dominion, rule and teaching authority over others, women cannot be ordained because they cannot exercise dominion.[4]

This Thomistic tradition is represented in the recent Vatican teaching that women cannot be ordained because they cannot represent Christ. However the Vatican "Declaration on the Question of the Admission of Women to the Ministerial Priesthood" undercuts the earlier anthropological basis of this teaching. It attempts to separate the question of women's civil equality in society from ordination. It asserts that the Catholic Church (the Magisterium) has always supported women's civil equality, but that the question of women's ordination is not a question of civil equality or "civil rights" but belongs to a separate higher plane of sacramental relationships to God.

This assertion that the church has always supported women's civil equality is historically false. In fact the Vatican and several national episcopacies were opposed to women's suffrage or civil equality, when suffragists, women and men, were struggling to win this reform of women's subordinate status in society in the late nineteenth and early twentieth centuries.[5] This anti-liberal history of the Catholic Church is conveniently forgotten.

The Catholic Church accommodates to the new status quo of women's civil rights in society by forgetting its own past teaching and practice. But it attempts to remove the question of women's ordination to another plane unconnected with women's civil rights or standing in society.

Women are said to be unable to be ordained, not because of any inferior status in nature or society, but because of a sacramental "mystery". The historical fact that Jesus was a male demands that another male must represent him. This is a question of "appropriate" matter or of symbols needing to "look like" what they symbolize.

"Sacramental signs", says Saint Thomas, "represent what they signify by natural resemblance." The same natural resemblance is required for persons as for things: when Christ's role in the eucharist is to be expressed sacramentally, there would not be this "natural resemblance" which must exist between Christ and the minister if the role of Christ were not taken by a man. In such a case it would be difficult to see in the minister the image of Christ. For Christ was and remains a man.[6]

It is difficult to know what is really intended by such a statement of "natural resemblance". Surely bread and wine do not "look like" a male human being, but have always been understood to represent Christ. The attempt to split the question of whether women are equal in creation (image of God) from whether they are Christomorphic or image Christ seems to be based on an untraditional disjunction of nature and grace or society and sacrament. Although citing Thomas Aquinas as their authority, such a division is quite foreign to his thought.

For Thomas, women's inability to image Christ and to be ordained has no other basis than his belief that they were non-normative or defective humans who cannot have autonomous standing or exercise leadership in society. Once this anthropology is rejected for a belief in women's equality in nature, then Thomas's teaching that women are not Christomorphic also disappears. The present Catholic teaching attempts to retain the conclusions of Thomas's thought without his premises. This does not work, which is the reason why the present arguments lack credibility. One must therefore conclude that the classical view that women lack full human standing and personhood lurk covertly behind the present teaching that women cannot be ordained because they cannot "image" Christ.

An issue of ideology — and idolatry

In the first version of her paper Porcile made much of the fact that the existence of the female ovum was not "discovered" until 1827. Before that it was not known that women contribute "50%" to procreation (does nine months of gestation count for nothing?). Therefore it was understandable that before this was known women would be defined as an inferior or secondary member of the human species. Porcile seems to think that the previous doctrine that women were only passive incubators of the male seed is simply a matter of scientific ignorance that now has been corrected.

But surely the matter is more complex than this. The Aristotelian false biology did not express just scientific ignorance. Rather it enshrined an androcentric ideology that reflected the patriarchal legal situation of women as instrumentalized creatures of male domination.

The belief that the male alone provides the formative potency in procreation, and women provide only the matter that is to be formed, does not derive just from naive observation of male semen, the female ovum being invisible. In fact, naive observation does not make a ready connection between the semen ejaculated in the sexual act and impregnation. Anthropologists have suggested that early human societies for many millennia may have not understood this connection or else ignored it. They regarded women as giving birth by themselves, with the help of spirits.[7] This focus on women as the primary procreators coincided with a period in human consciousness where the female as mother was the primary symbol of cosmic potency or divinity.

The lowering of regard for female potency in procreation corresponds with the increasing subjugation of women to male domination. This culminated in the Aristotelian view that women contribute nothing formative in procreation. It is perhaps not accidental that the female ovum was discovered in 1827 at precisely the time when the patriarchal doctrine of women's passive subordination to male domination was shifting to the new doctrine of women's equal but complementary relationship to man in society.

Porcile's account of Catholic teaching on women and sexuality lacks any element of ideology critique. She never suggests that this teaching might have been shaped by patriarchy as a particular social system and ideology. She seems to assume that the Catholic Magisterium stands outside of and above any social and historical context. Her claim that the Catholic Church alone possesses a concept of final teaching authority seems to assume that this teaching authority has a privileged capacity to discern truth unconditioned by social ideology and historical context. This capacity to discern truth unconditionally is extended not only to the interpretation of scripture, but also to the interpretation of nature or natural law. The Catholic Magisterium can discern how other thinkers, both in this church and outside it, have fallen into error because they have been biased by the social practices and ideologies of their times. But it doesn't or cannot succumb to these errors or biases itself.

This view of the Roman Catholic magisterium undoubtedly reflects its own self-concept. But it is a scarcely credible viewpoint. All human knowledge is a finite social construct. We can only know "in part" from our social context. What we know and how we know it is always somewhat biased by unconscious self-interest. This recognition that all knowledge is partial and biased corresponds not only to modern understanding of the sociology of knowledge, but also with the basic Christian anthropology that confesses that all humans are finite and sinful. To stand outside the social historical context and to possess unconditional truth is to be, not human, but divine.

The Roman Catholic doctrine of the infallibility of the magisterium seeks to place one institution, one group of men, in their official teaching capacity, outside this human situation. It denies that these men in this role are subject to finitude and sin. By implication they cannot repent or admit error and sin and are in no need of forgiveness. To put it colloquially, "being infallible means never having to say you're sorry". This is idolatry. It makes the Catholic Magisterium God.

A crisis of credibility

This discussion of infallibility in the context of a response to a paper on Catholic teachings on women and sexuality is not irrelevant. In fact infallibility has become the major stumbling block to rethinking traditions, especially on women and sexuality. Oddly enough the present Vatican leadership has become far more concerned to enforce its teachings on birth control, abortion, homosexuality and women's non-ordainability, all of which are based on concepts of natural law, than traditional theological issues based on revelation. To put it another way, the defence of patriarchy has overshadowed the defence of Christian faith.

This connection of sexual teaching and infallible authority was made evident twenty years ago with the release of the papal encyclical *Humanae Vitae*. The traditional Augustinian teaching that made any separation of sexual pleasure from procreation, even within marriage, mortally sinful, was based on the belief that sexual concupiscence was inherently sinful and was forgiven or allowed only for its good end in procreation. This teaching was based on a fundamental discounting of the role of sex in lovemaking or the expression of love between the couple.

The reason for this discounting of love as a valid "end" of sexuality in itself was rooted in the devaluing of women. If men and women are not peers between whom a love relation of equals is possible, then sex cannot be seen as an expression of love. The sexual act was instrumentalized as a relation of subject to object. The male as subject either "used" woman as body rightly, for procreation, or wrongly, for selfish pleasure. Sex as a mutual relation of body-selves expressing mutual love was not considered.

In the twentieth century this narrow view of sexuality, originally shared by Protestants, began to be questioned. Once it was accepted that the expression of love was a valid purpose of sexuality, independent of procreation, the traditional arguments against birth control began to break down. Protestants in the United States rethought these traditions, and, in the 1930-50s, they accepted the morality of all medically safe methods of birth control within marriage.[8]

Catholic moral theologians adapted to this new moral valuing of sexual love, as well as to demographic arguments against the large family (that was resulting from modern medicine) by accepting the "safe period" method. This method was accepted as "natural", preserving the "integrity" of the sexual function, while barrier methods of contraception were rejected as unnatural, violating this "integrity".

However many Catholic couples found this method unworkable. It resulted in frequent failure and hence heightened anxiety about sexuality for those who could not afford another pregnancy. From a psychological and experiential point of view its "naturalness" was in doubt, since it required both a high degree of manipulation of the relationship based on the female fertile period, and also meant that the "safe period" fell primarily during the woman's menstrual period (a point Porcile never mentions).

These arguments based on experience of married couples began to influence moral theologians who, as celibate males, had tended to theorize about the "integrity of the sexual act" without the benefit of such experience. By the early 1960s the Catholic arguments that made a major distinction between the safe period method and other methods of contraception within marriage were losing their credibility, both for Catholic laity and for many moral theologians.

It was in this context of the crisis of credibility of the traditional anti-contraceptive teaching that Pope Paul VI called together a birth control commission to study the question. The commission attempted to create a genuine consensus of the church by bringing together bishops, medical and sociological experts and married people. The majority report (there was no official minority report, contrary to the impression held by many) concluded that within faithful and committed marriage there was no moral difference between safe period and other methods of contraception. However Pope Paul VI was unable to accept the conclusions of his own Birth Control Commission. Instead he reaffirmed the traditional anti-contraceptive teaching.[9]

Infallibility played a major role in the Pope's inability to accept what had become a new consensus of the "church". What the church had taught so long and so insistently could not be wrong. Hans Küng picked up on this connection of infallibility and the inability of the Pope to reform past teaching in his book *Infallible? An Inquiry* (1970). [10]

However the difficulty of reforming the error of long-held teaching is not the only question here. Catholicism has let other teaching, with an equally long and authoritative history, such as its teaching on the moral acceptability of slavery, slip away without much notice. [11] Why is there so much difficulty over birth control?

The need to move towards relationality

I suggest that the special inability to rethink this question reflects the peculiarities of the patriarchal and sexophobic traditions of the Catholic celibate hierarchy. Ownership of woman's body, particularly her fertility, must be seen as foundational to male control over women. This is doubly true for an ascetic clerical system which combines the anxieties of patriarchal control over women's bodies with a shunning of sexuality as morally debasing and sacramentally polluting of the "holy". It is this social and psychological context which has made it so difficult for the Catholic Church to let go of its anti-contraceptive teaching. It also helps explain the peculiar interconnection of rigid authoritarianism and sexual control over others who are thought of as inferior precisely because they are defined as sexual (married men, women, and homosexuals in descending order).

There are many other questions of sexual ethics that might be discussed in this response. I will focus on only one such area where anxiety is high in all the Christian churches (perhaps because it touches also on the clergy) and that is homosexuality.

Homosexuality has been traditionally condemned for some of the same reasons that contraception was condemned. It was sexual pleasure without procreation. By definition it took place outside legitimate marriage, since marriage was allowed only between heterosexuals. Thus it was fornication. It violated the "structure" of reproductive sexuality (wrong orifice) and hence was sodomy. Finally it violated patriarchal male-male relations by putting one of the male partners in the submissive position of the woman. This is an abomination. This is the chief reason why it was condemned in Hebrew scripture. [12]

The focus of hostility to homosexuality is on male homosexuality. Female homosexuality tends to be overlooked. Although, when it is noticed, it raises another anxiety for patriarchal males; namely, the possibility of female sexual (and social) autonomy of males altogether. All these arguments presuppose an instrumentalized view of both moral and immoral sex. They discount the possibility of sexuality as love. As we have noted, the underlying presupposition is that sexual relations are relations of dominance and submission, not mutual relations between peers to express love through pleasure.

In 1977 the Catholic Theological Society of America published a major study of human sexuality that explored an alternative ethic for addressing a number of questions of sexual morality, including homosexuality. The CTSA report suggested that Catholic moral theology should move from a legalistic to a relational sexual ethic. The basis of what makes sexual acts moral or immoral is the quality of relationality. Healthy relationality is not achieved all at once but is a question of moral development. The goal is to move towards relationships which are faithful, loving, mutual and life-enhancing, and away from relationships which are violent, unfaithful, deceitful, manipulative and exploitative.

The report suggested that homosexuality should be seen as a variant type of sexual orientation that occurs naturally in ten to twelve percent of the population. It was compared with left-handedness, as a minority, but normal and natural variant of human "wiring". Homosexuals, like heterosexuals, should be encouraged to develop committed relationships which are faithful, loving and mutual. The same basic ethic of moral and immoral relationality governs heterosexual and homosexual relationships.

These relational criteria of sexual morality threaten to blur the neat boundaries between sinful homosexual, unmarried or non-procreative sex, and moral heterosexual, married procreative sex. This did not mean a libertine ethic. In many ways the ethical criteria proposed by the study would be critical where patriarchal society has traditionally been lax. Much of married heterosexual sex would be judged as immoral because it is violent, exploitative, non-mutual and without regard for the equal human development of the female partner.

However a committed homosexual relationship, or an unmarried relationship which has not made a lifetime commitment, but is faithful, loving and mutual, would have to be seen as having positive moral value. This attempt to look at all sexual questions from the ethical criteria of the quality of relationality provides an important challenge to traditional Catholic sexual ethics.[13] Porcile's paper ignores the fact that there are not only dissenting practices among Catholics on sexual ethics. There are also comprehensive and carefully worked out alternative understandings of the ethical criteria for decision-making held by respected moral theologians.

Two other issues

Porcile's paper raises many other questions that call for further discussion, both in terms of historical tradition and ethical reflection. I will mention only two issues, and these but briefly. On the historical side she confidently dismisses any residue in Christianity of Jewish traditions of women's impurity during menstruation or after childbirth.* But in fact exactly these traditions were strongly reinstated in the 6th-9th centuries as the Christian ministry became redefined as sacramental priesthood. Women's bodily impurity in general, but especially during menstruation and after childbirth, was used to evict women ministers (deaconesses) from the sanctuary and from contact with the "holy".[14]

Although these traditions of female bodily impurity, over against a sacramental and male celibate, sacerdotal definition of holiness, have largely faded from consciousness, a residue still remains in Catholic practice. The custom of the churching of women expressed the tradition of women's impurity after childbirth. The continuing refusal of the Vatican to accept female altar servers, and the official insistence that female readers of scripture (allowable only in the absence of competent males) should read outside the sanctuary, reflect this tradition in which the holy is defined by the exclusion of the female body.

The one area where Porcile is ready to denounce a past Catholic tradition is in the quasi-gnostic negativity to the body of patristic ascetic culture. This ascetic anti-body culture she sees as happily overcome today in a culture that is much more Hebraic in its affirmation of body-spirit.

However I am less sanguine than she is about modern culture and its affirmation of body-soul unity. Much of the modern body and fitness culture, with its concern for diet and exercise, remains obsessively performance-oriented. The dream of the contemporary health and fitness devotee is total control over the body as a perfectly performing machine. The relation to the body is highly competitive. One constantly tries to outperform past "records". One suspects that the ultimate hope of this body culture is bodily immortality or the conquest of sickness and death.

---

* The reference here is to an earlier version of Maria-Teresa Porcile's study presented during the 1985 NGO Conference on the UN Decade for Women. In this version she briefly discussed some of the questions identified by the original group of researchers as pertinent to an understanding of religious attitudes towards women (such as pronouncements on menstruation, lactation, childbirth, etc.). She argued that in the RCC there is no such thing as a rite of passage at puberty (male or female), nor a sense of purity/impurity on account of blood or menstruation. On this point, the "offical teaching in regard to female bodily functions exists and is explicit whenever the relationship with another is involved".

I suggest that these attitudes towards the body are asceticism in a new guise. No more than in the time of St Anthony are we able to simply let ourselves be as bodily beings. We can neither be with our bodily pleasure, as a good in itself, nor can we accept our finitude, weakness and mortal natures. Instead we are constantly trying to transcend and negate our bodily natures, either through rejection of the body or through athletic perfectionizing of it.

The patriarchal traditions that seek to negate and transcend the mortality and finitude of the body are closely linked with the negation of women. The flight from the body, the woman and the world is finally the flight from mortality. Women become identified with the inferior realm of the corruptible body. They are scapegoated for sin which results in the mortality of the body. By seeking to negate and transcend women, men seek to negate and transcend their own mortality.

Catholic self-absolutizing of the magisterium and the negation of women and sexuality are inter-connected. The Catholic magisterium cannot reform its teaching on women and sexuality, because it cannot face its own finitude and corruptibility. To allow women to be moral agents of their own sexuality is to give up the whole patriarchal struggle to both own and control women's generative powers and also to stand outside the mortality of human life. For patriarchal men to acknowledge women as their peers is also to acknowledge that they too are prone to error and death.

NOTES

[1] Augustine, *De trinitate*, 7.7.10.
[2] Aristotle, *Generation of Animals*, 729b, 738a-b, 775a.
[3] Aquinas, *Summa theologica*, I, 92.
[4] Aquinas, ibid.
[5] The American Catholic hierarchy, led by James Cardinal Gibbons, opposed women's suffrage. A message from the Cardinal was read to the Anti-Suffrage Convention held in Washington D.C. on December 7, 1916. Papal opposition to all aspects of the movement for the emancipation of women can be found in Pius XI, *Casti Connubii*, (1930).
[6] *Declaration on the Question of the Admission of Women to the Ministerial Priesthood*, (1976), 27.
[7] Elizabeth Gould Davis, *The First Sex*, Baltimore, Penguin Books, 1972, 86-88.
[8] David M. Kennedy, *Birth Control in America*, New Haven, Conn., Yale University Press, 1970, 143-4.
[9] For the history of the Papal Birth Control Commission, see Robert Blair Kaiser, *The Politics of Sex and Religion*, Kansas City, Mo., Leaven Press, 1985.

[10] English translation published by Doubleday and Company, 1971.

[11] See John Francis Maxwell, *Slavery and the Catholic Church*, London, 1975.

[12] "You shall not lie with another man as with a woman. It is an abomination": Leviticus 18:22.

[13] Catholic Theological Society of America, *Human Sexuality: New Directions in American Catholic Thought*, New York: Paulist Press, 1977.

[14] See Susan Wemple, *Women in Frankish Society: Marriage and the Cloister, 500-900 A.D.*. Philadelphia: University of Pennsylvania Press, 1983.

Attitudes to Female Sexuality in the Anglican Church in New Zealand

Janet Crawford

This paper is a shortened version of one originally written in 1984-5. Since then there have been some significant changes in the Anglican church, which means that some of this material is now out of date. These changes include the publication of A New Zealand Prayer Book/He Karakia Mihinare o Aotearoa in 1989 which moves much further in the direction of inclusive language and also contains some important changes incorporating more women in the calendar. Another important development occurred in November 1989 with the election of the first woman diocesan bishop in the Anglican communion. There has also been a greater commitment to partnership between Maori and Pakeha which may well result in important changes to the Constitution of the church.

Feminist groups in a number of places are developing new forms of liturgy and ritual and new theological perspectives which are often related to female sexuality. The church is beginning to look at the issues of sexual harassment and violence against women. This is an area of major concern to many women which the church in the past has failed to address.

This paper then reflects the church of the eighties rather than the church of the nineties, the church as it was at one moment in the recent past rather than it is at the present. What it will become in the future of course remains to be seen.

Introduction

There is no one authoritative source to which one can turn to determine what Anglicans teach and believe on such matters as female sexuality and bodily functions, for Anglican authority is dispersed and much of its teaching is not explicit, but implied in its worship. Also the Anglican church is by nature comprehensive, and on all except essential matters of faith there is room for diversity and considerable difference of opinion. To the best of my knowledge this is the first time there has been any research on this topic, at least in relation to the church in New Zealand, and so this paper is very much a first exploration into a field where much work remains to be done.

New Zealand society has undergone rapid changes in recent years and there have been corresponding changes in the church. Many of these changes are related to the position and status of women. In this paper I have focused on teaching and attitudes in the Anglican church in the period from 1970 to the present. I am conscious that there are many omissions and many questions left unanswered, but I have tried to focus on those points which seem most significant. As a Pakeha (person of European descent) I have concentrated on the Pakeha church. Undoubtedly research based on the Maori section of the church would yield much interesting material and somewhat different results, but this lies outside my scope and competence.

I have done my best to be a faithful interpreter of the Anglican church in New Zealand, but all conclusions and opinions are my own and as such I alone am responsible for them.

Authority in the church

Since the beginning of organized European settlement in New Zealand in the 1840s the Anglican church (officially titled the Church of the Province of New Zealand) has been the largest Christian denomination, a fact which clearly reflects nineteenth century immigration patterns. According to the most recent census (1981) 25.67 percent of the New Zealand population declared themselves to be Anglicans, followed by Presbyterians with 16.5 percent and Roman Catholics 14.4 percent. It is accepted that such figures bear little resemblance to church attendance or level of commitment and there is no doubt that a considerable number of Anglicans are merely nominal members of the church.

The Anglican church in New Zealand still has some cultural and emotional ties with the Church of England from which it originated. However it is an autonomous member of the Anglican Communion. Over the years it has developed its own liturgy and its own form of government and it disagrees with the Church of England on some important issues as, for example, the ordination of women and the remarriage of divorced people.

The doctrine and sacraments of the church are established in the "fundamental clauses" of the constitution which cannot be changed. Basically, in these clauses the Authorized Version of the Bible, the Book of Common Prayer, the Ordinal and the Thirty-nine Articles are understood as containing all that is essential, authoritative and unalterable for the Anglican church. Authority in the church is embedded in a synodical structure and a decision-making process which is essentially democratic, with an inbuilt system of checks and balances.

The Anglican church in New Zealand, in keeping with the Anglican tradition and ethos, is comprehensive and pluralistic, containing in one body different traditions and perspectives such as catholic, evangelical and charismatic. So far liberals, radicals and conservatives have all been able to co-exist in the one church, in spite of much diversity of opinion.

Women in the church

According to the Constitution and Code of Canons of the Church of the Province of New Zealand women and men are fully equal in all aspects of church life. Since 1922, "the terms Layman, Vestryman, Synodsman, Parishioner and man shall be held to include persons of either sex". (Canon V, Title B, 22). This means that elected and appointed offices are open to all lay people, irrespective of gender.

Since 1976, there has been no distinction between women and men with regard to ordination. The bill proposing the ordination of women to the priesthood was approved by the General Synod in that year, following some years of discussion. It was then legally challenged on the grounds that the decision represented a departure from the doctrine and sacraments of the Anglican church in New Zealand as defined in clause 1 of the constitution, but this change was not upheld by the tribunal appointed to consider it. The Constitution was amended to state that, "Women are eligible for the diaconate and priesthood and there shall be no impediment by reason of sex to any such ordination" (Constitution, clause 30).

Thus constitutionally all offices and orders in the church are open to women and men although this does not mean in fact that women are represented in equal numbers, or in proportion to the number of women in the church. Generally speaking, women and men participate equally in the lower levels, while men still dominate at the higher levels of authority and decision-making. Thus, for example, at the parish level women are well-represented, many vestries being composed of men and women in roughly equal numbers. The number of women representatives on diocesan synods has risen steadily from 4 percent in 1962 to 23 percent in

1978. Figures for 1985 are not available, but one can assume that this increase has continued. However, the highest authority in the church, the General Synod, is still heavily male-dominated, as the following table shows.

1984 General Synod

	Male	*Female*
House of Bishops	18	0
House of Clergy	33	0
House of Laity	31	10

The first women were ordained to the priesthood in December 1976 and although there is a continuing increase in their number, they are still a small minority (approximately 5 percent) of all ordained clergy. The Anglican church in New Zealand made the decision to ordain women as an autonomous member of the Anglican Communion which recognizes that some member churches ordain women and some do not.

As yet there has been no research on the results of this change in the church's practice. A real evaluation will not be possible until more time has lapsed and there are more women priests. However, personal observation, discussion with other women priests, and the results of a small survey carried out in 1984,[1] all lead me to suggest that women priests do make a difference in both sacramental and pastoral ministry, and particularly that women priests are experienced as *affirming* other women. In the words of one woman priest, "My presence has encouraged other women to know, acknowledge, and rejoice in their own strengths". Following are some of the points which have been made concerning the significance of women priests:

a) Male and female priests together show a model of male-female complementarity and equality instead of just preaching about it. They symbolize the God in whose image we are created, male and female.

b) The presence of women priests challenges traditional sex-role stereotyping and particularly the traditional linking of sin with women's sexuality.

c) Women priests bring a new dimension to theology. As women, their life experiences are significantly different from those of men and their theologizing on them brings a new light to issues such as conception, labouring to give new life, birth and nurturing new life.

d) A clergy couple at the altar may be experienced as an affirmation of marriage and a pregnant priest as an affirmation of sexuality and motherhood.

e) The pastoral ministry to women may be greatly enriched when the priest is able to personally identify with women's experiences. Many women find it easier to share sexual and marital problems with a woman.

f) Women priests often find it easier than men to touch other people, particularly women and elderly people, and so they affirm the importance of bodies and physical contact.

In a church which affirms the equality of women and men, women priests appear to have an important symbolic role. The effects of this are not easily measured.

Worship in the church

It is commonly asserted that to know what Anglicans believe, one must experience Anglican worship. At any Anglican service in New Zealand today there will be no physical separation between women and men. People sit where they wish, and children are not separated from their families (although they may perhaps attend a separate Sunday School during the service, or be placed in a creche). There is no space in the church which is denied to women. Laywomen will generally be involved with laymen in such activities as leading prayers, reading lessons, serving at the altar, and administering the communion chalice. Where there is a choir it will contain male and female choristers, except in a few cathedrals which continue the tradition of an all-male choir. In a small but increasing number of churches services will be led and sacraments performed by a woman priest. There are no particular conventions or traditions regarding women's clothing in church. The last such convention, the wearing of a hat in church, has virtually disappeared in recent years, though it is still retained by some elderly women.

For the purposes of this discussion, Anglican services may be divided into occasional services and the liturgy of the eucharist.

A. Occasional services

The main occasional services are those of Christian initiation, marriage and funeral, all of which occur at significant points in the human life-cycle. For many nominal Anglicans these services may be their main points of contact with the church and of course those who are not Anglicans often attend these services.

1. *Christian initiation*: The total rite of Christian initiation comprises baptism, confirmation and first communion. In the case of an adult, the total rite takes place on the one occasion, while for those baptised as infants confirmation (or the rite of Episcopal Reception and Commissioning as it is now called) follows some years later.

The services generally used are those entitled Christian initiation 1976. These new services contain no fundamental change from the doctrine in the services for baptism and confirmation in the Book of Common Prayer (BCP) which may still be used (although such use is increasingly rare). There are, however, some small, but significant differences with reference to sexuality.

In the BCP there seems to be an implied linking of sin and sexuality in two places. The first occurs in the preamble to Baptism, where the priest states the reason for baptism as: "forasmuch as all men are conceived and born in sin; and that our Saviour Christ saith, None can enter into the Kingdom of God, except he be regenerate and born anew of Water and of the Holy Ghost ..."

In Christian initiation 1976 all reference to being conceived and born in sin is omitted and the priest cites the scriptural text alone (John 3:5).

Secondly, in the BCP the candidate or his/her godparents promise to renounce "the devil and all his works, the vain pomp and glory of the world, with all covetous desires of the same, and the carnal desires of the flesh".

In the 1976 services the promise is simply "to renounce evil and resolve to follow Christ".

Confirmation used in some senses to approximate a puberty rite, with children generally being confirmed at around thirteen years old. Girls used to wear white dresses and veils for the service. Now it is permitted under certain conditions for children to be admitted to holy communion before confirmation and confirmation is usually delayed till a later age, sixteen or upwards. The custom of white dresses and veils seems to have vanished.

2. *Marriage*: Under New Zealand statute, a marriage solemnized by a minister of religion who has been duly registered with the Registrar General of Marriages is a marriage in civil law. Couples may be married in a church service, in a registry office, or in a non-religious service performed by a registered officiating minister. Anglicans require that in a church marriage one of the couple must be baptized.

The form of solemnization of matrimony in an Anglican church may be according to the Book of Common Prayer, the 1928 Prayer Book (a modified version of BCP), or one of the three services offered in the newer Christian Marriage Services (1976). In practice the BCP is probably almost never used, the 1928 service is used sometimes, and the vast majority of marriages take place according to one of the 1976 services. Each form of service falls into three parts, namely introduction, marriage and prayers. The following points are significant for this study.

In the introduction to the 1928 Prayer Book service, the priest states that:

a) marriage is an honourable state, instituted by God;
b) it symbolizes the mystical union between Christ and his church;
c) it was supported by Jesus;
d) it is not to be entered upon lightly;
e) the threefold purpose of marriage includes the "increase of mankind", the hallowing and directing aright of "the natural instincts and affections", and the mutual support and comfort of the marriage partners;
f) God has placed limits on who may marry.

In the 1976 services there is a general written introduction which states that marriage is a relationship "blessed and sustained by God", and that it is therefore "a solemn, lifelong and public covenant made between a man and a woman". The introduction to the first form of service states that marriage is:

a) a gift of God;
b) it best makes known to us the union of Christ with his church;
c) God intends that husband and wife should be united in heart, body and mind and find in their union "the stability necessary for family life and the care of children";
d) the couple should seek each other's good in "a union of strength, sympathy and delight".

The introduction to the second form of service is briefer and more general, stating that, "God has created us in his image, male and female he has created us. It is in his love we are drawn to each other."

The third form states that, "In marriage husband and wife belong together, providing mutual support and a stability in which their children may grow."

Thus, in the 1928 services all references in the BCP to "carnal lusts and appetites", "the procreation of children", and "a remedy against sin and to avoid fornication" are omitted and in the 1976 services the emphasis is on mutual support and love, with no reference to the "increase of mankind" and the hallowing of "natural instincts and affections".

In the marriage part of the 1928 service, the couple exchange vows, promising to serve, love and honour and keep each other, in sickness and in health, as long as they both live, and in addition the woman promises to *obey* her husband. The woman is given to be married by her father (or a friend). The man puts a ring on the fourth finger of the woman's left hand and says,

> With this ring I thee wed, with my body I thee worship,
> and with my worldly goods I thee endow...

The priest proclaims that they are man and wife.

In the 1976 services the couple exchange identical vows and there is no provision for the woman to "obey". In the first form, there is an instruction that "The father or friend of the bride may place her right hand into that of the bridegroom", but this is omitted in the other two forms and the question, "Who gives this woman to be married to this man?" is entirely omitted. There is provision for a mutual exchange of rings with identical words to be said by the man and the woman. After this they are pronounced to be husband and wife.

After the marriage there are prayers for the couple. In the 1928 service there is a prayer which "shall be omitted, where the woman is past child-bearing". The prayer asks that the couple may be granted "the heritage and gift of children". This is followed by a prayer based on scriptural texts. After a reference to the fact that marriage symbolizes the spiritual marriage of Christ and his church it continues:

> Look mercifully upon these thy servants, that both this man may love his wife, according to thy Word (as Christ did love his spouse the Church, who gave himself for it, loving it and cherishing it even as his own flesh) and also that this woman may be loving and amiable, and faithful to her husband, and in all quietness, sobriety and peace, be a follower of holy and godly matrons.

If the service is followed by holy communion, then two Bible passages could be read, namely Ephesians 3:14 and John 15:9. If there be no communion, nor sermon declaring the duties of man and wife, there shall be read some portion of scripture, or the priest shall say the Exhortation provided in the Form of 1662.

This "Exhortation" on the duties of husbands and wives is based on Ephesians 5 and 1 Peter 3. Husbands are exhorted to love and honour their wives, wives to submit to their husbands.

In the 1976 services there is a considerable choice of prayers. There is no prayer that the couple may have children, but optional prayers that they may be good parents to any children they may have. There is no equivalent of the 1928 prayer which implies separate roles for husband and wife. Approved non-scriptural lessons may be read, providing that there is at least one New Testament reading. Suggested Bible readings are:

Genesis 2:18-24	Man and woman
Ruth 1:16-18	Faithfulness
Matthew 5:3-10	The Beatitudes
Matthew 22:35-40	The Great Commandment
John 2:1-11	Jesus at a wedding
John 15:9-12	Dwelling in love
Romans 12:1-21	Gift from God
1 Corinthians 13:4-7	Hymn to love
Ephesians 5:21-33	Duties of man and wife
Colossians 3:12-17	Signs of love
1 Thessalonians 3:11-13	Purpose of love
1 John 4:7-12	Love made perfect

In general one may say that couples marrying in the Anglican church today have considerable freedom of choice, within certain parameters. Most choose the modern forms of service, which are based on an understanding of marriage as the union of equals and which emphasize mutual love and support. In these forms of service women are no longer "given away", they do not promise to "obey" nor are they exhorted to "submit" to their husbands. Childbearing is no longer stated as a purpose of marriage, and no mention is made of "natural" (sexual) instincts. There is more emphasis on equality and less on sexuality. The custom of brides wearing white and a veil is still followed though increasingly brides break with the tradition. For most it is one of the "trimmings" associated with a church wedding and has little or no significance (i.e. white is no longer associated with virginity).

3. *Thanksgiving after the birth of a child*: This service has replaced the BCP service known as the thanksgiving of women after child-birth, commonly called the churching of women. The change in title reflects the change of emphasis and no doubt also changing circumstances.

The BCP service is very much a service of thanksgiving for deliverance from danger and death, from "the great pain and peril of child-birth". In the BCP it comes between services of the burial of the dead and "A commination or denouncing of God's anger and judgments against sinners"! There is no thanksgiving for the child, and no mention of the father except that the woman may be accompanied by her husband, "if he so desire". The service took place in the church.

The modern thanksgiving service may be used in the maternity hospital, singly or with a group, or with a group of families, privately or in the church. It is usually used privately and probably not very frequently. Both parents are included in the prayers, but the service is specifically for the mother. The introduction suggest that she will want to give thanks for *the care you had during your pregnancy, the strength you knew in childbirth, the skill and tenderness of the nurses and doctors, the safe delivery of your child, the joy of being a mother*.

In the brief prayers the parents give thanks to God "for this new life, for our share in your act of creation, for this child born among us", and the minister prays for their home and family, and for the baby.

It is interesting to note that the old BCP service itself replaces a much older order "for the purification of a woman after childbirth, before the door of the church". This service was based on Leviticus 12, according to which a woman who has given birth is "unclean" and must be purified before she can enter the temple. This notion of "uncleanness" does not remain in the BCP service, but many women still have an idea that it is a purification rite. They are not familiar with the actual service, but the old tradition of female impurity lingers on.

4. *Funerals*: The 1928 Prayer Book Order for the Burial of the Dead and the 1980 Funeral Service do not discriminate at all between women and men. The only variation is that in the 1980 book one of the suggested Old Testament readings is Proverbs 31, the praises of a woman, and this would obviously be read only at the funeral of a woman.

5. There are other occasional services such as those for use with the sick and ordination services, but in none of these is there any significant distinction between men and women nor any references to sexuality.

B. The liturgy

At present the Anglican church uses several liturgies of the eucharist. The oldest is the BCP service of holy communion, dating from 1662. However, to a large extent it has been replaced by the New Zealand Liturgy 1970 (NZL) and this is the service with which most Anglicans are familiar. In most churches the celebration of the NZL is the main Sunday service and it is also used on other occasions, such as weddings and ordinations. Although the structure and language of the rite differ quite considerably from those of the BCP holy communion service, the changes do not intend any change in eucharistic doctrine. In 1984 the General

Synod authorized for experimental use the services contained in the Liturgy of the Eucharist 1984. These alternative eucharistic liturgies continue the work of revision which always endeavours to conserve traditional Anglican doctrine, while taking account of present developments in liturgical knowledge and the needs of the contemporary church.

As NZL 1970 is the most frequently used liturgy and the most familiar order of service, so it is also the one which to a higher degree than any other influences the ideas and attitudes of Anglicans. In this liturgy there is no overt or intended discrimination against women, but it has been extensively criticized, mainly by women but also by some men, for its use of exclusive and sexist language, i.e. language which implies that the male is the norm and thereby excludes women. Since 1970 the question of exclusive and inclusive language has become increasingly a matter of concern, debate and change in society and the male-oriented, androcentric language and imagery traditionally used by the church is no longer acceptable to a growing number of Christians.

Inclusive language

Within the Anglican church the issue of inclusive language was first raised in public during the General Synod of 1978 when a motion was moved asking that in all subsequent work on the revision of the church's services of worship an endeavour be made to avoid the use of sexist language. The motion gained considerable media attention and when it came before the Synod, the Synod disposed of it quickly by using a procedural motion to pass to the next business. This meant that there was little debate and the motion itself was not voted on. According to the mover: "The impression gained was that the Synod, composed of fifty-eight men and four women, was glad of a way to avoid discussing the matter."[2]

The matter did not rest there, however, as more and more women began to insist that language which ignored women effectively implied that women were inferior beings. Exclusively male imagery for God also came in for criticism for reinforcing the concept of a masculine God and ignoring the fullness of the One in whose image human beings are created, "male and female". Many expressed their opinion that the language of NZL 1970 was quite inappropriate, insensitive and even offensive.

According to one piece of research, "the NZL 1970 has around 305 male titles, nouns and referent pronouns. There are three female references: the word 'women' comes once, 'Elizabeth our Queen', and the 'Virgin Mary'". [3] Women and men in the congregation were addressed as "brethren" and asked to pray for "all men". They were told that "man" was made in God's own image, that Jesus Christ was born "as man", "for us men". Their prayers were addressed to God, "Almighty Father, Judge of all men", "Almighty God", "Father" and "Lord". The impression given by such language is that God is male and that maleness is the norm for human beings. The sexist language of much scripture and hymnody reinforced this impression.

By 1984, people's consciousness about language had generally risen considerably and as a result a number of changes took place. In his address to General Synod in 1984, the president devoted some time to a discussion of "Christian anthropology", pointing out that both male and female image God equally and that though in history male and female have become alienated, in Christ their relationship is restored. He also gave examples of feminine imagery for God and Christ in the Bible and drew attention to the work of the Prayer Book commission on inclusive language.

After this beginning the General Synod later passed a motion to the effect that all future legislation and motions will be written in deliberately inclusive terms. It also received the report of the Provisional Commission on Prayer Book Revision. This report contained a section titled "Beyond Sexist Language" which began with this quotation from *Liturgy* (Vol. 3, No. 2):

> Liturgy, the church's most important act, can and often has been a source of injustice when it renders any person as of less human worth than any other or when it refuses to recognize the full personhood of some within the body of Christ.

The General Synod also approved for experimental use the liturgy of the eucharist 1984 and these forms will be used increasingly in parishes in the next few years. The introduction to this states: "In our liturgical revision we seek to broaden the range of words and concepts used, rather than to limit them. We have struggled to present material which will not alienate any group within the church. We have sought to go beyond sexist language, into that of inclusive language, where the God-given dignity of all members of the human race must be reflected by the language in which we worship."

Some examples from NZL 1979 and 1984 revised version show the sort of linguistic changes that have been made.

New Zealand Liturgy 1970	1984
men, brethren	people, brothers and sisters
for us men	for us
you... made man in your own image	you formed us in your own image; male and female you created us
to be born as man	to share our human nature
Father, Son and Holy Spirit	Creator, Redeemer and Giver of Life (used only once)
Jesus Christ our Lord	Jesus Christ our friend and brother
Almightly God, God our Father, etc.	merciful God eternal God
(These phrases are still used, but are complemented with others)	God of love Redeemer God God our creator Most Holy Giver of life living God

C. *The New Zealand Calendar*

In accordance with the tradition of the early church, the Anglican church appoints certain days each year "for the commemoration of those among the faithful departed who, by reason of martyrdom or otherwise, has offered a conspicuous example of heroic Christian faith and virtue". In the New Zealand Calendar 1980 there are 158 days on which individuals or groups of Christians may be commemorated by using appointed readings and prayers. Twenty individual women are named in the Calendar:

1. Agnes, child martyr at Rome. A child martyr, the patron of young girls.
2. Perpetua and her companions, martyrs. Companions in perpetual felicity.
3. Catherine of Siena, teacher of the faith. Faith and works.
4. Dame Julian of Norwich, mystic. A writer of the divine love.

5. Mother Edith, foundress of the community of the sacred name. The mother foundress of the first religious order in New Zealand.
6. The Visitation of the Blessed Virgin Mary. A joyous visit.
7. Henry Williams and Marianne Williams, missionaries. Two pioneer missionaries of New Zealand.
8. Saint Mary Magdalene. A woman's witness.
9. Anne, mother of the blessed Virgin Mary. Consecrated family life.
10. Clare of Assisi, abbess. Holy poverty.
11. Saint Mary, the Virgin, mother of our Lord Jesus Christ. Blessed among women.
12. Rose of Lima, mystic. An ardent lover of Christ.
13. Monica, mother of Augustine of Hippo. Persevering in prayer.
14. The birth of the Blessed Virgin Mary, mother of our Lord. The chosen handmaid of the Lord.
15. Teresa of Avila, teacher of the faith. Wise obedience.
16. Margaret of Scotland, queen. A virtuous woman.
17. Hilda, abbess of Whitby. The religious life.
18. Elizabeth of Hungary, princess. To serve the needy is to serve Christ.
19. Cecila, martyr at Rome. The patroness of music.
20. Lucy, martyr, Syracuse. A patron of the blind.

On about twelve other occasions groups of saints, martyrs and founders are commemorated and these would probably include women though this is not usually obvious from the language used. This imbalance in the number of women and men suggests that women are considered of less significance in the history of the church. Also it provides few models and little encouragement for contemporary women in their Christian vocations.

D. The Lectionary

The Anglican church uses, like many others, a lectionary, i.e. an ordered arrangement for the reading of the Bible. This means that certain portions of scripture are appointed to be read at Sunday worship and also for weekday services and daily offices throughout the year. In fact at present there are several lectionaries authorized for use and consequently there is no uniformity. The following comments are based on the Three-Year Cycle of Readings which is becoming increasingly popular as an ecumenical lectionary and is used in many Anglican churches.

The basic structure of the lectionary is Christocentric and the readings are centred around Christ's birth, death and resurrection, celebrated in the great liturgical festivals of Christmas and Easter. The lectionary gives three readings for each Sunday, one from the Old Testament, one from the writings of the apostles in the New Testament, and a gospel reading. Of these the gospel reading is central, the Old Testament lesson being chosen to complement or comment upon it. During the Easter season sections from the book of Acts replace the Old Testament lesson. The sermon or homily is usually, but not necessarily, based on the gospel. Each synoptic gospel is read in turn, Matthew in year A, Mark in year B, except for five weeks when the "Bread of life" sermon from John is used; Luke in year C. The Gospel of John is given a special place during Christmas, Lent and Easter. The other New Testament readings give a semi-continuous selection from some of the epistles. Throughout the whole lectionary there is a good deal of selectivity, as is inevitable in any scheme in which the Bible is not read in its entirety.

The year 1985 is year B and therefore Mark is the synoptic gospel which is used. A study of the readings appointed for Sundays, Christmas and Easter shows the following passages which involve women as central characters or address women's concerns:

Mark	3:20-25	Jesus says, "Whoever does the will of God is my brother, my sister, my mother."
Mark	5:21-43	Jairus' daughter and the women with a haemorrhage are healed.
Mark	10:2-16	Teaching on marriage and divorce.
Mark	12.38-44	The widow's offering.
Mark	16:1-8	The women at the empty tomb.

and also

Luke	1:26-38	God's call to Mary.
Matt.	15:21-28	Jesus and the Syro-Phoenician women (a parallel to Mark 7:24-30 which is omitted).
John	12:1-11	Jesus anointed by a woman (parallel to Mark 14:3-9).
John	20:1-9	Jesus appears to Mary Magdalene (parallel to Mark 16:9-11).

The basic structure for the other New Testament readings in year B is that 1 Corinthians 6-11, 2 Corinthians, Ephesians, James and Hebrews 2-10 are read. Once again a certain selectivity occurs and we find that almost all of 1 Corinthians 7 (Paul's teaching on marriage) is omitted, although vv. 29-31 and 32-35 are included. Also omitted is 1 Corinthians 11:2-15, the passage in which Paul teaches that woman's head is man and that she must keep her head covered. Ephesians 5 is included, including vv. 21-32, where wives are told to be subject to their husbands.

Thus in year B there are a total of nine gospel readings concerning women. Some teaching on women and marriage is deliberately omitted from the epistles. The pattern in years A and C is similar. Because the Old Testament is not read as a continuous narrative (and the Old Testament lesson is not always read) women are spared most of the misogynistic Old Testament passages. The laws of purification and holiness in Leviticus are not read, for example, nor such "texts of horror" as the stories of Jephtha's daughter (Judges 11), the rape of a concubine (Judges 19), and the rape of Tamar (2 Samuel 13). On the other hand, no mention is made of important women of faith such as Miriam, Deborah, Huldah, Rahab and the Hebrew midwives. Added to this is the fact that so far the several versions of the Bible authorized for reading in church are all written in non-inclusive, androcentric language. Masculine nouns, pronouns and imagery dominate.

The Anglican church is proud of its tradition of regular and extensive reading of the Bible in public worship. However, for a number of women today the Bible is itself problematic, a book written by men for men, which has little to say that is affirmative of women. There is a growing body of literature on women and the Bible which addresses the theological and hermeneutical questions from various perspectives.[4] It is true that for many, perhaps a majority, of women the Bible remains an unquestioned source of faith and one from which they draw comfort and hope. However, there are others for whom the reading of the Bible serves to increase their sense of marginality and inferiority.

E. Sermons

In the Anglican church sermons may be preached by ordained clergy and by licensed lay readers. This means that the great majority of sermons are preached by men. Sermons are not usually printed, collected or published, and therefore it is virtually impossible to do any research on them, and not possible to make a comparison between sermons preached by men and those preached by women. This would be an interesting area for future research. The variety of theme and content in sermons would undoubtedly reflect individual understandings and attitudes from the most conservative to the most liberal. Some women and men question the use of the sermon at all, seeing it as an authoritative, one-sided means of communication which puts the preacher "six feet above contradiction" and reduces the congregation to passive listeners.

Anglican worship is not "free", that is, it consists of a number of authorized services for different occasions and the celebration of the eucharist according to an authorized liturgy. This means a degree of uniformity, though there is also room for considerable variation. Anglican worship is undergoing a process of change, aimed at producing services which will be faithful to Anglican tradition and doctrine while at the same time authentically expressing the life and concerns of the church in New Zealand. The actual experience of Anglican worship may differ quite significantly from place to place, depending largely on the attitudes of the priest and the traditions of the parish.

It seems that in general there is nothing in Anglican worship, with the exception of some biblical passages, which is specifically negative towards women or to sexuality, female or male. Moreover considerable changes have been made recently as, for example, in the marriage services, to express contemporary understandings of women and to emphasize equality and mutuality of the sexes. However, on the other hand there is little in Anglican worship that is specifically affirmative of women and sexuality. The question of inclusive language and imagery is probably the major area of concern and much work remains to be done in this area.

Some ethical questions

Marriage and divorce

There have been fairly rapid changes in New Zealand society in the last two decades, not least in regard to marriage. Although traditional ideas of marriage are still upheld by many and the majority of New Zealanders still choose to marry and raise families, there are a number of variations from past norms and traditions and for an increasing number of people a family is no longer a married couple and their children living in a nuclear household. *De facto* relationships and ex-nuptial births are more frequent and more acceptable than in the past. There is a definite trend for young couples to live together before marriage and marriage for them is often the result of a decision to have children. Fewer couples are choosing church marriages: in 1981 only 54% were married by a minister of religion.

During this century there has been a progressive liberalization in divorce legislation, with major changes taking place in the 1920s and 1960s, and culminating in the 1980 Domestic Proceedings Act which established the sole ground for dissolution of marriages as the breakdown of marriage, evidenced by the spouses' having lived apart for two years. Divorce has become progressively more available and more socially acceptable and the rate of divorce has increased. The rate of remarriage after divorce has also increased.

In the present understanding of marriage no distinction is made between male and female roles and responsibilities. The sexual act is understood as part of a wider relationship, the physical expression of love and not solely for procreation. In fact, although the importance of children and family life is emphasized, responsible family planning is encouraged. Decisions about birth control, the size of families and so on are for individual couples to make and they are called to be responsible in their decision-making, "to guard against selfishness and covetousness, and to be thoughtfully aware of the world into which the children are to be born. They ought to make all such decisions as part of their life of prayer and of pursuit of the guidance of God."[5]

This teaching on sex within marriage is fully in accord with Anglican thought as expressed by the Lambeth Conference of 1958, which stated the traditional Anglican understanding that sexuality itself is good, a gift of God.

> But the procreation of children is not the only purpose of marriage. Husbands and wives owe to each other and to the depth and stability of their families the duty to express, in sexual intercourse, the love which they bear and mean to bear to each other. Sexual intercourse is not by any means the only language of earthly love, but in its full and right use, the most intimate and the most revealing; it has the depth of communication signified by the biblical word so often used for it, "knowledge"; it is a giving and receiving in the unity of two free spirits which is in itself good (within the marriage bond) and mediates good to those who share it. Therefore it is utterly wrong to urge that, unless children are specifically desired, sexual intercourse is of the nature of sin. It is also wrong to say that such intercourse ought not be engaged in except with the willing intention to procreate children.[6]

The canon also states the responsibility of all members of the church to uphold Christian standards of marriage in society and in their own marriage, and the special responsibility of the clergy for preparing couples for marriage and for ministering to those experiencing marital difficulties. Responsible marriage should include explanation of the church's teaching on the nature of marriage and also teaching on the biological, psychological, spiritual and sociological factors in marriage.

There is no reliable data on the effect of these regulations. Very few parishes seem to exercise any planned programme for marriage preparation or enrichment and individual clergy vary greatly in their skills and intent in this area. Similarly the amount of support actually given to couples and families varies considerably, but in general is probably rather inadequate. On the other hand, couples and families experiencing difficulties may be reluctant to seek support or help, or may choose to turn to other agencies or helping professions.

In spite of its teaching that marriage is a lifelong exclusive union of one man and one woman, the Anglican church in New Zealand today allows both divorce and remarriage of its members. Of course the church could never prohibit divorce among its members, as this took place according to civil laws over which the church has no jurisdiction. It could however, prevent the remarriage by the church of divorced persons and until recently did so. Thus there has been a change in Anglican attitudes and teaching on divorce, and this is fairly closely related to changes in legislation and social attitudes generally. Similar changes have taken place in the main Protestant churches as well. In general they have all "progressed from dissatisfaction with the liberality of the 1920 divorce legislation through a more tolerant attitude in the late 1930s, to recent positions of broad tolerance within their general doctrines of marriage".[7]

After more liberal divorce legislation was passed in 1920, the Anglican church in 1922 associated itself with a decision of the 1920 Lambeth conference that marriage was indissoluble. At the 1940 General Synod, a major report was presented on marriage and divorce, stating that marriage was in principle lifelong and indissoluble, but that when the bond had already been broken by the physical unfaithfulness of one or both parties a decree of divorce merely recognized the fact. Thus adultery was accepted as ground for divorce and the church continued to deny remarriage to divorced women and men whose former spouses were still living. On the exceptional ground that a divorced person could have obtained an ecclesiastical nullification of marriage a bishop could grant a licence for a remarriage to take place in church, but no Anglican priest could be compelled to solemnize such a marriage.

In 1970 the Anglican church considerably modified its restrictions on remarriage and implicitly accepted irretrievable breakdown of marriage as the ground for divorce. Title G Canon III part IV: Marriage of divorced persons states that such marriages may be solemnized provided that there are good and sufficient grounds to believe that:

a) any divorced person intending marriage sincerely regrets that the promises made in any previous marriage were not kept; and

b) both parties to an intended marriage have an avowed intention to abide by the life-long intent of the proposed marriage.

Any priest can, however, on conscientious grounds refuse to solemnize the marriage of a divorced person.

Basically the Anglican attitude and teaching uphold the biblical and traditional view of marriage as a lifelong union while at the same time acknowledging that marriages do break down for reasons of human weakness and sinfulness, and that to end a particular marriage by divorce may be a lesser evil than to force it to continue. In these circumstances the church's concern is to be pastoral rather than judgmental and therefore it emphasizes the possibility of God's forgiveness and a new beginning.

A typical example of Anglican thought is to be found in the Report of the Commission of Enquiry on Marriage and Divorce, Christchurch Diocese, 1978. In its introduction the Commission stated that it "wished to avoid a judgmental approach which the church has too often seemed to adopt in relation to divorce and marriage breakdown". It acknowledged a number of factors contributing to change in traditional family patterns and to marriage breakdown and that Christian expectations of marriage differ in certain vital respects from both traditional and modern expectations.

Both of these see marriage basically as an arrangement of convenience — either for wider society in its search for stability, or for individuals in their search for fulfilment.

The Christian expectation on the other hand sees value in emphasizing both the longevity and the quality of relationships in marriage. It looks for love and loyalty in marriage. But the motivation is not convenience — it is the kingdom of God, a pattern for society which God is working out.[8] The Report acknowledges that church members experiencing marriage difficulties often find it difficult to share their problems within the Christian fellowship for "too often Christians have given the impression of being untouched by human frailty". The tendency is often for church members to fear the judgment of other Christians, to withdraw from active membership, and to disregard the Church as a useful counselling agency. To some extent this reaction may be due to "the historical reluctance of the Church to accept divorce". The report insists: "There should be active teaching and counselling within the Church to promote the sanctity of the marriage bond, yet those who have tried and failed should not be condemned."[9] It emphasizes the role of the church in preparation for marriage, in providing support and counsel during marriage, and in counselling and encouraging those whose marriages have ended in separation or divorce.

In sum therefore the teaching of the Anglican church emphasizes the importance of Christian marriage and family life while allowing for divorce and remarriage. In its teaching the church makes no distinction between male and female roles and responsibilities and generally upholds an ideal of mutuality in male/female relationships. Individual Anglicans may, however, hold other views. The Church is concerned to be forgiving rather than judgmental, but on the other hand it is frequently experienced as inadequate in its actual support of marriage and family life.

Abortion

Abortion has been the subject of intense public controversy in New Zealand in recent years. The 1970s saw a growing movement for liberalization and reform of the laws concerning abortion while at the same time there was considerable opposition to any liberalization. "Pro-choice" groups such as the Abortion Law Reform Association of New Zealand and the Women's National Abortion Action Campaign were pitted against "pro-life" groups, the most prominent of which was the Society for the Protection of the Unborn Child (SPUC).

In 1977 the passing of the contraception, sterilization and abortion act, together with the crimes amendment act changed the law considerably. The legislation had the effect of widening the grounds on which abortions could be legally obtained while at the same time bringing abortion firmly under state control. The changes in legislation have not stopped controversy. They are seen by conservatives as too liberal and by radical feminists as enforcing state control over women's reproductive functions.

As far as the Anglican church is concerned, there is no canonical condemnation of abortion and in fact it is not mentioned in the Canons at all. Thus when abortion became a matter of public debate the Anglican church had no authoritative teaching or position on the matter and it became a subject for debate and discussion within the church. One can assume that individual Anglicans held attitudes at all points on the spectrum from most conservative to most radical, but it seems likely that the majority were in favour of some liberalization of the law. The National Research Bureau carried out public opinion polls in 1972, 1974 and 1976 and concluded: "Those with no religious affiliations were the strongest supporters of liberalization while among the various denominations the most liberal were the Anglicans".

The Association of Anglican Women in 1976 made submissions to the Royal Commission on contraception, sterilization and abortion, basing them on the views of over one thousand individual members. Most thought serious threat to the physical or mental health of the mother should be sufficient reason for a legal abortion while only 128 favoured abortion on request. They emphasized the need for better education for family and parental responsibilities and supported readily available, free contraceptives for women and counselling on contraception for teenagers.

To assist in informed debate and discussion the Provincial Public and Social Affairs Committee, a body responsible to the General Synod, set up a special committee to prepare a report on abortion. This committee was made up of thirteen people representing a number of disciplines and professions, including theology, philosophy, medicine, psychiatry, law and social welfare. The report of this committee came down in favour of what is best described as a situation ethic i.e. doing the most loving thing possible in particular circumstances. It pointed out that Christian morality goes beyond obedience to the law and that Christian ethics centres in a faith relationship with God-in-Christ. It pointed out that the Bible, the basic Christian resource, is interpreted in different ways and does not directly address many contemporary issues such as abortion. The committee concluded: "Our report will disappoint those looking for an authoritative decision either to follow or to attack, it will possibly enrage many who will look to the Church for a lead and expect that lead in terms of definite answers and directions. But the Church is called to be the servant not the master."[10]

The same attitude was taken by a Statement for Discussion issued by the Provincial Public and Social Affairs Committee the following year. According to this Statement: "On the abortion issue there is no one position which can be labelled specifically Christian although, of course, some positions may be more in line with Christian insights and emphasis than others."[11]

Following the legislative changes in 1977 abortion has been discussed at a number of diocesan synods as efforts have been made to persuade the church to express a firmer opinion either for or against abortion. It seems to be an issue on which church members continue to be divided, but the following points from synod debates and resolutions give a fair indication of majority opinion at the present time.

a) The church is concerned about the number of abortions taking place and is generally against further liberalization of the law and particularly opposed to abortion "on demand".

b) The present rate of abortion is seen as evidence of insufficient education and support for parents, married or unmarried.

c) The church needs to teach and affirm the unique value of each human life.

d) The church should act with compassion, offering care and support to women with unwanted pregnancies and creating an accepting environment for unmarried women who choose to keep their children.

e) The church should respect conscientious conviction and follow the law of love in caring for those considering abortion

The attitude of the Anglican church is perhaps best summed up in a statement from Wellington Diocese (1982) that, "the pastoral responsibility of the Church includes the loving acceptance of the woman who has had an abortion, as befits those who live by grace and not under law".

Human birth technology

New questions relating to human sexuality have recently arisen with developments in human birth technology, particularly in-vitro fertilization (IVF) and artificial insemination by donor (AID), and new possibilities for genetic engineering. As yet there is no legislation in New Zealand regarding these matters, but medical research is continuing and already several babies have been born as the result of an IVF programme. There is increasing public interest and debate about the implications of such technology and, as might be expected, public opinion is divided. The Anglican church, in common with other churches, is now studying the issues involved, so that "help can be given to church members in relating Christian teaching to these matters". [12] It is unlikely that the result in the Anglican church will be an authorative statement or an addition to the Canons. Rather there may be guidelines to assist Anglicans to make up their own minds and provide freedom for them to make conscientious decisions.

Homosexuality

In New Zealand homosexual acts between males are illegal while female homosexual acts are not. Thus male homosexuals are discriminated against by the law and socially, while lesbians experience varying degrees of social discrimination. An attempt to liberalize the law regarding male homosexuality in the 1970s failed, but made the whole issue of homosexuality a matter of public debate and considerable controversy. At present a bill to decriminalize homosexual acts between consenting males is being considered by Parliament and is arousing considerable controversy in the country at large. Inevitably the Church became involved in the debate over homosexuality in the 1970s, but it was unable to speak with united voice.

Homosexuality is not the subject of any canonical statement, but it is clear that until recently Anglicans shared in the almost universal condemnation of homosexuality and homosexual behaviour. At present the situation is more complicated as revealed by a number of studies and reports which the church has produced in the last ten years. As the background to these was the illegality of male homosexuality, the reports tended to focus on questions of law reform and on male homosexuality, but nevertheless they reveal certain general attitudes which apply to homosexuality in both sexes, and which distinguish between morality and legality or illegality. There was a general distinction made between homosexual *persons*, i.e. those with a sexual orientation to persons of the same sex, and homosexual *activity*, i.e. sexual acts.

The most liberal attitude expressed was that homosexuality is "natural" and therefore good and a gift of God. Therefore homosexual behaviour is an allowable option and homosexual relationships should be regarded as a Christian option and subjected to the same general criteria as heterosexual relationships e.g. faithful, loving, honest. According to this view, the *quality* of relationships is paramount.

The most conservative attitude held that all homosexual acts are always wrong. Those who held this traditional viewpoint believed that through the power of God some homosexuals might change and be enabled to enter a fulfilling heterosexual marriage. Those for whom this was not possible were called to live as celibates.

Undoubtedly the Anglican church continues to uphold heterosexual marriage as the Christian norm and undoubtedly an unknown number of Anglicans are homosexuals, male and female, celibate and sexually active, public and concealed.

A statement by a priest recognizes the differences existing in the church and gives a typically Anglican response to homosexuality: "As a company of Christ's people we should accept those who hold another view from our own in a spirit of Christian tolerance — which is not something that tolerates anything because it doesn't care which is right, but a spirit which accepts that as human beings we never know everything about anything and that people who hold different views may be accepted in the spirit of Jesus."[13]

Conclusions

The Anglican church in New Zealand, in common with the wider Anglican tradition, is generally affirmative of human sexuality which it understands to be a gift of God and therefore good. However, any teaching on, or discussion of, human sexuality is usually in the context of relationships and the morality or immorality of particular forms of sexual activity. Little attention is given to female sexuality and bodily functions. Negative attitudes of the past have largely disappeared, but they have not been replaced with positive attitudes. The stages of the female life-cycle are ignored, apart from marriage and pregnancy. Within the church important aspects of female sexuality, such as menstruation, pregnancy and menopause, are not mentioned. There seems to be no affirmation of what is specifically uniquely female. Little if any attention is given to distortions and mistreatments of female sexuality such as occur in rape, incest, pornography, and other forms of violence against women. This is not to say that the Anglican church in fact condones such acts, but by its silence it seems to imply that they do not exist or are unimportant.

As far as sexual relationships are concerned, the Anglican church continues to uphold heterosexual marriage as the Christian norm and to emphasize the importance of family life. Little consideration is given to those who for any reason do not fit this norm: those who do not or cannot marry, the divorced and widowed, the childless, those of homosexual orientation, and disabled people. The alternative to marriage is celibacy, but there is little positive teaching on this and the sexual desires and needs of unmarried people, male and female, are ignored.

Changes in the church have led to greater equality of women and men and to increased participation by women. Constitutionally and theologically the church teaches that women and men are equal, equal recipients of God's grace at baptism and equal members of the church. Women and men are equally eligible for all offices and orders within the church. However, the church remains male-dominated in its leadership and decision-making. Discussion and statements on questions such as abortion are made by synods and committees on which women are a minority. Although more women are now achieving some theological education, the academic study and teaching of theology is still male-dominated and androcentric. The questions and concerns of women, such as questions to do with female sexuality, are not yet part of the agenda. This androcentric bias of the church is reflected and expressed in the language and imagery of its worship, although now some changes are taking place in this area. However, the tradition of God as "Father" has undoubtedly reinforced the attitude that the male is the norm.

The Anglican tradition emphasizes the freedom and responsibility of individuals to make up their own minds and to act according to conscience. The role of the church is to help people to make decisions, not to tell them what they must do. Within the church there is room for diversity and differences of opinion on all except matters of faith.

Such differences stem from different ways of interpreting the Bible and applying its teaching to contemporary situations. So, for example, some Anglicans believe that biblical injunctions that wives should be submissive to their husbands are historically and culturally conditioned and no longer applicable while others believe that they are divine commands which are eternally valid. Generally speaking the church in its official decisions in recent years has tended to be fairly liberal in its interpretation of the Bible, thus allowing for such changes as the ordination of women and the remarriage of divorced people.

The clergy have a powerful role in the transmission of the church's tradition and in the formation of attitudes. They are authorized by the church to preach, teach and counsel and in so doing they inevitably impart their own theological perspective which may be anywhere between ultra-conservative and very radical. Some recent research has revealed some of the current diversity in what Anglican priests believe and presumably teach. For example, in answer to a question about the acceptability of remarriage of divorced persons 80.7 percent were in favour, 13.1 percent against and 6.2 percent uncertain. Sixty-seven point two percent agreed with the biblical condemnation of homosexual acts, 24 percent disagreed and the remainder were not sure. Regarding abortion, 13.3 percent thought it was morally wrong, 77.2 percent thought it should be permissible on certain grounds, and 9.5 percent thought it should be available on request. [14] Such diversity is part of the nature of the Anglican church.

The power of the clergy lies in their moral authority for they have no juridical authority over lay people. The worst sanction which they can apply is to refuse holy communion to a person who is, in the words of the Book of Common Prayer, "an open and notorious evil liver". This happens extremely rarely and must be authorized by the bishop. Thus clergy have considerable freedom to transmit their own belief and attitudes, but lay people are free to disagree with them. In practice what usually happens is that those who disagree strongly with a particular point or who feel uncomfortable in a particular congregation will simply leave and join another congregation or in some cases another denomination — or they may even leave the church altogether. As all churches in New Zealand are organized on the basis of a voluntary compact people belong because they want to.

The relationship between religion and society is complex. Certainly Christianity played an important role in the development of Pakeha culture in New Zealand. Today society is increasingly secular, the Christian population is declining, and the churches have little influence except on their own members. The Anglican church has changed and is changing, not least in its attitudes towards women and female sexuality, and we can expect this process of change to continue. However, it seems that rather than initiating changes which influence society, the church changes in response to changes in society and in social attitudes. As women have achieved greater independence, recognition and status in society, so in the church. As society has discarded negative teachings on sexuality, so has the church. But the church has not yet developed a theology which is truly affirmative of female sexuality and it remains to be seen if this is possible.

NOTES

[1] Joyce Marcon, "Some Experiences of Priesting of Women in New Zealand", unpublished paper presented to ARC/NZ, 1984.
[2] Edward A. Johnston, "Sexist Language in the Liturgy", unpublished paper, 1978.
[3] Danby Dawn, "Caution - Low Visibility", Report to Anglican Provincial Prayer Book Revision Committee, August 1983, in *Vashti's Voice*, No. 21, November 1983/January 1984.
[4] See, for example, Elizabeth Schüssler Fiorenza, *In Memory of Her*, London, SCM Press, 1983.
[5] Code of Canons, Title G Canon III, I 1(e).
[6] A. Stephenson, *Anglicanism and the Lambeth Conferences*, London, SPCK, 1978, p. 209.
[7] R. Phillips, *Divorce in New Zealand*, London, OUP, 1981, p. 49.
[8] Report of the Commission of Enquiry on Marriage and Divorce, Christchurch, 1978.
[9] *Ibid.*
[10] Report on Abortion by the Provincial Public and Social Affairs Committee, 1974.
[11] Statement of Discussion: Provincial Public and Social Affairs Committee, 1975.
[12] Waikato Diocesan Synod resolution, 1984.
[13] Personal correspondence from the Rev. E.A. Johnston.
[14] Peter Drury, The Religious Role and Beliefs of Anglican Clergy and Their Socio-Political Correlation, M.A. Thesis, University of Canterbury, 1983.

Sexual Ethics
and the Church
A Response

Carter Heyward

I shall respond to several major themes in Janet Crawford's paper which pertain most directly to the interplay of sex, gender and power as this power-dynamic continues to shape Christian theology as well as to set the conditions for women's lives. I have divided these "major themes" into two categories for the purpose of this analysis: (1) those themes laid as the very foundations of Christian anthropology and theology; and (2) those which, reflecting Christian anthropology and theology, have shaped Christian ecclesiology. (There are related themes which I see also as important from an Anglican perspective; e.g., what are the "fundamentals" upon which Anglicans, in our "comprehensiveness", must agree? The limits of my response will not permit their treatment here.)

1. Re-imaging Christian life: sexuality, marriage, monogamy, and the moral aegis of women

One of the methodological problems in attempting to study an issue like "homosexuality" or "marriage" is that, like a domino, once touched it affects everthing else. Perhaps there is some intuitive "knowledge" of this in the realm of religious consciousness, for religious people often seem especially resistant to acting upon any issue apart from the many others upon which it would seem to touch. This is used, too frequently of course, as a rationale for doing nothing about anything. But the inclination to reach towards the whole, an inclination both conservative and radical, I believe, is embedded in wisdom. We cannot examine the foundations of our lives in piecemeal fashion and come to any authentic apprehension of who we are, as a whole people or as individuals with integrity.

"Homosexuality" cannot be explored as a critical moral issue if we separate it from explorations of heterosexuality, bisexuality, sexuality period. As scores of denominational study commissions have discovered in the United States, an ethical study of homosexuality (is it right or wrong, and under what conditions?) pushes quickly into questions about sex and bodies and biblical authority and commitment and faithfulness. We discover rapidly (unless we are biblical fundamentalists, which most Anglicans are not) that, as a moral issue, "homosexuality" is merely one lens through which we find ourselves examining the much wider panorama of sexual ethics and sexual theology. If we are genuinely interested in an ethics or theology of sexuality, we wind up facing basic issues in our own lives, facing one another and facing ourselves, with such questions as: Are our bodies really good? naturally good? precious gifts of God? If so, is the erotic energy that moves between us a fundamentally good energy? Is sexual touching, basically, a good and moral act? What distorts this goodness? Which dynamics in our life together violate, or pervert, this goodness? Could it be that the burden of ethical proof is really upon us to discover under what circumstances sex is wrong (abusive, violent, degrading, compulsive) rather than, as has been historically the case among Christians, under what circumstances sex is right?

If we are open to the possibility of envisioning a sex-positive, rather than a sex-negative, ethic, we find ourselves having to re-examine at least one significant dimension of the Christian understanding of marriage: to provide an arena in which sexual expression is morally legitimate, good. If, as an expression of love, and even commitment, sex is good, what does this do to the traditional Christian view of marriage, even in its most current evolutions (e.g., the 1976 Christian Marriage Services)?

One respondent to Janet Crawford's questions about marriage (not included in her paper) as "life-long and monogamous" wrote "lifelong, yes, monogamous, no." Several other respondents were ambiguous on the subject of monogamy. If they are to be honestly reflective not only of what is happening among, but also of what may be good for, God's people, Christian sexual ethics cannot simply dismiss as "un-Christian" or "wrong", the possibility of sex outside of marriage or of non-monogamous commitments. Rather, an honest, responsible ethical study of sexuality is likely to lead from affirmation of our bodies/ourselves towards a sex-positive ethic which includes the responsibility of discerning and acting in relation to those sexual relationships which are rooted and grounded in love, commitment and faithfulness. But is it possible to be "committed" to more than one person at a time? Of course it is, but to be *sexually* committed, and faithful? If so, what covenants or expressed-commitments of mutual fidelity might we envision to do justice not only to our lives as individuals-in-relation-to-particular-others but also to the larger community/world of sisters and brothers with whom we are always responsible for helping to sustain right relation?

Many theologians and ethicists in the United States (e.g., Beverly Wildung Harrison, Rosemary R. Ruether, Paula M. Cooey, Toinette Eugene, Rita Nakashima Brock, to name only a few) suggest that the *anti-sexual* bias of Christian life and practice is linked, inextricably, with the church's *anti-female* foundations. If this is so (as seems beyond dispute, not only in Christianity, but to some extent in all patriarchal, androcentric religions), the connection between the church's teachings on, for example, homosexuality, monogamy, and marriage cannot be separated from its views on procreative choice, including abortion. For the latter have constituted historically the realm in which Christian fathers (literally and figuratively) have exercised authority over women's bodies and, thereby, women's lives.

Women's sexuality and women's moral aegis have converged in "the abortion issue", in the United States as in New Zealand, to form a moral battleground. The struggle, at its core, is between those, on the one hand, who really do think that irresponsible (i.e. sexually active) women need to be punished (pay with pregnancy for their mistakes) and those, on the other, who would choose to celebrate both women's sexuality and women's ability and right to make sexually-responsible decisions, and mistakes, without being punished by church or state in the form of coerced childbearing or sterilization.

The church historically has taken the shape of a misogynist (woman-hating), erotophobic (sex-fearing) institution. Re-imaging Christian theology and anthropology on the basis of a profound respect for women's lives and moral agency, as well as of an affirmation of sexual pleasure, play and integrity, would move us towards startling, fresh, sensual apprehension of the power and love of an incarnate God in our midst.

We can move in this direction only insofar as many of us attempt together to live, work, and love at the intersections of the many so-called "issues" (e.g., homosexuality, marriage, divorce, abortion). For what we discover together at such intersections are ways in which the power (the ability to make things happen) is used and abused among us. And, as Christians, we can come to see more clearly that our fundamental ethical business is to help generate (live, teach, preach, pass on) the conditions for the creative, liberating use of power in our love and work.

2. Re-imaging the church: women's ordination and inclusive language

I purposely addressed above several basic issues of Christian life in the world of God, e.g., the realm of sexuality. If attended honestly, such themes will open us to better understanding the significance of women's ordination and the language and images of our lives, including our worship. Like each of the other matters raised here, there are intrinsic connections between the words and symbols of our liturgies and the persons whom we call to minister *with* us in various ways.

Like many women, I was aware long before I was ordained an Episcopal priest that many of the opponents to women's ordination comprehended more fully than some of the proponents what actually is at stake theologically in the ordination of women, especially perhaps in the "higher" liturgical traditions (such as the Anglican). Our opponents frequently would accuse us of trying to tear apart "the essence of catholic faith", whereas our proponents characteristically would respond, in our defence, "That's absurd. Women's ordination is simply a matter of justice." Certainly women's ordination was, and is, a matter of justice, but justice-making is seldom simple. And, in an ecclesial tradition literally established (over several generations) on patriarchal, androcentric principles, justice-making for women involves instigating a radical transformation of, yes, the essence of catholic faith: God himself is indeed transformed in this process, and *she* becomes our Lover, and Friend, our Mother and Sister, the still small voice, the bush on fire with God, one who still can be Father and Brother as well (sometimes).

The language must change because our experience changes, our experience of creative power, of liberation, of blessing and forgiveness, of prophetic witness and pastoral care, of courage and compassion, of that which *is* our power in right, mutual relation — that one which is our Liberator; he who is our Comforter; she who is our God.

This is what is happening today in Christian community wherever two or three are gathered together in praise of women's lives as sacred lives and of woman's creative, liberating power as the power and love of God.

Janet Crawford's carefully researched paper presents the social location within which, in New Zealand, the small but growing, spirited, and irrepressible movement among women (and some men) has begun. God bless the revolution! Make us strong and gentle and passionate, fiercely committed to justice-making with tenderness, humour, and the faith to move mountains!

Contributors

Elizabeth Amoah (Reformed), who is on the staff of the department for the study of religions at the University of Ghana, has done considerable research on women and religion in Ghana, with special reference to women and "spiritual churches".

Marie Assaad (Coptic Orthodox) was a WCC deputy general secretary and moderator of Unit III on Education and Renewal from 1980 to 1986.

Elisabeth Behr-Sigel teaches philosophy at the Graduate Institute of Ecumenical Studies in Paris, and is co-editor of *Contacts*, a French review of Orthodoxy.

Janet Crawford (Anglican) teaches at Knox College, Dunedin, New Zealand. She has been a consultant to the WCC's Sub-unit on Women in Church and Society and, as a member of the Faith and Order Sub-unit, has worked on the WCC study on the Community of Women and Men in the Church.

Blu Greenberg is a writer and lecturer on contemporary Jewish issues. She is the author of *How to Run a Traditional Jewish Household* and *On Women and Judaism*.

Riffat Hassan (Muslim) is associate professor and chairperson of the Religious Studies Program at the University of Louisville, Kentucky, USA, where she has taught since 1976. She also teaches occasionally at the Louisville Presbyterian Theological Seminary.

Carter Heyward (Episcopal) is professor of theology at Episcopal Divinity School, Cambridge, MA, USA.

Pnina Navè Levinson, a Jewish scholar, taught at Heidelberg University and School of Education, Federal Republic of Germany, from 1976 to 1986, and has authored publications in Hebrew, German and English.

Nicole Maillard (Orthodox) has studied Protestant theology and is a journalist and teacher in France.

Junko Minamoto, formerly a lecturer in Shin Buddhism at Ryukoku University, Japan, has written many papers on feminist movements in Japan and Japanese Buddhism.

Anca-Lucia Manolache is a theologian who works as legal adviser, documentalist and editor in the Orthodox Church of Romania and at the Bible Institute.

Vasudha Narayanan (Hindu) is associate professor in the department of religion at the University of Florida, Gainesville, USA.

Maria-Teresa Porcile-Santiso is a Roman Catholic theologian from Uruguay who is currently working with the Bible Society.

Rosemary Ruether (Roman Catholic) teaches at Garret Evangelical Theological Seminary, in Evanston, Illinois, USA.